Consciousness

Consciousness Sutras

Principles of Becoming Conscious

An Experiential Map of Inner Evolution

Ovidiu Brazdău

TransPersonal
Press

TransPersonal Press
(*a Kaminn Media imprint*)
272 Bath Street
Glasgow G2 4JR
Scotland
transpersonalpress.com

A CIP record for this title is available from the British Library.

ISBN 978-1-912698-10-3 (print)
ISBN 978-1-912698-11-0 (ebook)

Edited by Joya Stevenson
Text design and layout by Thierry Bogliolo
This book was typeset in Calluna.

Printed, bound and distributed by Ingram Spark

Contents

"To put out a manifesto you must want: ABC
to fulminate against 1, 2, 3
to fly into a rage and sharpen your wings to conquer and dis-
seminate little abcs and big abcs; to sign, shout, swear, to organize
prose into a form of absolute and irrefutable evidence, to prove
your non plus ultra.[...]

How can one expect to put order into the chaos that consti-
tutes that infinite and shapeless variation: man?[...]

I speak only of myself since I do not wish to convince; I have
no right to drag others into my river, I oblige no one to follow me
and everyone practises his art in his own way, if he knows the joy
that rises like arrows to the astral layers, or that other joy that goes
down into the mines of corpse-flowers and fertile spasms."

—Tristan Tzara, in 'Dada Manifesto 1918'.

Foreword

The consciousness sutras are a compilation of principles, describing conscious experience and inner evolution. They are intended as experiential guidelines for psychologists, transformational counselors, life coaches, and anyone on a transformational journey.

The sutras and the commentaries have been created using my previous research—'Psychology of Becoming Conscious' and 'Entheogenic Insights', available in the 'Becoming Conscious' collection at www.consciousness-quotient.com/becoming-conscious. This text also includes previously unpublished research results, especially the conceptual meta-research on conceptual convergence of conscious experiences and inner evolution, undertaken for the development of the Consciousness Quotient concept and the CQ-i assessment tool.

This book is the result of 28 years of explorations and research, ignited by reading and seeking to understand Patanjali's Yoga Sutras through personal practice. My growth journey toward maturity and inner harmony has been a long and messy process, with many ups and downs. Amazing insights and openings unfolded, simultaneously with stressful entrepreneurial failures in Romania, which forced me to go deeper within myself, to be truthful, compassionate, more flexible, and adapt to life as it is.

I am thankful to my family, for their unconditional love and support, and to all the people who provided insights, support, inspiration, and ideas for this research; my colleagues from the Consciousness Quotient Institute and Info-Sanatate project, the researchers from the Dayalbagh Educational Institute in Agra (India), my former students in Bucharest, and people who shared their research and transformational experiences during live discussions, or through books, blogs, or video channels.

The following people are included with quotes that clarify and describe certain topics: Walter Russell, Anirban Bandyopadhyay, Mircea Steriade, Mae-Wan Ho, Peter Walla, Tamas Madl, Bernard Baars, Stan Franklin, Marc Wittmann, Sona Ahuja, Cristian-Dan Opariuc, Valita Jones, Sadhna Sharma, Sperry Andrews, Keith Fiveson, Swami Sivananda, Todd Duncan, Jack Semura, Carlo Monsanto, Charles Alexander, Les Fehmi, Abraham Maslow, Vyasa, Daniel Yetman, Corey W. de Vos, Susanne Cook-Greuter, Terri O'Fallon, Kim Barta, Abigail Lynam, Jana Dixon, Ester Albini, Liz Long, Linda Silverman, Osho, Elaine Aron, Steve Bearman, Matt James, Kazimierz Dabrowski, Beena Sharma, Alison Crosthwait, Satprem, Sri Aurobindo, John Welwood, Kaissa Puhakka, Stanislav Grof, Jeff Warren, Robert Monroe, Carl Zimmer, Heather Lonczak, Tara Jenkins, Valita Jones, Simma Lieberman, Frederic Laloux, John Stewart, Scott Kiloby, Raluca Ciobanu, Janet Adler, Mike Johnson, Simon Baron-Cohen, Andrea Olsen, Caryn McHose, Paula Sager, Patanjali, Timothy Leary, Ralph Metzner, Richard Alpert, Michael J. Winkelman. I am grateful for their work. I also thank experts from the American Center for the Integration of Spiritually Transformative Experiences and the Conscious Capitalism movement.

For this book, an easy-to-read citation style has been used for the quotes from books or scientific papers. For quoted text included in the commentary, source numbers are grouped using the sutra numbers. Dashes, hyphens, and punctuation marks have been standardized to facilitate reading; breaks in quoted texts are marked with square brackets [...]; occasionally, commas and words enclosed by brackets have been added to the quoted texts to explain complex scientific ideas and meanings (there are about 20 such additions to the quoted source materials). Some words and phrases, which are highly relevant to some specific topic, have been emphasized using italics.

How to read this book

The consciousness sutras clarify and describe the structure and the layers of conscious experience, and their dynamics during inner evolution, while providing various first-person methodologies for their exploration. The text includes multidimensional perspectives and highly experiential descriptions from a first-person perspective; due to this complexity, some phrases may require more than one reading. You could take short pauses while reading, to reflect on how collective mechanisms generate your personal conscious experience. If some ideas don't make sense at first, please continue reading, and allow your mind to slowly form the puzzle, until a coherent big picture emerges. Some pieces of the puzzle will reveal themselves later, after you understand why all the pieces are related to one another, and how they work together to create the conscious experience.

Please consider this compilation of ideas to be my subjective perspective on how inner evolution could unfold.

Good journeys!

Principles of Becoming Conscious

Chapter One

Conscious Experience

1. Consciousness is a generic concept, an umbrella term, that describes the ability to experience life on multiple *self-reflective* levels. This guideline is focused on conscious experience, the subjective experience of being awake and alive.

2. The conscious experience is an outcome of the natural evolution of life. It provides the means to observe, self-reflect, and partially influence automatic behaviors and patterns, enhancing adaptability to life processes and generating evolutionary diversity.

———

In Western culture, the concepts of consciousness and states of consciousness have been debated across different scientific communities, including psychology and cognitive science, philosophy, neuroscience, psychiatry, and physics. Still, the terms 'conscious' and 'unconscious' are quite challenging to define and use, and some researchers prefer to use the terms 'explicit or implicit', instead of 'conscious or unconscious'[2]. In spiritual traditions around the world, various methods have been used to explore or influence conscious experience, such as yoga, meditation, dance, shaking, singing, sleep and light deprivation, fasting, medicinal plants, and entheogenic extracts.

3. Conscious experience is generated by the *adaptive processing* in our body, its cellular life and energy, the electromagnetic, gravitational, and other fundamental forces and processes, and their *rhythmic balanced interchange*. Conscious experience emerges from the functioning of the whole body, not just the brain. The interactions between all cells, organs, and systems of the human body are reflected in specific ways in conscious experience.

Walter Russell, in 'The Secret of Light', says: "I have but one law for all My opposed pairs of creating things; and that law needs but one word to spell it out, so hear Me when I say that the one word of My one law is Balance. And if man needs two words to aid him in his knowing of the working of that law, those two words are Balanced Interchange. If man still needs more words to aid his knowing of My one law, give to him another one, and let those three words be Rhythmic Balanced Interchange.[...] By disobeying the law, [man] is but hurting himself while on his journey, but he must make the journey and must balance every unbalanced action while on the way."[3]

4. The human body is interconnected through complex chemical and biological systems, and also through resonance chains on various frequencies. The resonance chains form *synchronic nested-rhythms networks* that define the brain-body architecture. These resonance-based architectures provide the structure for local-global *information exchanges* and high-speed regulative processes throughout the body.

——

Anirban Bandyopadhyay's research suggested that the brain-body architecture has 1030 fundamental frequencies: "We are proposing an integrated model of the whole brain and the body from 10^{15} Hz to 10^{-15} Hz, where 12 ranges of frequency bands and associated components are outlined along with major carrier type (ions for proteins and neurotransmitters for neuron firing, etc.) and interactions (electrical, mechanical or electromechanical). In our model, the entire human brain-body system is made of 1030 primary frequencies."[4a,b]

5. The rhythmic, balanced interchanges can *coalesce* in different combinations of frequencies, forming dynamic resonance structures. These structures adapt the human body dynamics to life dynamics, through multi-frequency and multi-rhythmic adaptive

processing. The resonant adaptive processing is embedded in the architecture of the mechanical and electrochemical exchanges, developed by the 60+ trillion human and bacterial cells that form the human body. *Cognition, intelligence, attention*, and *awareness* provide a glimpse of this multi-layered adaptive processing.

————

Mircea Steriade in 'Grouping of Brain Rhythms in Corticothalamic Systems' explains: "Different brain rhythms, with both low-frequency and fast-frequency, are grouped within complex wave-sequences. Instead of dissecting various frequency bands of the major oscillations that characterize the brain electrical activity during states of vigilance, it is conceptually more rewarding to analyze their coalescence, which is due to neuronal interactions in corticothalamic systems. This concept of unified brain rhythms does not only include low-frequency sleep oscillations, but also fast (beta and gamma) activities that are not exclusively confined to brain-activated states, since they also occur during slow-wave sleep. The major factor behind this coalescence is the cortically generated slow oscillation that, through corticocortical and corticothalamic drives, is effective in grouping other brain rhythms."[5a]

In 'Quantum Jazz: Liquid Crystalline Water Music of the Organism', Mae-Wan Ho writes: "What is quantum jazz? It is the radical wholeness or coherence of the organism that profoundly transforms our view of health and disease. The organism is thick with coherent activities on every scale, from the macroscopic down to the molecular and below. I call the totality of these activities 'quantum jazz' to highlight the immense diversity and multiplicity of players, the complexity and coherence of the performance, and above all, the freedom and spontaneity.

Quantum jazz is played out by the whole organism, in every nerve and sinew, every muscle, every single cell, molecule, atom, and elementary particle. There is no conductor or choreographer. Quantum jazz is written while it is being performed; each gesture, each phrase is new, shaped by what has gone before, though not quite. The organism never ceases to experience her environment, taking it in (entangling it) for future reference, modifying her liquid crystalline matrix and neural circuits, recoding and rewriting her genes.

The quantum jazz player lives strictly in the now, the ever-present overarching the future and the past, composing and rewriting her life history as she goes along, never quite finishing until she dies. But her script is passed on to the next generation—not just to her biological offspring, but the species as a whole. Each generation rewrites, edits, and adds to the score, making it unique."[5b]

6. Life's adaptive processing develops in progressive steps. Around 80 to 90% of the processing develops automatically, entirely outside of our awareness, while regulating the functioning of our body. The other 10-20% of life's adaptive processing creates three awareness types. Primary processing, from 20ms (milliseconds) to 100ms after the stimulus onset, generates *basic* awareness. Secondary processing, from 100ms to 300ms, creates *pre-conscious* awareness, and tertiary processing, from 300ms to 600ms and beyond, generates *conscious* awareness through cognition.

——

Peter Walla, in 'Non-Conscious Brain Processes Revealed by Magnetoencephalography (MEG)', writes: "Findings revealed by MEG and other methods clearly demonstrate that only a little fraction of brain processes related to even high cognitive functions such as our self are associated with consciousness. Or in other words, much of our even highest cognitive functions do happen non-consciously. It almost seems as if we mainly run non-consciously with only bits and pieces entering the stream of consciousness.

It may be reasonable to believe that around *80 to 90% of our daily activities are controlled outside our own awareness.* However, we should not make the mistake to underestimate consciousness as it arises now [...] while reading these lines. Consciousness still seems to be inevitable to appreciate a lot of what we are so much used to. The appreciation of music and art, the ability to love and to feel happy are just some of them. In fact, the more we learn about how dominant non-conscious processes guide our behaviour the more we learn to appreciate what our individual consciousness actually means to us."[6a]

From a psychological-experiential perspective, and for practical purposes, the chronology of adaptive processing that generates conscious awareness can be summarized using three stages:

The first stage occurs from 20-50ms to 100ms after the stimulus, when primary processing generates basic awareness. In this initial stage, information that 'something' is there exists, but the information about 'what is there' is not yet processed. In this interval, the attention is automatically oriented toward stimuli. Some studies reveal that auditory stimulation might attract attention 20ms to 50ms after stimulus onset, while visual processing and non-conscious recognition of visual stimuli could arise later, 50ms-100ms after the stimulus onset.[6b]

The second stage emerges from 100ms to 300ms after the stimulus, when secondary processing creates degrees of *pre-conscious awareness*, while more information is being processed, using early local recurrent and late top-down feedback processes.

Still, at this stage, there is no conscious awareness of what the stimulus is. The earliest emotional processing occurs in this interval, generating *pre-conscious emotions*, which may automatically influence our behavior, especially when there is a life-threatening situation. Semantic processing (i.e., understanding words) also begins as a pre-conscious process, together with spatial perception about the possible 'location in space' of the stimulus ('in the body or outside it'). The self-identity processing (identifying that 'it is about me') starts at the earliest between 200ms and 300ms.[6c]

The third stage, from 300ms to 600ms and beyond, is when tertiary processing generates degrees of *conscious awareness* through cognition about the stimulus. In this stage, neural decision-making takes place, by selecting one option out of the multiple possibilities generated in the previous stage of processing. During this stage, the localization of the stimulus in space is decided; i.e., the source of the stimulus, its 3D positioning, either in the body or outside of it. Olfaction (smell) is processed between 200ms and 500ms after the stimulus onset, followed by more complex processing between 600ms and 900ms.[6d]

Conscious awareness, and how it unfolds, is still being debated and researched by neuroscientists. For instance, Tamas Madl, Bernard J. Baars, and Stan Franklin, in 'The Timing of the Cognitive Cycle', write: "We propose that an initial phase of perception (stimulus recognition) occurs 80-100ms from stimulus onset under optimal conditions. It is followed by a conscious episode (broadcast) 200-280ms after stimulus onset, and an action selection phase 60-110ms from the start of the conscious phase. One cognitive cycle would therefore take 260-390ms. [Our] LIDA timing model is consistent with brain evidence indicating a fundamental role for a theta-gamma wave, spreading forward from sensory cortices to rostral corticothalamic regions. This posteriofrontal theta-gamma wave may be experienced as a conscious perceptual event starting at 200-280ms post stimulus."[6e]

7. Reflective self-awareness ('mental presence'), involving cognition and perception of time, needs at least 1-3 seconds to evoke the *nowness* experience, the localizing of an event in time as happening 'now'. However, through *witnessing awareness*, which re-

quires minimal categorization and cognition, humans could have a continuous 'raw' part of the conscious experience, subjectively felt as a *fresh 'being in the now'*. Witnessing awareness begins to unfold from basic and pre-conscious awareness (below the 300ms threshold), while *mindfulness* is available later, after cognition gets involved in processing and the 'nowness' experience is generated. That's why some contemplative experiences, with a significant witnessing component, are perceived as 'atemporal', or 'with no self-identity', while usual mindfulness experiences feel more like this: 'I am observing reality here-now'.

————

Some researchers consider that the experience of now integrates *successive processing units*, titled functional moments. These moments in the range of milliseconds could provide a basis for the conscious experience of *nowness*, the direct experience of what is occurring 'in the now'. However, at least 1-3 seconds of processing are needed for generating a fully conscious experience of the present moment—this means that a person is fully aware of oneself as an individual, differentiated from the surrounding objects, there is a temporal localization of events ('happening in the now'), and choice making is available.[7a]

In 'Moments in Time', Marc Wittmann writes: "The reported limits in duration reproduction and short-term memory do not point to absolute and static boundaries—correspondingly, mental presence has no fixed duration—but to a gradual dissolving of representation with increasing duration. Related to this temporal characteristic, mental presence is related to the fact that once attended objects slowly phase out of experience over time; that is, the phenomenally experienced sliding window of mental presence co-occurs with the constant loss of memory contents. The moving window of presence is related to the constant sequential input of a sequence of perceived events, which each fade out of working memory one after the other after some time. Mental presence is a *temporal platform of multiple seconds* within which an individual is aware of herself and the environment, where sensory–motor perception, cognition, and emotion are interconnected features of representation leading to phenomenal experience.[...]

Regarding specifically the continuity of experience across experienced moments, working memory related to semantic and episodic content might bind together the sequence of temporal segments of nowness that leads to the experience of mental presence. The experienced moment is defined as what is occurring now as immediate experience. It is also a prerequisite for interpersonal communication between two individuals—made possible by synchronizing the moments of individuals, thereby creating shared moments of presence for effortless interaction—an essential feature in music, conversation, and dance. However, the experience of a self acting in its environment, remembering the past and planning the future, necessitates an integration interval—as has been related to mental presence, exceeding the postulated 3 seconds time window of the experienced moment. Continuity of experience only unfolds as mental presence, which is a floating window of feeling present and acting at present."[7b]

Other researchers suggest that we should also consider different mechanisms for adaptive processing, alongside neuronal processing: a faster adaptive processing could be mediated by microtubule 'vibrations', which could provide another basis for the 'raw' subjective experience of 'being in the now'.[7c]

8. To be conscious means to have a degree of *witnessing awareness* and a degree of freedom of choice when thinking, feeling, sensing, and interacting with people and the environment. An essential element of conscious experience is intentionality, which allows a person to choose deliberately what behavior to enact and what attitude to allow and select. From a temporal unfolding perspective,

conscious experience is a *flowing 'window to reality'*: it includes *fresh components* (generated by witnessing, with not as much choice available) and *delayed components* (generated by witnessing, cognition, and other aspects of processing, with greater freedom of choice available). The weight of these two components, in the overall conscious experience, is highly dynamic; some experiences can be 'more fresh' (when witnessing has more weight), while others can be 'more delayed' (when cognitive processing has more weight). There are also various other combinations, generated by the layers of conscious experience and sub-systems.

Witnessing awareness is usually described as the 'I am experience', the observer experience, 'just being' (as opposed to 'doing'), awareness of awareness itself, no-mind, pure consciousness, fundamental awareness, or non-symbolic awareness. The first-person reports describe the witnessing awareness mode as a constantly fresh look into the present moment, as a new 'zeroth-person' perspective, where there is only a present-centered experience.[8]

9. *The witnessing awareness mode* is a part of a meta-reflective intelligence system, generated by the body's adaptive processing. When a part of attention is focused on the attentional stream itself, it generates *meta-attention*, and then *meta-awareness*—the awareness of awareness streams, creating a framework for awareness flows. While the feedback loop is added to the meta-processing of awareness, the witnessing awareness mode is activated, as an evolutionary response that supports the continuity of the feedback cycle. There is no need to sit in meditation to 'achieve' the witnessing awareness mode. Witnessing is available as a conscious choice, and it can be habituated through practice.

Witnessing is neither a conceptual structure mediated by language, nor a superego (or higher self) that analyzes what presents itself in the inner experience. It is simply a mirroring process, active in all life processes on Earth, translated into our psyche as the experience of being alive and wide-awake.[9]

10. Witnessing awareness is an evolutionary feature, slowly developing in humans and other life forms, enhancing the conscious experience. This advanced *feedback processing* also develops in humans as *meta-cognition* (cognition about cognition), *meta-emotions* (secondary emotions, generated by primary-reactive emotions), and other types of meta-reflective processing. The witnessing experience seems directly connected to the early local recurrent and late top-down feedback processes in our brain, as well as all feedback mechanisms in our body, which maintain homeostasis and provide adaptation and support for life processes.

11. Witnessing is a *fluid experience*, a dynamic process, not a static 'component' of the conscious experience. It flows moment to moment. As life's intelligence evolves, this perceptual ability also evolves, becoming richer and more complex. However, this evolutionary feature is at its earliest stage of development in humans, and it seems to reach its full potential in the post-autonomous stages of inner growth, through in-depth inner work and long-term efforts to de-automatize the psychological system and educate the attentional mechanisms.

12. Attention is the part of life's intelligence that monitors and enhances the adaptive processing of stimuli from various sources, internal and external. While monitoring the global workspace of automatic processing, attention selects the stimuli that have or need *increased processing*. After selection, the body's intelligence increases their processing through various mechanisms, including awareness and cognition. Thus, a *conscious experience* related to the stimuli is generated.

――

Through witnessing, it is possible to attend to certain information flows unfolding in all three stages—basic, preconscious, and conscious. The feedback loops that regulate attentional mechanisms happen in all stages; still, we can only *intervene intentionally* in the automatic *attentional configuration* while the processing is in the third stage. In this stage, cognition is involved; and choice making and meta-attention (attention to attention) are also available, usually through attention training.

However, it is possible to alter some parts of the automatic attentional structure which regulate the second (pre-conscious) stage, but it doesn't happen instantly. It takes two steps to do it: first, the attention style is changed, in the conscious stage, by using cognition and repetition; then, while allowing a few months for these changes to habituate and become automatic, the intentional control is progressively reduced and handed over to the automatic processing.[12]

13. The conscious experience is enhanced by *dividing attention* to include narrow focus and global focus, at the same time, and also the immersed and objective ways simultaneously.

———

We can have an *objective* style of paying attention, looking at things as if from outside, as an objective/detached observer, or we can be *immersed/absorbed* in the experience, being in contact with all the objects in our attentional field. In the transformation process, it is necessary to break the addiction to *narrow* focus (tunnel vision) and to use a type of attention named *diffuse/wide* attention (global vision), or attention to the big picture. Through practice, all this flexibility of attention (narrow/wide, objective/immersed) can be included simultaneously in the attentional configuration.[13]

Usually, when we talk about meaningful emotional experiences from the past, they tend to attract our attention and make us re-live the past, forgetting about the present. Through practice, we can learn to divide the focus and simultaneously keep both the past and the present moment information.

An exercise: begin to tell a story from the past, including all the emotional aspects, while paying attention to the present-moment environment. And try to stay both in the present and in the past. This will help you differentiate between the information sent to you by memory engrams and the information sent to you by here-now stimuli. Then, include them together in your conscious experience.

14. During adaptive processing, *perspective filters* are naturally created as coherent patterns of various information flows, such as awareness, cognition systems, attentional streams, memory, sensory perception, energy patterns, and self-identity. These patterns are then used to attend to the present moment.

15. *Perspective-taking* is the process a person uses to filter reality via various vantage points, or lenses, which select information sources and create meaning.

———

The perspective is our vantage point of view, a specific way we use our resources to look around. A broader perspective means to see a larger context, a higher complexity. The perspective provides inner configurations, similar to a set of lenses with various colors and opacity levels; these configurations 'modulate' the perceptual field and, as a result, the conscious experience may be larger or smaller, more profound or not, with more or less flexibility.[15]

16. The perspective-taking generates highly subjective knowledge about reality, as it is conditioned by personal experiences, body functioning, group experiences, culture, and civilization habits.

17. Organic life on Earth developed collective patterns of functioning through the evolutionary process, reflected in human inner experience as collective root tendencies. These natural tendencies organize the adaptive processing in our body layers, generating various *functional patterns* inside the conscious experience, common to all humans.

Further reading: 'An Exploratory Analysis of Collective Patterns of Conscious Experience Using a Self-Report Questionnaire', by Ovidiu Brazdău, Sona Ahuja, Cristian-Dan Opariuc, Valita Jones, Sadhna Sharma, Carlo Monsanto, Sperry Andrews, and Keith Fiveson, available at www.ncbi.nlm.nih.gov/pmc/articles/PMC8414250.

"This study is an exploration of collective patterns of conscious experience, as described by various psychological models, using a self-report questionnaire: The Consciousness Quotient Inventory (CQ-i).[...] A set of 237 items covering major aspects of the subjective conscious experience was selected to detect the phenomenal patterns of subjective conscious experience. An exploratory factor analysis on a large sample (N = 2,360), combined with our previous meta-research on conceptual convergence of conscious experiences, revealed that these experiences appear to have 15 patterns common to all of us.[...]

In this research, our approach was focused on studying the conscious experience, not the philosophical concept of consciousness. From the psychological perspective, the conscious experience is just another variable that describes first-person experiences. We did not analyze theories of consciousness or propose a new theory of consciousness; instead, we indexed the repertoire of experiences already classified as 'conscious/explicit'. In our view, consciousness is a natural stage in the evolution of life on Earth, so, instead of proposing a 'unified theory of consciousness', which is beyond our capabilities, we followed the procedure described by the assessment standards: indexing first-person reports using a new questionnaire, adapting it to comply with the assessment standards, creating a list of experiences and situations, asking individuals to reply if their personal experience includes these situations and how often, then gathering a statistically significant sample, and detecting the patterns that already exist in human experience. Our purpose was to treat the conscious experience as a variable and find a way to use it in psychological assessment, to support the psychological research on consciousness by providing more sub-variables/scales."[17]

18. Root tendencies are barely accessible to our conscious awareness. Still, through in-depth self-exploration, it is possible to attend to their flows and adjust their effects in our inner life through conscious interventions. The collective root tendencies provide the initial structure for the personal *vāsanās/samskaras*, identified and described by Advaita, Yoga, Buddhism, and their practitioners; vāsanās/samskaras are sub-conscious drives and psychological imprints that automatically influence our thoughts, emotions, and behavior.

Swami Sivananda explains: "Vasanas are very subtle. Just as the sprout or flower exists in the seed, the vasanas lie dormant or latent in the heart. They agitate the bed of samskaras. Through agitation of samskaras or subtle impressions, memory of pleasure comes. Through memory of pleasure, desire arises. When desire arises, the senses begin to function in conjunction with their leader—the mind.[...] A mind that is filled with impure vasanas tends to bondage, whereas a mind that is destitute of Vasanas tends to freedom. Mind is no mind when the Vasanas are destroyed. You become mindless. When you become mindless, intuition dawns, and you are endowed with the eye of wisdom. You will enjoy indescribable peace."[18]

19. From an experiential, first-person perspective, there are *three essential layers of reality* we can attend to, through the body: physical-material, energy, information, all taking place in space, as a container of these three layers, generating *multidimensional dynamics* inside the conscious experience. These reality layers are reflected in the human experience as interpenetrating body layers.

Space, matter (including cellular life), energy, and information seem to be fundamental forms of bookkeeping. These layers are interconnected and interpenetrating; their dynamics unfold in connection with one another, and they are permanently in motion. Their dynamics develop due to their embedded laws of motion, while 'the whole' allows various degrees of liberty for their mutual exchanges.

Todd Duncan and Jack Semura in 'The Deep Physics Behind the Second Law: Information and Energy as Independent Forms of Bookkeeping' explain: "We pursue the notion that the second law is ultimately a restriction operating directly on the dynamics of information, so the existence of this law can be traced to the need for a system of 'information bookkeeping' that is independent of the bookkeeping for energy. Energy and information are related but independent, so the dynamical restrictions for one cannot be derived from those for the other.[...] When energy and information are exchanged between two systems, the dynamics of energy exchange does not uniquely determine the information exchanged."[19]

20. *Physical Body layer* consists of physical matter and its organizations in cells, organs, and systems of cells. Their dynamics are reflected in our inner experience through various external and internal senses, including sound, vision, touch, smell, internal organ sense, hunger, thirst, suffocation, pain, temperature, body position, balance, spatial orientation, movement, muscle and organs tensions, blood pressure, connectivity with other life forms, or other specific body processes.

21. *Energy Body layer* includes the energy exchanges that occur in our physical body, owing to various forces or phenomena, e.g., chemical forces, electromagnetism, gravity, body heat, food processing, breath. The energy body is the result of life processes, doing 'work' to maintain the functioning of a human being, perceived in various ways, e.g., emotions, feelings, flowing sensations, vital energy, sexual drives, cognitive energy, kundalini waves, energetic effects from human interactions (or from other

life forms and nature), and various other energy-related sensations and perceptions.

22. *Information Body layer* incorporates various types of information exchanges between the cells and cell systems, as well as complex adaptive processing, such as awareness, cognition, attention, perspective-taking, language and meanings, intelligence, social and interpersonal information exchanges, connections with the intelligence of other life forms, and information from various resonance dynamics of life on Earth.

23. A good *multi-modal integration* enhances the conscious experience. Multi-modal integration refers to a harmonic integration of awareness related to body layers (physical, energy, and information). Memory and self-identity are embedded in all layers. That's why, during the inner evolution process, one has to consider working with the patterns in all three body layers. The integration process is supported by a global attentional style, which keeps various flows of awareness together, in a synesthetic-like style.

————

The most common integration pattern is the psychosomatic integration resulting from interactions between the mind, body, and emotions. These are some patterns of pre-emotional responses, as described by Carlo Monsanto: "Fear-control (controlling)—distrust, restless, controlling, tension, stiffness, cramp, contraction, stinging cold/sudden temperature change, electric-like sensation, giddiness, nausea, bloated (aversion); Sadness-anger (victimizing)—burning, uncomfortable heat, prickly/oversensitive, irritated, swollen, inflammation; Rejection-disassociation (isolating)—heavy, blocking, pressing, disconnecting, absent, lethargic, too much sleep, constantly feeling tired; Powerlessness (paralyzing)—a combination of all three pre-emotional responses: feels painful, blocked, tensed; as if paralyzed. Other pre-emotional patterns are feverish (processing), vibrating (balancing), and happy (flowing)."[23]

This is one of the exercises developed by Carlo Monsanto, that increases the psychosomatic integration: "Close your eyes. Begin by noticing everything occurring inside your body. Can you feel the difference between the left and right side of your body? One side may feel heavier or larger, more present or absent, shifted moreforward, up, or down; more or less tense, painful or heavy. Now, witness what you sense in the left side of the body and then the right. Allow yourself to notice all that you can sense physically and emotionally. By being aware of everything, all at once, our mind attaches to 'space'.

By recognizing and acknowledging what you sense, experience is transformed, and the mind becomes quieter. As your mind stops searching for resolution, it calms down. The key here is not to react to, but to recognize and acknowledge what is noticed. Through fully conscious awareness, which is neither internal nor external, and a heightened form of discernment, you learn to recognize these pre-emotional responses. Be open to see how what you sense and feel is transformed as you bring more awareness to what you feel. Within your mind and body, notice everything that's calling your attention. If you feel your emotions are overwhelming, you may also be able to notice that you're afraid of losing control over whatever you're not-yet used to 'allowing'. Notice if you resist and deny what you are feeling. Go through this process by simply noticing and allowing.

Are you able to notice what you think, sense, feel and intuit without 'trying' to change or solve it? Our mind remains restless if these pre-emotions are not adequately absorbed by choiceless awareness.[...] Restlessness disrupts our ability to focus. It makes us feel unsafe and insecure. What's more, our mistaken sense of reality may make us misinterpret our circumstances and relationships, imagining obstacles where there aren't any.

Notice how you are experiencing from a place that is always open and receptive. As you learn to see 'what is', without the need to change 'what is', you will notice how being a 'discerning embodied witness' reorganizes even the most troublesome responses, forever."[23]

24. Increasing the *clarity of discrimination* is essential for conscious experience. Clarity of discrimination refers to selecting/discriminating various stimuli, facets, and subsystems of the conscious experience. It also means perceiving and responding to differences and multiple changes in the inner and outer environment.

———

Discrimination is an embedded feature of life's adaptive processing, usually running in the background and appearing in conscious experience only when necessary. 'Clarity of discrimination' seems to have strong conceptual links with concepts such as viveka (Sanskrit concept meaning 'discernment or discrimination') and *sati sampajañña* (a concept from Buddhism, usually translated as 'clear comprehension').[24]

25. There are a variety of inner configurations available to humans, generating common states of consciousness, such as the waking state, relaxation, dreaming, deep sleep, transitions before or after sleep, daydreaming, creativity, trance states (zone/flow), or rare states such as lucid dreaming, high-energy experiences (*kundalini* spikes), *samadhi*, each of them having various stages of depth and variations.

26. Using witnessing awareness, we can attend to some structures and contents of the body's adaptive processing even while dreaming or experiencing deep sleep. These inner configurations are known as witnessing dreams, witnessing deep sleep, and *turiya*. In the Upanishads, turiya is described as the fourth state of consciousness that could run in the background of all states, such as

waking, sleeping, dreaming, or samadhi. Turiya is generated by a specific configuration of the witnessing awareness mode.

——

Through witnessing, it is possible to keep a 'raw' self-reflection even during deep sleep, which is perceived as an echo of the 'I am' experience, without content, that could be described in this way: 'I am aware, but there is no content in awareness, just awareness of empty awareness'.[26a]

Charles Alexander, in 'Dream Lucidity and Dream Witnessing: A Developmental Model Based on the Practice of Transcendental Meditation', says: "Ordinary waking and sleeping is a cycle: you're awake, you're asleep, you're dreaming, you're in deep sleep, you're dreaming again, and eventually waking again.[...] The Vedic tradition proposes that underlying these changing states of consciousness, and from which they arise, is an unchanging continuum of pure consciousness.[...] A unified field of consciousness from which the diverse changing states of consciousness arise. This unified field of consciousness is described as transcendental consciousness or a fourth state of consciousness, distinct from waking, dreaming and sleeping. It's said to have the character of restful alertness. That the individual is, at the same time, very settled, as he or she would be in sleep or dreaming, including deep sleep. On the other hand they're increasingly wakeful and alert within. So that it also shares the attribute of enhanced alertness, as in the waking state.

This fourth state of consciousness combines these dual characteristics in one state by being increasingly awake and aware and yet in a very settled, silent state, both metabolically and phenomenologically/psychologically. This state is said to be purely content free.[...] 'All that it is' is a simple experience of 'Self' or 'am'ness; an experience of one's inner being. It's a state of being. It's a state of knowingness, rather than a state of knowing particulars, like I am a boy or I am a girl, or I've done this or I will do that. All that is transcended, and all that's left is consciousness as a field, aware of itself, alone without anything else in that awareness: no thoughts, no feelings, no perceptions."[26b]

27. Conscious experience is enhanced if the perspective is trained to include attention to space, as a permanent part of the attentional structure. This creates a new type of awareness, known as *spatial awareness*, sometimes described by mystics and philosophers as the void-like nature of conscious experience.

———

In 'Attention to Attention', Les Fehmi writes: "Appropriately shifting emphasis from narrow to diffuse and from objective to absorbed styles of attention, to the feelings of pain and body and *space* simultaneously, dissolves even the most extreme pains. Most notable among pains that have dissolved in response to this technique are those in relation to birthing, kidney stones, interstitial cystitis, endometriosis, ulcers, irritable bowel syndrome, back pain, headaches, colitis and phantom limb pain. It is not unusual for this pain-dissolving attention technique to bring about long-term remission of symptoms. In addition, emotional pains such as anxiety, panic, depression, feelings of guilt, loss and failure also have dissolved."[27]

28. By consciously using the *perspective*, the *attentional* structures, and the connection with *space*, we can participate in the present moment with more richness, connecting with multiple layers of reality in creative ways.

29. The natural events in our lives create specific patterns of thinking, feeling, sensing, and acting. In time, they habituate as a psychological self-identity, a unique personality. *Self-identity* is a habituated way of experiencing life.

In the Consciousness Quotient construct, Global Self-Identity includes traits, skills, and abilities related to identity, self-system, one's image of life, self-awareness, the ability to see oneself as objectively as possible, flexibility in self-related thinking (e.g., the ability to make and appreciate jokes about the way we are), self-compassion, self-kindness, and awareness of goals/direction in life. It also includes meta-skills related to post-autonomous stages of inner growth and psychological maturity, such as awareness of self as a construct, awareness of subpersonalities, being aware and connected to the feeling of 'life flowing through', non-reactivity to inner experiences, sense of wonder regarding everyday activities, serving as catalyst for other people, 'use of language' awareness, overall flexibility and acceptance of various types of experiences, and good present-moment awareness.

The self-identity is a fundamental part of our inner life, a dynamic structure that can be changed and adjusted. It is an intelligent tool that transforms its own shape through preferences and choices, reinforcing its strength through the repetition of preferences and choices.[29]

30. Specific and repeated events in our lives form a web of patterns that activates in specific circumstances, generating *subpersonalities*, mini-identities adapted to that specific event/topic.

31. In the inner evolution journey, observation of the subpersonalities is the premise for becoming an authentic human being. In time, we can integrate all the subpersonalities into one *fluid identity*, and we can live in contact with the totality of ourselves in each moment. To do this integration, first we need to notice the subpersonalities and then create a system of life-values that can apply to all subpersonalities. Using this method, we get a coherent structure that allows us to be authentic all the time, while adapting our behavior to each specific context.

32. The *Consciousness Quotient* is a composite psychological construct, including traits, skills, and abilities that allow us to explore and optimize the conscious experience.

The everyday Consciousness Quotient is the habituated level of being conscious that is experienced in the morning, one hour after waking up and after having had a refreshing sleep, without being exposed to any significant stimulus (coffee, TV, radio, music, talking, or psychological stress, social interactions, food). The Consciousness Quotient model (version 2020) includes the following patterns and facets of the conscious experience: perspective-taking, clarity of discrimination, quality of experience, spirituality-harmony, global self-identity, language use, physical self, energy self, cognition self, non-conceptual self, social-relational interconnectivity, inner growth, multi-modal integration, habitual patterns, awakening skills.[32]

33. An *enhanced Consciousness Quotient* means a higher degree of witnessing awareness and being less automatic in thinking, feeling, sensing, and interacting with people and the environment, together with a higher degree of choice when initiating a behavior. It also means a better capacity for connecting with life and experiencing fresh aliveness through the body.

The Consciousness Quotient Inventory (CQ-i) is a self-assessment tool that evaluates patterns of behaviors, attitudes, attentional styles, and the usage of conscious skills, awareness, and the capacity to 'feel awake and alive', providing a complex exploration of conscious experience. The CQ-i was developed through 18 studies across 17 years (2003-2020) and provides standardized ratings using the already familiar style of the Intelligence Quotient and Emotional Quotient (mean = 100). CQ-i scores are classified into six intervals with inclusive labels, selected to reflect the evolution in the capacity for being conscious.

The 6-level classification is the same for the global score and the scales scores: emerging (significantly below average); basic (moderately below average); balanced (average range); well-balanced (average range); enhanced (moderately above average); heightened (significantly above average).[33]

The Consciousness Quotient Inventory assessment is available online. A descriptive summary of the results is available at no cost, providing the minimal information needed to understand your results (www.consciousness-quotient.com).

Chapter Two

Inner Evolution Drives

34. Life on Earth is a continuous flow of change; collective adaptation and evolution unfold continuously in every human being, driven by internal and external circumstances.

35. Inner evolution happens when *unexpected* events, whether personal, social, or planetary, require adaptation to new circumstances.

36. Along with the temporary drives requiring adaptation to unexpected issues in life, ten evolutionary drives can generate and sustain accelerated *transformative waves* in individuals.

37. Giving birth to life
   This evolutionary drive provides the energy for the procreation and education of human descendants.

38. *Connect and align*
   The drive to comply and align to group values and beliefs (including religious ones), by conforming and adjusting to collective cultural values and civilization rules, and achieving group ideals.

39. *No more!*
   This drive sustains the evolutionary processes, ignited by life issues such as dramas, traumas, failures, or conflicts. It relates to 'cleaning' and healing the effects of unbalanced actions from the past, becoming aware and integrating personal or transgenerational patterns, or solving personal problems.

40. *What's this?*
   This is the evolutionary drive toward understanding and generating new knowledge and wisdom.

41. *Being human*

This is the drive toward developing a healthy identity, sustaining the journey toward maturity, realizing autonomy, self-actualizing, finding unity, and adopting Being-values.

————

The Being-values were introduced by Abraham Maslow, in his studies on human evolution and maturity. These values are indicators of psychological health; Maslow named them 'meta-needs', to distinguish between 'ordinary' need motivation, based on deficiency, and the motives of self-actualizing individuals.

"*Wholeness* – unity, integration, tendency to oneness, interconnectedness, simplicity, organization, structure, dichotomy-transcendence, order.

Perfection – necessity, just-right-ness, just-so-ness, inevitability, suitability, justice, completeness.

Completion – ending, finality, justice, 'it's finished', fulfillment, destiny, fate.

Justice – fairness, orderliness, lawfulness.

Aliveness – process, non-deadness, spontaneity, self-regulation, full-functioning.

Richness – differentiation, complexity, intricacy.

Simplicity – honesty, nakedness, essentiality, abstract, essential, skeletal structure.

Beauty – rightness, form, aliveness, simplicity, richness, wholeness, perfection, completion, uniqueness, honesty.

Goodness – rightness, desirability, oughtness, justice, benevolence, honesty.

Uniqueness – idiosyncrasy, individuality, non-comparability, novelty.

Effortlessness – ease, lack of strain, striving or difficulty, grace, perfect, beautiful functioning.

Playfulness – fun, joy, amusement, gaiety, humor, exuberance, effortlessness.

Truth – honesty, reality, nakedness, simplicity, richness, oughtness, beauty, pure, clean and unadulterated, completeness, essentiality.

Self-sufficiency – autonomy, independence, not-needing-other-than-itself-in-order-to-be-itself, self-determining, environment-transcendence, separateness, living by its own laws."[41]

42. *Sattva*

This drive motivates and sustains the journey toward harmony and freedom, usually through spirituality. Sattva is one of the three tendencies of nature ('gunas'), described by Eastern philosophies as the quality of 'being light' (as opposed to restlessness and heaviness). Sattva also refers to goodness, positivity, truth, serenity, balance, and peacefulness. The other two tendencies of nature are *rajas*, oriented toward passion, activity, and motion, and *tamas*, related to confusion and inertia.

The three tendencies of nature are described by Vyasa in the *Bhagavad Gita*, in the dialogue between Krishna—one of the deities from the Hindu pantheon—and Arjuna, the main character of this epic saga. The following quote is an excerpt from chapter 14, and it was edited for fluency. In this text, *jiva* refers to the individual soul, *prakriti* to nature, *purusha* to spirit or universal soul; the nine gates are the eyes, ears, mouth, nostrils, anus, and genitals.

"Whatever forms are produced, in all different wombs, the great Prakriti is their mother, and the Purusha is the father. [The three Gunas are] Sattva or goodness, Rajas or activity, and Tamas or inertia. These three Gunas bind the imperishable soul to the body.

Of these, Sattva, being calm, is illuminating and ethical. It chains the embodied being, the Jivatma or Purusha, by at-

tachment to happiness and knowledge. Rajas is characterized by intense, is born of desire and attachment, and it
binds the Jiva by attachment to the fruits of their work.
Tamas, the deluder of Jiva, is born of inertia, and it binds
by ignorance, laziness, and sleep.

Sattva attaches the individual to happiness, Rajas to action, and Tamas to ignorance, by covering the knowledge.[...] When the lamp of knowledge shines through all
the nine gates of the body, then it should be known that
Sattva is predominant.

Greed, activity, restlessness, passion, and undertaking of
[selfish] activities, arise when Rajas is predominant. Ignorance, inactivity, carelessness, and delusion arise when
Tamas is predominant.[...] The fruit of good action is said
to be Sattvika and pure, the fruit of Rajasika action is pain,
and the fruit of Tamasika action is ignorance.

Knowledge arises from Sattva, desires arise from Rajas, and
negligence, delusion, and ignorance arise from Tamas.[...]
When visionaries perceive no doer, other than the Gunas,
and know That which is above and beyond the Gunas, they
attain Nirvana. When one transcends the three Gunas, one
is freed from birth, old age, disease, and death."[42]

43. *Feel alive*
This is the evolutionary tendency to immerse oneself in the experience of being alive.

44. *What's beyond?*
This drive generates evolution through curiosity and exploration.

45. *Support and protect life*
This is the collective drive to take care of life in all its forms.

46. Innovate and share
This is the evolutionary drive to generate innovative ways of being and living.

47. These evolutionary drives run in the background of conscious experience and shape the individual's inner journey toward fulfilling its evolutionary goal, which supports collective evolution.

48. The transformative waves generated by these drives could extend over *many years or decades.*

49. A transformative wave begins with a *challenge*, when an issue is presented to the global workspace of conscious awareness, followed by some *chaos* when new information is flooding inner experience. Then the wave reaches a *peak*, when the 'chaos' is structured into *new patterns*, generating a *shift* (unfolding as insights, energy re-arrangements, ecstatic states, new perspectives, awakenings, decisions, etc.), usually followed by *integration*. This will eventually lead to a new structure of personality (self-identity) or new ways of being alive. It can be unhealthy to enter the new personality before the transformative wave has slowed down naturally.

––––

Occasionally, a *premature re-entry into consensual reality* (expressed as 'that's it, I'm done with this process') can destabilize automatic processing and overload conscious processing. This can generate temporary side-effects such as hypersensitivities, thinking loops, emotional instability, psychosomatic issues, psychosis-like mental content, paranoid thoughts, delusions, depersonalization, or exaggeratedly positive side-effects (e.g., 'all is love', 'all is light'). If this is the case, remember that the conscious content is just 10-20% of all the processing, and it is healthier to allow life's intelligence to carry on by itself, rather than trying to 'control' the process too much. Instead, you might adapt more quickly and temporarily change certain components of your lifestyle to support the transformation. Eventually, when the evolutionary wave reaches its destination, the transformative energy will slow down by itself.

50. A transformative wave ends when that specific adaptation is acquired, the specific need has been satisfied, and the evolutionary seed unfolds. Multiple rounds of chaos/adaptation cycles could occur before the drive is satisfied. Some evolutionary drives are active for a very long time, or through the entire life of an individual, and their effects could be mistakenly considered as 'stable personality traits'.

51. It's natural for these drives to be depleted if the change requires a broad adaptation that cannot be acquired in one or a few transformative waves. Sometimes a drive may activate again, generating another attempt to synchronize. Sometimes it remains inactive, and the drive energy is 'reassigned' by life's intelligence to follow the natural pace of collective evolution.

52. More than one drive may be active simultaneously in an individual, at a given time, generating inner experiences with enhanced complexity and aliveness. For any individual who wants to understand what's emerging now in the inner life, it is helpful to become aware of these active transformative waves, noticing whether the wave is peaking, or the energy is before or after the peak.

———

Water fasting for a few days may be helpful during intense transformative waves, oriented toward cleaning and healing, followed by healthy and nutritious food. Due to intense internal re-arrangements occurring during the wave's peak, one's energy consumption may be higher than usual. A lot of water is needed to support the homeostatic processes of the body. If the transformative wave is oriented toward clarity and harmony, avoiding meat and processed food is a good choice. If the wave generates too much cognitive activity that overloads the mind, intense physical activities are helpful. If the mind is hugely overloaded, it is helpful to introduce meat and physical activities in nature. Other methods that have proven helpful for managing aliveness levels, and organizing 'chaos' into 'patterns', are writing in a journal, working with dreams, and expressing content through arts, singing, and dancing. If possible, introducing naps or a polyphasic sleep routine allows a better management of the energy consumption/regeneration cycle. Still, polyphasic sleep seems to reduce dreaming time, so it needs to be used carefully.[52a]

During some peaks of transformative waves, the patterns of brain functioning may be altered, and transitional states usually appearing before or after sleep could emerge during daily activities, adding an extra layer to conscious experience; this may feel unusual for individuals not accustomed to these altered states of consciousness.

Daniel Yetman in 'What is Hypnagogia, the State Between Wakefulness and Sleep?' writes: "Hypnagogia is the transitional state of consciousness between wakefulness and sleep. It's the opposite of hypnopompia, which is the transitional state that occurs before you wake up. During hypnagogia, it's common to experience involuntary and imagined experiences. These are referred to as hypnagogic hallucinations. Up to 70 percent of people experience these hallucinations, which can appear in the form of sights, sounds, or even feelings of movement. Muscle jerks, sleep paralysis, and lucid dreams are also common during the hypnagogic phase.[...] Some people purposefully try to induce hypnagogia to stimulate creativity. Thomas Edison and Edgar Allan Poe are among the creatives who have used this technique."[52b]

Chapter Three

Developmental Maps

53. Inner evolution has two main components: *inner growth* (growing up) is a journey toward maturity, by learning to develop a harmonic, healthy, and fluid self-identity, while the *awakening journeys* (waking up) add new depths and facets to our conscious experience of being alive, open and connected with ourselves and life.

——

In the beginning, the theories and research of Western psychology have focused on the evolution of personality, from basic levels to self-actualization, which was considered to be the most mature evolutionary stage. These approaches are found in the works of Piaget, Freud, Erikson, Kohlberg, and Maslow. Advancing on these paths, a new series of theories and researchers describe 'trans-personal' and post-autonomous stages of inner growth. These approaches are found in the works of Graves, Kegan, Loevinger, Wilber, Beck and Cowan, Washburn, Wade, Grof, Torbert, O'Fallon, and Cook-Greuter.[53a]

Corey W. de Vos, in a comment on 'A New Republic of the Heart: The Art and Practice of Sacred Activism'—a book by Terry Patten and Ken Wilber, writes: "We often talk about the 'Four Ups' of integral living: Growing Up, Waking Up, Cleaning Up, and Showing Up. The first three all have to do with our 'inner work', the often-grueling personal work we do within our own consciousness and closest relationships. But the fourth—Showing Up—is where the fruits of our labor truly begin to ripen, where all of our accumulated knowledge, personal growth, spiritual practice, and shadow work become a limitless source of strength, presence, and wisdom, allowing to us engage the many di-

mensions and challenges of our world in a far more meaningful and impactful way, from becoming a better parent,
to becoming a better leader, to becoming a better citizen
of the world.

After all, if our practice does not help us to show up more
fully in the world, if it does not compel us to enact real
change within each of our own spheres of influence, if it
does not equip us to directly confront the many terrors and
tragedies of our collective unfolding with fearless compassion and skillful action, then what's the point? If the sum
total of our practice cannot benefit the world around us,
exactly what (or whom) are we practicing for?"[53b]

54. Inner Growth, the journey toward psychological maturity and
a fluid self-identity, unfolds in *developmental stages*, from birth to
adulthood, while one's mental frameworks/worldviews evolve
from egocentric (me) to ethnocentric (my family, my group), so-
ciocentric (my community, my nation), worldcentric (all of us),
planet-centric (all beings, the Earth), and cosmocentric (all that
exists, the universe). Caring, love, respect, and deep connection
with nature and life are available at any stage of development.

————

In the Consciousness Quotient model, inner growth is related to the evolution of personality, paradigm shifts, un-
learning and learning (through pain or by open learning),
openness, the language updating process, accepting criticism, abandoning old perspectives and embracing new
ones, noticing resistance to change, learning after peak experiences, detecting the cognitive biases related to learning (e.g., confirmation bias), resilience, awareness of one's
level of inner growth, and an ability to sustain new patterns
of thinking/feeling while old habits slowly lose their grip
(awareness of the process of neuroplasticity).[54]

55. Developmental psychologists have identified *specific characteristics for each stage*, which seem to be similar among all the people

at that specific stage of inner growth and maturity, in all cultures. The healthy transition through stages develops in a *logical sequence*. Later stages are reached by transitioning through the previous stages, incorporating their perspectives, structures, and patterns into a larger, more flexible, and connected self-identity. Later stages are not happier or more adjusted; each stage has its challenges.

————

In 'Nine Levels of Increasing Embrace in Ego Development: A Full-Spectrum Theory of Vertical Growth and Meaning Making', Susanne Cook-Greuter explains: "Ego[/Self] development is a theory of the consolidation at various levels of identity formation (translation, horizontal expansion) as well as of potential transformation from one view of reality to a broader, more inclusive one. It describes a sequence of how people's mental models of reality evolve over time. Each new level contains the previous ones as subsets. This is best illustrated with a set of Russian dolls, each nested within another[...]. Thus, each new level is both a new whole with its own coherence, and—at the same time— also a part of a larger, more complex system.[...] Derailment in development, pockets of lack of integration, trauma, and psychopathology are seen at all levels. Thus, later stages are not more adjusted or happier."[55a]

These are the inner growth stages, and the estimation of the population on each stage, based on Cook-Greuter's research on the adult US population:

Symbiotic stage:
  – all infants

Preconventional: ~10%
  1. Impulsive
  2. Self-Protective (Opportunist, Self-centric)

Conventional: ~75%
  3. Conformist (Diplomat, Rule-Oriented, Group-centric)
  4. Expert (Self-conscious, Skill-centric)
  5. Achiever (Conscientious, Self-determining)

Post-conventional: ~12%
6. Individualist-Pluralist (Self-questioning)
7. Autonomous (Self-actualizing, Strategist)

Post-autonomous:
8. Construct-aware (Ego/Self-aware): <2%
9. Unitive (Ego/Self-Transcendent): < 1%

Terri O'Fallon observed that the post-autonomous stages could be refined even further. She proposed four stages for post-autonomous development; however, due to the rare occurrences of such stages in individuals across the globe, these stages are still debated by the developmental research community. These are the post-autonomous stages, according to Terri O'Fallon:

– Construct-aware (Ego/Self-aware)
– Transpersonal
– Universal
– Illumined.[55b]

56. During inner growth, individuals become increasingly aware of the psychological mechanisms that generate their inner experience, while expanding from *concrete contents* of inner experience (e.g., facts, events, social interactions, sensations, thoughts, emotions), to *psychological-philosophical contents* (e.g., how thinking happens, why emotions occur, how self-identity develops, the use of paradigms, philosophical processing), to *continuous real-time attending to meta-reflective processing*, such as witnessing awareness, meta-attention, meta-awareness, meta-cognition, meta-emotions, self-identity and subpersonalities dynamics, perspective-taking mechanisms, collective awareness.

––––

Terri O'Fallon and collaborators, in 'The Validation of a New Scoring Method for Assessing Ego Development Based on Three Dimensions of Language', write: "[Each tier] specifies the general type of object one is aware of. By object we are referring generally to anything one can focus one's awareness on and refer to, including physical things, subjective experiences, processes, properties, abstract ideas, etc.

Concrete stages apprehend concrete objects of which there are two types. First are phenomena that are perceivable through a direct experience of the exterior senses. Examples include cars, a church, or rules in sports and card games. Second are those same phenomena that one can experience through their interior senses (visualization, interior hearing, and interior feelings or emotions).

Subtle stages apprehend more abstract objects, including phenomena that one cannot form distinct and accurate images of, or hear sounds about, or touch as they do with their exterior or interior senses. Examples include brainstorming, reasoning, contexts, complex adaptive systems, models, values, determinism, democracy, and square roots. Entrance into the Subtle tier corresponds roughly to the transition from Piaget's Concrete Operational to Formal Operational thinking and includes abilities in the arena of abstract, logical, and systematic reasoning.

MetAware stages apprehend even more subtle objects such as the capacity to examine one's awareness of concrete and subtle objects to clearly determine the previously assumed constructions of the mind such as word meaning, boundaries, and the reification of time and space. MetAware 'objects' are more similar to processes or properties that are perceived to permeate, pervade, or underlie reality or experience. Examples include what has been called witnessing of consciousness or experiencing ideas or identity formation in the mind as it happens (and thus experiencing the emptiness aspect of the self or the meaning-making processes). Fullness is a characteristic as well as emptiness, for instance, experiencing a sense of oneness, life energy, or beauty pervading everything."[56a]

In 'Seven Perspectives on the Stages Developmental Model', Kim Barta writes:

"The first tier is concrete.[...] This is based upon our concrete senses of sight, sound, touch, taste, smell, and movement. We can also see the extensions of these with tools like telescopes and microscopes, radio waves, and others; these are all just tools to extend the capacity of our concrete senses. As we move through,[...] we can perceive subtle awarenesses too, helping us move into the subtle tier. However, our subtle awarenesses, like imagination, are still based upon concrete items. For example, we can visualize a tree, or a house or a friend, or running through the streets with a friend. But we won't be able to visualize a strategic plan or the dynamic of how memes and emotional energy are passed through the family system.

The second tier is the subtle tier. In the subtle tier, we sense subtle objects. These subtle objects are different from concrete objects.[...] In the subtle tier, we can witness the passing of memes and emotional energy from one person or group to another and how those memes and energies affect people as they are moved around. In the concrete tier, we can think or cognate about anything. But we can't meta-cognate. We cannot analyze and think about our thinking itself. We can have rich emotions, but we can't have meta-emotions, feelings about feeling. In the subtle tier, we can think about thinking, feel about feeling, think about feeling, and feel about thinking. It is this meta-capacity of thoughts and emotions that signals a clear shift into the subtle tier.

In the third tier, the MetAware tier, we are able to sense MetAware objects. This is a perception of mind awareness itself without concrete or subtle objects at all. We may include them, but we may exclude them as well, just like in the subtle tier when two philosophers talk about the nature of thought, neither may ever mention a concrete object. So too, when in the MetAware tier, one can experience mind without a concrete object or even a subtle object. The mind is tuned to awareness of mind vs. thought.

Each tier can hold the previous tier but within a larger whole. In each tier, our senses get more refined. They are more able to perceive finer sensorial stimuli. This does not mean our concrete senses themselves get more refined. We may go blind and deaf and still be able to sense these more refined sensorial stimuli. Yet, with a twist of irony, it is these same concrete senses, fading away in the concrete world, that are still the seed of our more refined subtle and MetAware sensorial capacities. There is still sight, sound, touch, taste, smell, and movement. Just in a different dimension of awareness."[56b]

57. A person at a more mature stage can understand earlier worldviews, while an individual at an earlier stage cannot understand someone whose center of gravity is at a more mature stage.

58. Most of us simultaneously live within multiple stages; e.g., a sub-personality may be in stage 4 and another one in stage 5. We can feel, act, and react authentically from a unified perspective only after the inner harmonization process has reached a certain maturity.

59. In the journey toward maturity, there are two steps in each transition through developmental stages: *vertical development*, a structural shift in meaning-making, and *horizontal development*, an exploration of the world using the same configuration of being-thinking-feeling-sensing-acting-relating. Both are important and necessary for a healthy evolution of personality.

———

Horizontal development is needed to integrate the vertical configuration upgrades. After people change their ways of meaning-making, it is necessary to use the new way, until it habituates. Neurons need time to form new neural networks, and during this time, both ways are available. Prioritizing and using the new ones: this is the challenge.

Susanne Cook-Greuter in 'Nine Levels of Increasing Embrace in Ego Development: A Full-Spectrum Theory of Vertical Growth and Meaning Making' says: "Most growth in adulthood seems to occur within a given stage, variously described as lateral or horizontal development or 'translation' in Wilber's terminology. The current way of viewing the self and reality is refined, enriched, and modified to include more diverse domains, more contexts and detail, and to establish more connections among them. We learn new skills, new methods, new facts, even new ways of organizing knowledge. The later the stage, the more room for such horizontal expansion exists while the current stage or mental model of the world remains the same. Although rarer, vertical development also occurs over a lifetime. In that case, the whole previous meaning system is transformed and restructured into a new, more expansive and inclusive self-theory and theory of the world."[59]

60. Occasionally, during *peak experiences* or 'altered states of consciousness', a person can temporarily access configurations specific to more mature stages, but without being able to influence the flow. After the peak experience ends, such people tend to interpret the meaning of the peak experiences through their habituated perspectives. Although our psyche allows short-term 'vertical jumps' during peak experiences, these jumps are rare, as many peak experiences facilitate the processes of letting go, connecting, opening, allowing, fluidifying, or awakening experiences, which usually do not transform self-identity structures.

————

A peak experience could be highly transformative and create a structural change in self-identity structure[60], reorganizing the meaning-making patterns, especially if that peak experience is the last piece in the puzzle during a transformative wave. What is the differentiating marker between someone stabilized in a configuration, and someone who is temporary there during a peak experience? It could be *the associated emotion*. For example, a person who temporarily jumps from 4 (expert) to 8 (ego/self-aware) during a peak experience usually floats there by chance on some kind of non-patterned energy release, maybe on a euphoric energy spike. For a person habituated to stage 8, the body-mind is accustomed to this configuration; spikes of energy such as bliss or joy do appear in stage 8, but naturally and occasionally. It is essential to remember that as a potential, all structures, stages, and types of inner configurations are available all the time to everyone, as long as the collective evolutionary process has made them accessible.

61. Even after a stage is habituated, a *regression* of the self-identity center-of-gravity to an earlier stage may happen, due to stressful life events. In these situations, the self-identity returns to the last stable configuration. This is a healthy defense mechanism.

62. Understanding and learning about developmental stages, and consciously using these transformation maps, may reduce the inherent suffering during inner growth by facilitating smooth transitions toward maturity and inner harmony.

––––

These are some features of the main stages of inner growth, as described by Abigail Lynam:

"*Conformist stage* – Late 2nd person perspective: In relationship with another. 'See others seeing them' concretely. Concerned about socially expected behavior, approval, avoids conflict, loyalty to chosen group. Wants to belong. 'One right way' thinking. Can't question group norms. Uses hierarchical thinking to distinguish between levels of morality and appropriateness (good-better-best).

Expert stage – Early 3rd person perspective: Stands back and observes two others interacting and 'objectively sees what is happening' on a subtle interior level. Beginning recognition of one's own ideas separate from social groups. Interested in expertise, procedure, and efficiency; what's logical. Has a hard time prioritizing ideas because they are all good. Black or White thinking; knows the answer and only sees one side of an argument. Tends towards perfectionism."

Achiever stage – Late 3rd person perspective: Interested in rational scientific analysis, success within a system, thinking about thinking. Prioritizes ideas for effectiveness and goal-oriented results. Either/or thinking. Tends to talk at, rather than with. Critical reflective thinking is useful for being more effective in completing tasks and achieving goals.

Individualist-Pluralist stage – Early 4th person perspective: Stands back and sees that the observer is situated in a social context, and therefore subjective. Can see others seeing them on a subtle level. Reciprocal. Knows others can see things in them that they can't see in themselves and has the courage to delve into what others may see, even if they don't like what they hear. Has a hard time prioritizing contexts—relativism. 'Both/and', 'it depends' thinking. Metacognition.

Autonomous (Self-actualizing) stage – Late 4th person perspective: Understands and prioritizes interior and exterior contexts, sees developmental unfolding, shapes contexts to support development of self and others. Works with dynamic systems and paradox, linking theory and practice. Sees that what they judge in others is held within themselves. Interpenetrative, one within the other, paradoxical thinking.

Construct-aware stage – Early 5th person perspective: Stands back and see the previous pattern of observing observers observing, awareness of the constructs we hold, the complexity of meaning-making, witnesses the emptiness of words and illusion of meaning. Has a hard time prioritizing constructs."[62a]

In her research, titled 'States and Stages: Waking up Developmentally', Terri O'Fallon describes some of the developmental confusions specific to various stages of development. These need to be understood in order for a person to evolve. Here are a few examples:

"*Conformist stage:* confuses individual thought and action with collective thought and action. They think that they are making individual decisions and taking individual actions, but their thinking and actions are conformed to their identified group.

Expert stage: 'Who am I?' The individual confuses their Conformist collective identity with their Expert individual identity. They are beginning to make individual decisions and take individual action but cannot identify this difference with the collective thought and action taken in the Conformist stage.

Achiever stage: confuses the 'fantasy/visualizations of the future' with reality. They visualize a goal in the future and believe that it represents the reality that they will reach once the goal is achieved. When they reach their goal, they find that the reality is not the same as their visualizations of the future.

Individualist-Pluralist stage: confuses individual subtle insights/awareness with collective synchronicity. Their group discussions are long and nuanced, and eventually they see a decision emerge. They often label this as synchronicity and do not recognize the process of eliminating thoughts achieved by the group discussion, or the subtle insights that are conditioned in them from subtle social conditioning (social construction of reality). They cannot differentiate between the experience of being socially constructed and their own individuality."[62b]

63. If a person is interested in using the developmental stages map as a *tool for self-evolution*, it is most efficient to do it step by step, while seeking to understand the next two stages of inner growth. One should also do inner work to cultivate the new psychological structures and worldviews, inviting the transformation, rather than trying to reach the later stages of development directly. This process can be facilitated by transformational counselors, who

have been trained in vertical development, evolutionary mentoring, and transformative methodologies.

64. During transitions toward maturity and autonomy, a repeating pattern has been observed. First, the person opens up to a new way of functioning, but they see it as a personal development (*it's about me*). In the next step, they see this new way of functioning in other people, and realize that it is a collective feature (*it's about us*).

65. Non-conceptual experiences (pure consciousness, unity consciousness, transcendental states) are available across various developmental levels; they do not belong to a 'higher' developmental level.

66. Along the inner growth process, a simultaneous evolutionary process could emerge, described as *awakening journeys*. Awakening journeys consist of a continuum of openings and insights about the functioning of life and nature. Each awakening is a transformative experience, felt as a transition toward a more complex and deeper awareness.

67. Awakenings are natural evolutionary processes, each one making a specific contribution to the collective self-reflection process. People all over the world have the same types of openings/awakenings, with a subjective flavor added by their preferred frames of reference.

68. There are various types of openings that can be described as awakenings. An awakening is an opening to new ways of functioning, providing new ways of *being alive and connected* with life.

> Here are some examples of awakening journeys: Awakening from the collective culture-civilization hypnosis; The 'I am' experience: activation of the witnessing awareness; Conscious embodiment - the reconnection with the body energy and body perceptions; Awakening to the energy

flows and kundalini awakening; Vibrational awakenings: from erotic to ecstatic, enstatic and beyond; Interconnectedness awakening - the shift from individual to collective awareness; Awakening the heart and the experience of unconditional love as deep resonance; Awakening of the multidimensional awareness; Consciously using automatic perspective mechanisms to create a framework for conscious awareness content; Flow awareness and the modulation of life events; Inner eye vision: merging of the inner mental space with the real physical space; Entheogenic awakenings; Awakening the voice; The overview effect; Space awareness (spaciousness, spatial/depth perception); Awakening the passion of being (awakened aliveness); Spiritual awakening; Embracing the curiosity for life; Information awakening; Harmonic resonance awakening.

The descriptions of these journeys are provided in the Appendix.

69. In time, if this new opening is cultivated and consciously nurtured, it becomes an *awakeness skill*. In other words, it creates a habit (it *habituates*), supported by the neuroplasticity of the brain. After these neuroplasticity processes occur, the person can use the new awakeness skill without investing much attention. It becomes automated, thus creating the conditions for the next step in evolution.

70. Each person creates meaning from these natural openings based on their worldview. The individual's interpretation of these natural evolutionary processes is biased by their meaning-making structures, due to the inherent limitations of the language used by each framework (e.g., spiritual, philosophical, religious, pseudoscientific, scientific, etc.).

71. Awakenings happen either sequentially or, sometimes, simultaneously. New awakenings can occur even if previous openings have not been habituated. Each opening has various depths, and

it takes time to integrate it, anywhere between a few years to some decades. After integration, the new conscious awareness skills lead to lifestyle changes and new awakeness styles.

72. There is no 'final' awakening. Each awakening system triggers a deeper understanding of other systems, until multidimensional awakeness skills are acquired, and all the layers are harmonized and integrated into conscious experience. This process is species-wide, and it is a continuous process.

73. Awakenings can emerge within individuals at various developmental stages. Some awakenings are experienced in their essentiality at later stages, after the self-identity becomes more flexible.

74. Various opening experiences occur spontaneously during life, lasting from a few seconds to a few hours. Most people lack the education to recognize and cultivate them. When they are very intense, the opening moments could be considered peak experiences or altered states of consciousness.

75. Some evolutionary processes unfold in dramatic ways, which may be quite distressing for the people around them. The societal reaction is to confuse these transformational moments and to consider them as a kind of psychosis, schizophrenia, or bipolar disorder, which slows down the transformation process if one is required to use long-term medications.

76. Awakenings can be learned, cultivated, and invited into our lives, and habituated through practice. We just need to allow ourselves to be transformed in new ways.

77. Various *psychosomatic processes* accompany both the inner growth journeys—toward a mature and fluid self-identity, and the awakening journeys—which enhance one's connectivity with life. For in-depth information on psychosomatic dynamics, explore the following awakening journeys, described in the Appendix: Conscious embodiment - the reconnection with the body energy and

body perceptions; Awakening to the energy flows and kundalini awakening; Vibrational awakenings: from erotic to ecstatic, enstatic and beyond; Awakening the heart and the experience of unconditional love as deep resonance. Also, consider the 'chakras' model as a metaphor for energy dynamics, rather than as a technical description of the energy body.

78. During inner evolution, transformation ensues in all layers—physical, energy, and information. Each thinking pattern has a relationship with an energy pattern in the physical body or our emotional structure. Just intervening on one side, the body or emotions, will not produce a stable change. Visualization techniques, in which people imagine sending 'energy' to heal parts of the body, produce only placebo effects. To harmonize the cognitive and emotional imprints in the body, we need to use the body, not to visualize 'energies' in the body.

79. The psychosomatic process generated by life's energy intelligence, known as *kundalini*, has at least three parts: the first part seems to be *pranotthana*—the 'cleaning' process, when the body may be convulsing, moving uncontrollably, or sometimes performing perfect yoga asanas or spontaneous mudras. The second part is when the energy can *propagate smoothly* and increase the synchrony of rhythms and flows in the energy body layer.

———

Jana Dixon in 'Biology of Kundalini' explains: "Since kundalini awakening is most often just something that happens, we don't have a whole lot of say over how 'mature' we are when it strikes. However, by its very extreme nature, kundalini will force greater maturity and lucid adjustment to reality in order to survive. Along with the sense of danger inherent in the dissolving of one's known self, there is also a buoyant faith that arises from being so lit with Spirit and at one with the Universe. Kundalini arousal and the ongoing development of the nervous system make us more sensitive to the inner and outer worlds. The self-directed force of kundalini purifies accumulated stress caused by our past habits (samskaras) and traumas. Friction and difficulty during awakening occur not so much from the process itself, but from our conscious and unconscious interference with it due to not understanding what is going on.

Kundalini burns off much of the primary reactivity imprinted from our family of origin and early life experience. With kundalini, the opportunity for change is increased because our neurological slate is wiped relatively clean, but it depends on our will, faith and environment as to how far we can grow. If we do not change our habits to reflect the Self's true interests, we will continue to rebuild the conditioned reactive self we thought ourselves to be. We spend our entire lives thinking we are an entity that was created by our parents and culture, but are we really that entity? I mean they don't even know us; they only know their projections of us.[...]

Those who have had a childhood of abuse, neglect or dysfunction, tend to have more catastrophic awakenings because their systems are built for repression and dissociation. This is not always the case, but it is a pattern. One can imagine that the more loving-touch and self-validation the child receives, the more efficiently wired their nervous system will be, and the fewer psycho-somatic and emotional blocks they will have."[79]

80. The third stage of kundalini processing is when all types of energy are in synchrony, and there are no more significant/unsolved traumas or blockages. In this stage, the person can increase aliveness and combine high and low frequencies, without losing the high synchrony by generating 'heat' (or expansive energy flows). It's a transition from *ecstatic* to *enstatic*, usually occurring after the person develops the ability to allow high-frequency experiences, at the same time with low-frequency experiences; this is done by allowing the *increase of density* in the energy body experiences.

This transition is supported by a lifestyle that is oriented toward spirituality and harmony, while nurturing the *sattva* tendency in all layers.

————

If we take a point of view from inside the energy body layer, some energy-information dynamics become highly relevant:

1. There are two broad types of perceptions related to the energy's frequencies: the *static-vibrational energy*—with a high frequency and smaller wavelengths, oriented toward information processing, generating the experience of electric currents (or a high-frequency buzzing); and the *flowing-wave energy*—with a low frequency and large wavelength, oriented toward physical movement processing, generating the liquid flowing experiences, when the energy is felt like a wave flowing through the energy body.

From the high-resolution perspective, the low-resolution flowing movement seems slow, and its fundamental dynamics are intelligible. As a metaphor, let's say we look at a 100 Hz high-frequency vibrational layer and a 10 Hz low-frequency flowing layer. The computations inside the 10 Hz flowing wave provide 10x10=100 potential options to vibrate. But, the computations inside the 100 Hz vibrational energy provide 100x100=10,000 options to vibrate, as possibilities for flowing-wave patterns available at any moment. Thus, a high-frequency vibration can contain within the potential for various types of low-frequency vibrational patterns. When we experience extreme, high-frequency phenomena in our energy body, our conscious experience feels static-vibrational, increasingly alert, aware, and high resolution. We can see things vividly, with many details available to our mind's eye. When our conscious awareness has flowing-waves patterns, we tend to experience the world with a 'liquid-emotional' quality. An energy wave through a high-frequency layer is felt like an electric current, while an energy wave through a low-frequency layer feels more like a water wave.

2. The 1,000+ frequency layers in the human body harmonize either through local and neighbor-to-neighbor frequency resonance processing, or they can harmonize with the whole energy body through *global synchronization waves.* This global-sync wave shares the information from the local synchronies with the energy-information body layers, which adapt all at once after the local upgrade is received and distributed to the whole, perhaps using the *fascia-microtubule network.*

When we lie down and relax or receive a massage, some parts of the body may release tension, and we may feel a bubble of energy radiating as warm relaxation in that area. Usually, we feel this locally, but sometimes it feels like an explosion that expands through the entire energy body. This expansion is the 'global synchronization wave'. When it spreads throughout the entire energy body, it adds its local sync-ing pattern to the entire body, and inside we feel renewed and re-tuned.

Another example: when we relax the knee, if there are some tensions there, accumulated during the day—and the knee area is fine overall, the relaxation will just generate a local warming feeling as the tissues relax deeply. But, if a trauma is stored in the knee, complete relaxation is not possible at first. If, through practice, we can relax the tensions entirely, sometimes the knee relaxation can generate an upgrade in the global sync, through a synchronization wave that radiates from the knee to the entire energy body. This is like an explosion in the knee that expands in 3D, within the entire energy body layer, or flows through the spine upwards. If we consciously allow this synchronization wave to go through the physical-energy-information layers, there is a chance that it will generate an instant reconsolidation of memory. Thus, the traumatic memory will be harmonized easily, and fewer 'healing' cycles will be necessary.

3. *Energy is not transmitted from one person to another.* The energy patterns in one individual could generate similar patterns in the other individual, but each individual has his or her own energy body, locked to the physical body. In social and intimate interactions, each person modulates her or his own energy body, by non-consciously selecting various interconnectivity patterns from the persons nearby or the environment. There is a metaphor which says: 'there is a collective ocean in which we are drops of water, and the ocean of life mediates this interpersonal transfer'. This metaphor is not so helpful. The 'transfer' is local, and each individual is fully responsible for what he or she allows inside and what is shared with other individuals.

Imagine the human body as a shape, filled with a million marbles that oscillate at a high frequency, as if statically. And the oscillations are also involved in collective oscillations of sub-groups, by allowing various streams of resonating flowing waves to happen. The marbles inside a person have patterns of waves, which can be picked up through resonance by another person's energy body. Still, each person has her or his own set of marbles.

Let's use massage therapy process as a metaphor. The massage therapist, through the hands, invites the energy body of the other person to tune into certain patterns of waves. Through various self-tunings, if the energy bodies synchronize and pick up the patterns of another, the resonance connection becomes active, and the flowing waves begin exchanging information. This connection can be consciously improved if the therapist expands the awareness, to sense both types of energy simultaneously: static-vibrational and flowing waves. The buzz and the liquid flow at the same time, with all the frequency layers in between.

4. During inner evolution, we need to allow our energy awareness to refine itself and allow all types of resonance processes to participate in the energy body awareness, without fear. Through inner work, it is possible to facilitate

a global harmony, by allowing all types of processes and energies to move freely: active and receptive, high frequency and low frequency, vibrating and flowing. Some will increase, others decrease the density of the energy body, allowing global synchronization waves to unfold. These nuancing skills could be used to go deeper within, in a meditation session, or they can help manage high-energy kundalini spikes.

5. It may be that the fascia-microtubule network is one of the biological systems that support the interconnections necessary for conscious processing.

6. Let's consider the fascia-microtubule network as a biological 'antenna' that is sensitive to the collective information of life on earth. From this perspective, the fascia-microtubule network could be a background processing unit related to interpersonal empathy, telepathy, and various other interpersonal information exchanges, between humans or between any life forms with a fascia-like system.

In 'Myofascial Training', Ester Albini writes: "The fascial tissue is [...] a network that wraps around and separates every part of the body, creating a structural continuity that gives shape and function to all tissue and organs. The human body is a functional unit in which every region is in communication with another through the fascial network.[...] Think of the fascia as a close-fitting and semitransparent web that wraps us and connects us from head to toe, and acts as an external nervous system that processes and responds to sensory and mechanical stimuli.

The fascial tissue, which can be found throughout the body, surrounds and permeates blood vessels, nerves, organs, the meninges, bone, and muscles[...]. It is a semi-transparent network that starts from the skin and thickens in the fibrous tissue that surrounds muscles, bones, and internal organs. It is a continuous system that covers and crosses our body and accounts for 20 percent of our body weight.[...] The receptors responsible for our perception of the body are up to six times more abundant in the fascia than in the muscles. This is extremely important for accelerating the healing process, increasing well-being, and enhancing performance.

What is important to gather from this image is that the fascia is one piece; it is a three-dimensional web, and every inch of the body, including the bones, the organs, and of course, the muscles, are permeated by this web all the way down to the cells. Therefore, when you put your awareness into your fascial system, you are putting your awareness into your entire body as a whole. It is the most pervasive structure in the whole body."[80a]

Liz Long, in 'Fascia, Connections and Consciousness', says: "The fascial system is not simply a system of structure. It is also highly involved in mechanotransduction (when cells convert mechanical stimulus into electrical activity), hemodynamics (the movement of the blood), supporting the immune system, and creating an environment that allows for wound healing. It is highly innervated, especially with pain receptors, and it is a major contributor to proprioception.[...]

In my experience and what I've gathered from the reports of others, putting the attention in the fascial system allows the body to be sensed and moved as a singular connected whole. This awareness gives greater access to the 'in between' spaces, allows us to tone the organs, and gives us greater access to a sense of mechanical expansion and contraction. I currently hypothesize that the reason this awareness gives us those experiences is because the fascia literally exists all over the body and has its own motility. Motility means that something has its own contraction and expansion capabilities. That means that it is not just the cells of the muscles that contract and expand. Every place in the body that has fascia contracts and expands through the fascia itself."[80b]

Chapter Four

Transformative Learning

81. Transformative learning involves learning, understanding, opening, adjusting, adapting, and habituating to new ways of being alive.

82. The learning process during inner evolution requires an upgrade in the meaning-making structure; one must also grasp the basic *technical-experiential terminology* related to all body layers (physical, energy, information), their interconnections, and the transformative processes unfolding throughout. By understanding what's happening, the developmental transitions could advance more quickly, thus reducing confusion and suffering.

83. Developing *visual-spatial thinking* (thinking through spatial imagery), along with the *auditory-verbal* (sequential) thinking, provide an increased speed of processing and facilitate learning and understanding during inner evolution. An easy *access to both thinking systems* is helpful.

———

The auditory-verbal thinking style has evolutionary purposes. It is natural for children to talk out loud to themselves and, as they grow up, to internalize the out-loud speech. However, during inner evolution, thinking tends to transition naturally from words to imagery, due to an increased need for processing. When the high-speed processing through visual-spatial thinking is disturbed for various reasons, positive or negative (e.g., traumatic events or increases in energy flows), the inner speech may prefer the auditory-verbal processing style, which is narrower and more focused, as a coping mechanism.

Linda Silverman, in 'Upside-Down Brilliance: The Visual-Spatial Learner', explains: "Visual-spatial learners are individuals who think in pictures rather than in words. They have a different brain organization than auditory-sequential learners. They learn better visually than auditorially. They learn all-at-once, and when the light bulb goes on, the learning is permanent. They do not learn from repetition and drill. They are whole-part learners who need to see the big picture first before they learn the details.

They are non-sequential, which means that they do not learn in the step-by-step manner in which most teachers teach. They arrive at correct solutions without taking steps, so 'show your work' may be impossible for them. They may have difficulty with easy tasks, but show amazing ability with difficult, complex tasks. They are systems thinkers who can orchestrate large amounts of information from different domains, but they often miss the details.[...] Here are the basic distinctions between the visual-spatial and auditory-sequential learner:

Auditory-sequential learner – thinks primarily in words; has auditory strengths; relates well to time; is a step-by-step learner; learns by trial and error; progresses sequentially from easy to difficult material; is an analytical thinker; attends well to details; follows oral directions well; does well at arithmetic; learns phonics easily; can sound out spelling words; can write quickly and neat; is well-organized; can show steps of work easily; excels at rote memorization; has good auditory short-term memory; may need some repetition to reinforce learning; learns well from instruction; learns in spite of emotional reactions; is comfortable with one right answer; develops fairly evenly; usually maintains high grades; enjoys algebra and chemistry; learns languages in class; is academically talented; is an early bloomer.

Visual-spatial learner – thinks primarily in pictures; has visual strengths; relates well to space; is a whole-part learner; learns concepts all at once; learns complex con-

cepts easily, struggles with easy skills; is a good synthe-
sizer; sees the big picture, may miss details; reads maps
well; is better at math reasoning than computation; learns
whole words easily; must visualize words to spell them;
prefers keyboarding to writing; creates unique methods of
organization; arrives at correct solutions intuitively; learns
best by seeing relationships; has good long-term visual
memory; learns concepts permanently; is turned off by drill
and repetition; develops own methods of problem solving;
is very sensitive to teachers' attitudes; generates unusual
solutions to problems; develops quite asynchronously; may
have very uneven grades; enjoys geometry and physics;
masters other languages through immersion; is creatively,
mechanically, emotionally, or technologically gifted; is a
late bloomer."[83]

84. *Samyama* is a process of perfect and continuous fusion with the
object of attention, through absorption. This uninterrupted connection generates a real-time tuning of cognitive understanding and
other perceptions, leading to *prajna*, experiential-direct knowledge.

————

Technically, samyama is the concept used by Patanjali in
the 'Yoga Sutras' to describe an uninterrupted flow of attention toward the object of attention. Samyama facilitates the acquisition of information about the essential
nature, role, and purpose of the object of attention, in its
own context.[84a]

Prajna refers to 'knowing-by-being the object of attention'
while staying connected to its awareness flow continuously through samyama; thus, prajna is a very accurate
means to comprehend the 'innate features' and the 'unfolding styles' of the object of attention.[84b]

When the inner context is very dynamic, and the visual-
spatial thinking and the energy are very active, as in visionary experiences, it requires additional flexibility to maintain
an uninterrupted samyama.

85. Learning to practice samyama is helpful for finding the in-depth roots of developmental flows. Practicing samyama with various issues and topics that arise during inner evolution could provide insights for correct decisions, related to that specific issue.

————

> For some people, the transition to new contents brought about by spontaneous samyama is not so smooth, as they may experience spontaneous absorption in a landscape they see, or in a sound, causing 'black-outs' of a kind, when they may lose contact with external surroundings (if this occurs when they are driving, well, that's not okay). This could be a sign that the witnessing awareness is beginning to activate, and the person is experiencing a new way of connecting with life, based on full connection rather than thinking, feeling, or sensing through self-identity filters.

86. *A growth mindset* is essential for inner evolution. This includes openness, cognitive and emotional flexibility, and a willingness to accept feedback, criticism, and paradoxes. This mindset involves the frequent admission that 'I don't know yet' and an unconditional acceptance of life as it is. All these qualities need to be fueled daily when conscious transformation begins. In time, they will provide an automatic framework, catalyzing the inner evolution journey.

————

> We could ask ourselves, 'Is this what I am really experiencing, or is this just a frame I created for myself, a personal veil that I put on, automatically? Can I use other words that are more closely related to my inner experience? Am I labeling the experience using my current mindset, or am I using an old mindset that is blocking me from experiencing the present moment and what's new?'.

> Although receiving feedback is essential for inner growth, the individual's attitude toward feedback depends on their stage of inner growth. In the earlier stages, feedback can be experienced as threatening and may only be accepted from those considered authorities in the community or

field of study. These are the patterns in receiving feedback, observed by developmental researchers Susanne Cook-Greuter and Terri O'Fallon—as cited by Abigail Lynam:

"*Conformist* – receives feedback as disapproval, or as a reminder of norms; deflects feedback that threatens loss of face; unable to give feedback to others; cannot question group norms.

Expert – may take it personally, defends own position; dismisses feedback from those who are not seen as experts in the same field.

Achiever – accepts feedback, especially if it helps them to achieve their goals and to improve.

Individualist-Pluralist – welcomes feedback as necessary for self-knowledge and to uncover hidden aspects of their own behavior, to discover their authentic self.

Autonomous – invites feedback for self-actualization; conflict is seen as an inevitable aspect of viable and multiple relationships.

Construct-aware – views feedback (loops) as a natural part of living systems; essential for learning and change."[86]

87. In the inner evolution journey, we must defeat *psychological inertia* and modify the inner defense mechanisms that maintain self-identity stability. The self is a consequence of evolution; that's why the process of change is not gratified by nature with joy, but rather with fear and frustration. Some people tend to see this inertia as negative, or as if negative energies may 'attack them'. But, positive emotions (e.g., enthusiasm, joy, curiosity) are also released as an evolutionary support to overcome the inertia.

88. *Authenticity* and *radical honesty* are essential during inner evolution, to integrate the subpersonalities and create a workspace for the pre-conscious information to participate in the conscious experience flow. We cannot change the past; all we can do is ac-

cept everything and see the present as a result of our past actions. What we can do is become fully honest and authentic, and change the future by acting differently. It may be helpful to know that, during inner evolution, a pattern of experience shows up, known as the *mirror of karma*—when, in conscience, one re-evaluates past actions, and feelings of guilt and inadequacy may arise. In these situations, radical honesty and complete acceptance of all past actions are needed. Also, by connecting with friends or discussing such issues with a therapist, one can gain new perspectives on what has happened in the past, thus reducing the 'absolutist' tendency of self-judgment.

——

The 'mirror of karma' is an automatic flow that appears frequently throughout the inner evolution process; it occurs in night dreams, as an additional stream of thinking during everyday life, or during/after peak experiences and altered states of consciousness.

In 'The Psychedelic Experience. A Manual Based on the Tibetan Book of the Dead', Timothy Leary, Ralph Metzner, and Richard Alpert write: "The judgment vision may come: the Third Bardo blame game.[...] A judgment scene is a central part of many religious systems, and the vision can assume various forms. Westerners are most likely to see it in the well-known Christian version.[...] The Judge, or Lord of Death, symbolizes conscience itself in its stern aspect of impartiality and love of righteousness. The 'Mirror of Karma' (the Christian Judgment Book), consulted by the Judge, is *memory*.

Different parts of the ego will come forward, some offering lame excuses to meet accusations, others ascribing baser motives to various deeds, counting apparently neutral deeds among the black ones;[...] others offering justifications or requests for pardon. The mirror of memory reflects clearly; lying and subterfuge will be of no avail. Be not frightened, tell no lies, face truth fearlessly.

Now you may imagine yourself surrounded by figures who wish to torment, torture or ridicule you.[...] These merciless figures may be internal, or they may involve the people around you, seen as pitiless, mocking, superior. Remember that fear and guilt and persecuting, mocking figures are your own hallucinations. Your own guilt machine. Your personality is a collection of thought-patterns and void. It cannot be harmed or injured. 'Swords cannot pierce it, fire cannot burn it'. Free yourself from your own hallucinations. In reality, there is no such thing as the Lord of Death, or a justice-dispensing god or demon or spirit. Act so as to recognize this.[...]

If you are experiencing a vision of judgment and guilt, listen carefully:[...] this is the result of your own mental set. Your karma. No one is doing anything to you. There is nothing to do. Your own mind is creating the problem. Accordingly, float into meditation. Remember your former beliefs. Remember the teachings of this manual. Remember the friendly presence of your companions. If you do not know how to meditate, concentrate on any single object or sensation.[...] Recognize the illusory nature of existence and phenomena. This moment is of great importance.[...] Think of all these fears and terrifying apparitions as being your own ideal, or as the compassionate one. They are divine tests. Remember your guide.[...] Even though you fall, you will not be hurt."[88]

89. Usually, it takes more than one cycle of exploration to integrate an issue or a subpersonality that is unbalanced. Some brilliant and meticulous individuals, in a counseling or self-development process, tend to self-arrest themselves in a paradigm, just because they are ambitious to *solve an issue entirely*, before moving on to the next topic. They keep looking at causes and answers, with lengthy efforts, by diving again and again into personal and transgenerational material; they are looking for final answers or a final healing. But, even if we use our discriminative power extensively and do body work, some life issues are so intricate and complex that

the only way to 'solve' them for good is to *grow up as a whole* and become more mature with our entire being.

———

> Try this technique, proposed by Osho: before beginning a meditation, a ceremony, or an inner art session, say to yourself, 'Solved or not solved, I let it all go'[89]. And then, forget about this. Just dive in. Allow yourself to experience some time or hours of freedom, no matter your situation.

90. During inner evolution, everyone has times of high sensitivity. A *highly sensitive person* has an increased depth of processing. Such a person is over-aroused (i.e., easily aroused compared to others), has high emotional reactivity and empathy, and higher sensitivity to various stimuli. When people work with their emotional system using witnessing awareness, they discover new depths of sensitivity, experiencing full empathy and full connections with the target of the attentional stream.

———

> Elaine Aron explains: "If you find you are highly sensitive, or your child is, I'd like you to know the following: Your trait is normal. It is found in 15 to 20% of the population—too many to be a disorder, but not enough to be well understood by the majority of those around you. It is innate. In fact, biologists have found it in over 100 species (and probably there are many more) from fruit flies, birds, and fish to dogs, cats, horses, and primates. This trait reflects a certain type of survival strategy, being observant before acting. The brains of highly sensitive persons (HSPs) actually work a little differently than others'.
>
> You are more aware than others of subtleties. This is mainly because your brain processes information and reflects on it more deeply. So even if you wear glasses, for example, you see more than others by noticing more. You are also more easily overwhelmed. If you notice everything, you are naturally going to be overstimulated when things are too intense, complex, chaotic, or novel for a long time.

This trait is not a new discovery, but it has been misunderstood. Because HSPs prefer to look before entering new situations, they are often called 'shy'. But shyness is learned, not innate. In fact, 30% of HSPs are extroverts, although the trait is often mislabeled as introversion. It has also been called inhibitedness, fearfulness, or neuroticism. Some HSPs behave in these ways, but it is not innate to do so and not the basic trait. Sensitivity is valued differently in different cultures. In cultures where it is not valued, HSPs tend to have low self-esteem. They are told 'don't be so sensitive' so that they feel abnormal."[90]

91. Anxiety and depression are natural experiences, along the continuum of *aliveness*. When there is too much activation of life energy, people experience anxiety. When there is less aliveness, they experience depression. Learning to balance aliveness is essential for navigating inner evolution.

———

In 'Depression, Anxiety, and the Mismanagement of Aliveness', Steve Bearman explains: "Imagine depression and anxiety as opposite poles on a spectrum. Depression is characterized by a lack: low energy, low motivation, less meaning, less pleasure. Anxiety, on the other hand, is a kind of overabundance: too much energy, restlessness, hypervigilance, overactive thoughts.[...] Aliveness is the key to the entire system of depression and anxiety. Instead of asking what to do about depression, find out how to come more fully to life, how to liberate aliveness when it gets trapped. Instead of asking what to do about anxiety, learn how to withstand the relentless intensity of being alive."[91]

92. Transformative change requires noticing and observing patterns and understanding how these patterns connect and work together within systems. *Systems thinking* is a fundamental skill for a mature self-identity. Some of the systems which can be analyzed during inner evolution are the body, food, emotions, rela-

tionships with other people, the mind, the way we talk, and the self-identity. Perhaps the most dramatic transition during inner growth occurs when people begin to see their *self-identity as a system* and stop their compulsive identification with it, by expanding their perspective to include the self-identity as one of the many systems that create our inner life.

——

Systems thinking allows us to notice how certain patterns flow in association with other patterns[92a]. After connecting the dots, recognizing the next hierarchical system, and integrating previous 'polarities', we can go to the next level. This is like a jump from 2D to 3D. At the new level, the system becomes an object again, and we see it from outside. Then the process repeats until the object is integrated, and the system becomes a part of our everyday subjective experience. And so on, until we connect everything with everything. This associative mechanism is quite automatic and unconscious when the inner evolution engine starts.

Eventually, new associations emerge among ideas, objects, symbols, and archetypes, as the inner evolution process goes deeper and deeper. The final part of this beautiful associative drive involves the recognition that the associative mechanism itself is a system. One may get out of a never-ending fractal loop (or 'hall of mirrors'), by diving through life using witnessing awareness.

Terri O'Fallon, in 'The Evolution of the Human Soul: Developmental Practices in Spiritual Guidance', says: "The Construct Aware [person] moves into an early fifth person perspective. Previous perspectives have progressively backed off, taking a perspective on the previous one, but when one moves into Construct Aware, a different kind of realization begins to happen. The pattern of standing back to take a perspective on a perspective becomes present to them, and they begin to see a hall of mirrors, being able to take successive perspectives on perspectives at will.

Susanne Cook-Greuter calls this the fifth person perspective through the nth person perspective.

Some people experience this new person perspective through the actual envisioning of these multiple loops; others, who are more in a feeling mode, find themselves aware of their feelings looping in a somewhat wordless way. The fifth person perspective begins often when there is insight around projections in one's interior experience in the moment. The witness (awareness of awareness) is activated and it becomes aware, in the moment of projections arising. Judgments and thoughts about anything outside of the self are finally recognized as being projected from what is inside oneself; awareness of the mind and emotions making up these feelings, stories and judgments, loops back to one's own interior. At some point, all conceptions that seemed so solid within the subtle floor are experienced as an illusion, a mere ever-changing story; a construct made up by the subtle mind."[92b]

93. The switch from automatic pilot to conscious functioning requires an in-depth exploration of our ways of being and interacting. The process of inner evolution is a large-scale *re-programming* of certain automatic patterns that are available to conscious awareness.

———

Inner automation plays a crucial role in our everyday life[93]. Still, on our development journey, it is necessary to access our automatic programs and 're-write' certain aspects of them by adding 'the free will subprogram'. After that, they are free to become automatic again. It is as if the person could open the past memory systems-of-engrams, re-explore the situation, re-arrange the content by including the ignored materials, re-frame the meaning of the engram, and then close the engram. Thus, one lets the harmonized engram participate again in daily conscious experience, without paying attention to it. During the inner evolution process, we all discover blind spots in our autobiographical memories. Eventually, after years of practice, there are no more (significant) blind spots.

For people at the beginning of the inner journey, this may look like a state of hyper-vigilance or permanent self-reflection that requires continuous attention and energy. But after a while, the process becomes natural and automatic in a good way. In fact, awareness is always present in various degrees; there is no need to consume extra energy to pay attention. Attention naturally goes where it's needed, without consuming energy excessively.

94. Some automatic structures of the psyche are available for re-programming easily; some of them aren't, due to *non-conscious self-defenses* that make us negate, reject, or ignore certain experiences and their significance.

———

Some principles for working with automatic patterns are described by Matt James, in 'Conscious of the Unconscious':

"The unconscious mind preserves the body: one of its main objectives is the survival of your physical body. It will fight anything that appears to be a threat to that survival. So if you want to change a behavior more easily, show your unconscious how that behavior is hurting your body.

Runs the body: rather than telling the unconscious what perfect health looks like, try asking it what it knows and what you need for better health.

Is like a 7-year old child: needs very clear directions, and takes your instructions very literally. Therefore, if you say, 'This job is a pain in the neck', your unconscious will figure out a way to make sure that your neck hurts at work! The unconscious is also very 'moral' in the way a young child is moral, which means it is based on the morality taught and accepted by your parents or surroundings. So if you were taught, 'sex is nasty', your unconscious will still respond to that teaching even after your conscious mind has rejected it.

Communicates through emotion and symbols: to get your attention, the unconscious uses emotions. For example, if you suddenly feel afraid, your unconscious has detected (rightly or wrongly) that your survival is at risk.

Stores and organizes memories: the unconscious decides where and how your memories are stored. It may hide certain memories (such as traumas) that have strong negative emotions until you are mature enough to process them consciously. When it senses that you are ready (whether you consciously think you are or not!), it will bring them up so you can deal with them.

Does not process negatives: the unconscious absorbs pictures rather than words. So if you say, 'I don't want to procrastinate', the unconscious generates a picture of you procrastinating. Switching that picture from the negative to the positive takes an extra step. Better to tell your unconscious, 'Let's get to work!'.

Makes associations and learns quickly: to protect you, the unconscious stays alert and tries to glean the lessons from each experience. For example, if you had a bad experience in school, your unconscious may choose to lump all of your learning experiences into the 'this is not going to be fun' category. It will signal you with sweaty palms and anxiety whenever you attempt something new. But if you do well in sports, your unconscious will remember that 'sports equals success', and you'll feel positive and energized whenever physical activity comes up."[94]

95. The rejected/ignored content is what psychologists call *the shadow*. The shadow is an informational content that is *already available* to conscious awareness, but the *self-identity control* is acting as if the content doesn't exist, thus reducing harmony within the psyche. The shadow is usually created during childhood, through

unhealthy parenting styles, and propagates itself from childhood to adult life. The shadow can be transferred from parents to their descendants, if the adult doesn't do inner work. In the inner evolution process, it is necessary to access the shadow, and allow its contents and patterns to contribute to conscious experience.

———

In 'Seven Perspectives on the Stages Developmental Model', Kim Barta writes: "Shadows from our history inevitably create blind spots. These blind spots create holes in our current operational capacities.[...] We have three forms of resolution that are important to discuss. These forms of resolution of issues can work with both shadow issues and other issues that we have in our life.

'Height — The evolution solution' is about gaining greater heights to gain greater perspective upon the issue involved. By gaining height we can look down upon the issue, put it in perspective, so we can utilize multiple different shadow techniques to resolve the issue.

'Breadth — The dilution solution' is about utilizing our breadth. As we expand out wider, the material on which a shadow, or other issue, can hold onto becomes less and less until the shadow just has nothing left to hang onto and it falls away into oblivion.

'Depth — The dissolution solution' is a depth solution. Some people call this 'metabolizing' the issue. With the Depth solution, we go into the suffering deeply. We sustain the pain of the suffering until the suffering dissolves. By having the courage to drop into the depth of the suffering with courage and sustainability, we metabolize the issue until it dissolves into Pure Energy which can then be readily used by any aspect of consciousness for new purposes. To accomplish this journey successfully we need several capacities in place.

First, we need an unconditional loving witness that holds an unconditional loving environment within which we conduct our journey. Without this holding, when we dive into the darkness, we can get lost in it indefinitely. The more we swim in the lost space, the more we train the neural pathways to keep firing in those ways. As a result, we can actually accentuate the problem we seek to resolve. The unconditional loving witness prevents this problem. Sometimes the unconditional loving witness is held by another person: a friend, a lover, a therapist, a coach, a spiritual mentor. By having someone hold the unconditional loving witness space, we can drop into the depth of the suffering while being held in unconditional love. This external support can encourage us to sustain the pain that we would rather run away from, to understand it intimately, and to hold the tension until the distorted illusions are clarified and transformed.

The second thing we need, is courage. Courage is what allows us to take this journey in the first place. The third thing we need is endurance. Endurance gives us the persistence to follow through to the end until it is resolved."[95]

The shadow is integral to the psyche and an essential component for archetypal exploration. In Jungian-Senoi Dreamwork methodology, developed by Strephon Kaplan-Williams, inner work with the 'adversity' archetype is necessary, to gain a balanced archetypal structure. Fear is a natural response to intense 'adversity', and it takes some time to accept these fears and connect with adversity. Sometimes the masculine hero energy is needed; other times, the feminine heroine is necessary. We can look at fears as 'versions' of reality, so that the negative can be explored as a polarity.

For exploring certain deep automatic patterns, a method I use is to immerse myself deeply in the content, in a ceremonial way. For example, while exploring a fear, I allow some time (hours or days) to let my mind and emotions wander freely in contact with the particular content. During the inner art session, I write, dance, draw, go to work, and allow what is coming. In this ceremonial approach, setting a 'lifeline' for coming back is necessary. We need a person to help, who can bring us back to real life if the content becomes overwhelming.

96. De-automatization involves a new skill: to observe the *self-identity/ego defense mechanisms* and to skip using them, when they are not necessary. Allowing all kinds of experiences to flow through us is a natural way to integrate and accept them. If we interpret inner experiences that we don't like as 'negative', then conscious processing tends to bypass those parts labeled as 'negative'.

97. These are possible estimates for the rate of transformation: it takes at least six to eight months to change a habit; at least five years to transition from a developmental stage of maturity to the next, if the circumstances are favorable, or at least two-three years if the person is doing vertical transformative work under supervision; at least one or two years to integrate a transformative experience; and at least three to five years after an awakening experience. These are highly subjective estimates and depend on the time allocated to inner work and practice.

———

With daily inner work, perhaps a minimum of 10-15 years is necessary for an in-depth transformation that would include vertical transitions, awakening journeys, and the integration-habituation processes. In the first years, the daily inner work requires almost continuous self-monitoring. There will be 2-3 topics under observation in conscious awareness, and 3-4 topics running pre-consciously with minimal monitoring, while in the habituation process. And at least once a year, an intense transformative ceremony of 'letting go', when new contents are allowed into conscious experience.

With less time available for inner work, the evolutionary process could take decades or never reach maturity during one's lifetime.

98. People with a *high transformative potential* who decide to take a *positive disintegration* approach could advance more rapidly through transitions, but they also need time for integration.

———

Kazimierz Dabrowski developed a theory of positive disintegration: "Dabrowski's theoretical framework views psychological tension, anxiety, and depression as necessary for growth. He addresses five types of hyperexcitability: psychomotor—physical response to stimuli, often seen as hyperactivity; emotional—emotional hypersensitivity; imaginative/imaginational—intense fantasy life that sometimes disrupts reality; sensory/sensual—sensory hypersensitivity; mental/intellectual—highly active mind, or an exaggerated search for explanations and a tendency to intellectualize problems in everyday life. The person with a higher potential for development will experience growth as a loosening of the stable psychic structure accompanied by symptoms of 'psychoneuroses'. Dabrowski called this process 'positive disintegration'; he declares that psychoneurosis is not an illness, and he insists that psychotherapy is automatic when the person is conscious of his development.

To Dabrowski, real therapy is autopsychotherapy; it is the self being aware of the self through a long inner investigation, a mapping of the inner environment. There are no techniques to eliminate symptoms because the symptoms constitute the very psychic richness from which grows an increasing awareness of body, mind, humanity and cosmos. Without intense and painful introspection and reflection, development is unlikely. Psychoneurotic symptoms should be embraced and transformed into anxieties about human problems of an ever-higher order. If psychoneuroses continue to be classified as mental illness, then perhaps it is a sickness better than health."[98]

99. The inner evolution rate is substantially increased by adopting a *no-drama* attitude toward life experiences. Inner evolution generates fundamental changes in our inner structure and social-relational networks, and frictions could emerge. Allowing ourselves to adapt 'fast' could be a helpful strategy.

100. The practice of *inner arts* every night, before sleep, could enhance the rate of adaptation, by allowing daily echoes to be processed and integrated within conscious awareness. While the body transitions from wakefulness to sleep, an active witnessing could support the accelerated integration of daily issues. The simple act of contemplating the inner world, while transitioning to sleep and entering the dream mode, is a powerful and straightforward method that can be used by anyone who doesn't have the necessary time for a separate daily practice.

101. The *intention* is a lens through which we pre-define the perspective-taking process. The intention is composed of a choice and a commitment to action. It can be unhealthy to depend on intentions, because ultimately, intention is a way of 'controlling' the perception of reality. Rather than making an intention for 'something', it is more efficient to use broader intentions, such as 'I wish to live the experiences that I need in order to change', or 'I trust life, and I am heading towards where I am needed'. These statements should be followed by actions.

It's fine to use intentions for essential actions, from time to time, but in the end an internalized life-values system can be more useful, which allows us to set the direction of our lives and offers us space to relax during daily activities. In the groups who prefer a mindset such as 'we-create-our-world-and-we-manifest-abundance', who extensively use the intention as an everyday tool, there is a lot of attention and energy invested in the process of 'creating-the-world'. This feeds self-identity/ego control and blocks the natural fluidity of life. It's good to remember that we cannot change a stream with a stick; to change something in our lives, we need to immerse ourselves in life and change our actions, not just our perspective.

102. Daily practice is essential for supporting *self-directed neuroplasticity*. The concept of 'self-directed neuroplasticity' means that we can intentionally influence our brain functioning with the mind. We can embrace new ways of thinking, and feel them in our minds, by visualizing how we want life to be. Due to this stimulation, repeated over time, the brain will create new neural connections, and the anticipated experience becomes available for choice-making during everyday activities. Then, it's about practicing the new ways, until they become habitual.

———

Daily practice is essential for changing our default brain setting from 'reactive-survival' mode to 'responsive-natural' mode, allowing us a greater degree of choice about the way we live our experiences. We need to learn to reduce the 'reactive-survival' mode in our daily life, while stimulating and sustaining the responsive mode[102a]. While working to change the patterns, the old patterns and the new coexist simultaneously.

Here is a method that works well during these intermediate times: focus your attention on the *new* you wish to create, not on what you want to change—this is what is needed to reinforce new neural connections. With time, old patterns, that are not used anymore, will disappear, and the new ones, cultivated with care, will become the default mode. However, these new neural connections all depend on daily practice. The new synapses need to be sustained regularly, until they become permanent, or they will be lost.

Although self-directed neuroplasticity has positive and evolutionary effects, it also has side-effects when used for inner evolution: our brain creates new networks, but all these configurations are dependent on the context in which they were created. If we do meditation in the meditation room, the new patterns will be 100% available only when we are in the meditation room. That's why spiritual traditions also say that spiritual practice must be done all the time, to expand the reach and relevance of spiritual practice. In hesychasm, a spiritual tradition originating in eastern Christianity, it is said that the heart's prayer has to become active all the time in the disciple, not only during prayer.[102b]

103. In formal educational contexts, a *developmentally informed practice* can be helpful for learners, teachers, and educators. By adjusting the educational style to the learner's stage of maturity, better outcomes may be obtained during the educational process.

———

In 'Principles and Practices for Developmentally Aware Teaching and Mentoring in Higher Education', Abigail Lynam writes:

"Understanding one's own development as an educator, as well as the developmental diversity of students, can have a significant impact on how educators approach teaching, mentorship, and design learning experiences. Developmentally informed educators recognize the phases of development that students are likely to be in, and adapt their teaching accordingly. Recognizing developmental diversity, they adjust the outcomes, processes, and mentoring to meet the students where they are developmentally. Without this awareness and knowledge, educational programs are more likely to teach for particular forms of development, which provide an appropriate stretch for some students but not for others. In addition, educators may be more likely to project their own developmental needs onto students, teaching who they are, rather than who is in front of them.[...] Terri O'Fallon speaks to this when she says 'there is a different educational theory for every developmental perspective', making the point that educators operating from different stages of meaning-making are drawn to and enact different educational theories. There are multiple dimensions of diversity, including for example family backgrounds, learning styles, age, and ethnicity, all of which influence learning needs and interests.[...]

Developmental researchers and practitioners refer to developmental maps as a spectrum of compassion, because the maps can support increased understanding and valuing of multiple ways of being in the world. Each developmental phase, either active or latent as a capacity within each of us, offers both gifts and blind spots. The maps also offer insight into the developmental process—that there are times in a person's life where they are opening to new ways of seeing, times where they are stabilizing and integrating new insights, and times where they are learning to be active in the world with these new capacities. Learning is fundamentally a developmental process, and understanding more about these developmental patterns informs teaching and learning.[...]

Developmental psychology, while discovering patterns that appear to be cross-cultural, is also an approximation of complex phenomena that may never be fully understood. It is essential that this theory—like all theories—be held lightly, with the awareness that even while it offers insights, it is also partial in its understanding. The intention is not to box or limit people to a particular stage, but to support their liberation by understanding where they are and meeting them there in a way that can support growth and transformation. Additionally, as Susanne Cook-Greuter notes, these models and their stages 'are idealizations of how adults develop'. The actual lived and embodied expressions of these developmental stages are different from the idealizations. A foundational developmental ethic is that later levels are not intrinsically better than earlier levels, nor is someone a better person just for having a more complex meaning system.[...]

Description of the Person Perspectives and Implications for Teaching and Learning

Conformist – Students in the Conformist stage view the teacher as the ultimate authority. They expect and need highly structured learning environments to either conform to or rebel against. They want to know what the rules are. They are challenged to speak up individually in class except to get the answer to a question right. They struggle to think outside of the collective norms or to do group work. Individual feedback can be very threatening, and they are not likely to challenge the teacher directly. In following learning traditions, they value clear hierarchy. Status, appearance, material goods, reputation and prestige are also valued.

The next stage represents a shift from the concrete to the subtle tier. The third-person perspective gives rise to subtle 'I' stages, where a person realizes they have a subtle self—the thoughts, emotions, and independent mind of rational consciousness. It includes the receptive Expert and active Achiever stages. This is an I-oriented space again, but the 'we' is present and backgrounded. The 'We' that is present, however, is the concrete collective, groups and their norms and rituals, since no new subtle 'We' has yet been discovered. The 'I' that is formed is a new, subtle self, not identified with the body and concrete appearances, but with the thinking and feeling mind. This is a significant developmental shift and can be very disorienting in an individual's life and, as a result, takes time to stabilize. Although the shift into the subtle tier can occur in late high school or early college for some, others can live much of their adult life in this developmental stage, as is true of the late concrete stages and all of the subtle stages. Research suggests that a majority of adults in North America are between the Expert and Achiever stages. However, it appears that an increasing number of adults in Western European and North American contexts are moving into later subtle stages, including Pluralist.

Expert – Students at the Expert stage of development tend to be black and white thinkers and are likely to dismiss feedback from anyone not considered to be an expert in their field. They are awash in new ideas of their own, independent from the groups they identify with, but have a hard time prioritizing their ideas. This is a receptive stage, and so the individual is receptive to the newly arising subtle self or ego. They have a hard time reflecting on—or thinking—about their own thoughts and feelings, and may struggle with self-direction, time management, and completing assignments on time. This stage of development often emerges in late high school and early college students, although many adults in the Western world can live their whole lives in this stage of development. Authority and expertise are very important to this stage of development, as is an individual emphasis on figuring things out, and determining the 'right' and best way to do things.

Achiever – Achiever students are actively goal-oriented, think in either/or terms, are more single-system and results-oriented, and are establishing their skills and capacities as self-directed learners. Achiever learners accept feedback and will collaborate with others if it helps them to achieve a goal. They reflect on and evaluate their and others thinking to advance efficiency and value logical and objective processes to achieve results. They aren't yet aware of their own and others' subjectivity, nor that working harder will not necessarily yield the expected outcomes. The developmental capacities of this stage include independent objective thought, self-direction with an internal locus of control, and a sense of agency with goals and a future plan.

These reflect the conventional goals of college education in Western European countries. [Susanne Cook-Greuter writes]: 'Achiever is the target stage for much of Western culture. Our educational systems are geared towards producing adults with the mental capacity and emotional self-reliance of the Achiever stage, that is, rationally competent and independent adults'. However, this expectation in higher education has more recently shifted to a post-conventional, post-modern or pluralistic expectation with the critical deconstructive perspectives of the next stage of development.[...]

[Individualist]Pluralist – Students at Pluralist are likely to be interested in their own authenticity separate from society's expectations, seek creative and unique approaches to their work, are aware of social contexts (their own and others), want to hear everyone's voices, including faculty's, welcome feedback to discover their authentic selves, and may be strident about their pluralism and other socially critical ideologies. These students are both/and thinkers and recognize the subjectivity of objective perspectives.

Autonomous[Strategist] – Strategist students tend to be more complex systemic and paradoxical thinkers and are aware of and passionate about their own and others' transformation and development. They are action-oriented, interested in taking multiple perspectives, may be impatient with excessive sharing and processing, and may be critical of a mentor or program that is, in their own eyes, not transformative enough. They can step outside of systems and contexts and see how they have the capacity to shape contexts and systems, and thus are no longer subject to the experience of being created by contexts and systems. They also begin to see that the subtle things they see in others are also within themselves. This capacity to recognize projection is the mature or later part of the Strategist stage.[...]

Construct-Aware and Unitive[Transpersonal] – These students are aware of the constructed and developmental nature of perspective-taking, and they are flexible and adaptive in their communication and actions. Their thinking, which may be perceived as complex, includes both paradoxical and one-within-another ways of thinking. They may source their way of doing and being from a transpersonal experience of encountering a 'vibrant and alive' world. These students may not feel seen or understood, and because of the relative rarity of these stages, it is less likely that there would be other students or faculty with similar developmental capacities."[103]

104. Information categorized as 'intuition' needs to be carefully considered, and each individual has to decide whether the information is valuable or not. Sometimes intuitions are highly relevant, sometimes not.

105. For changing a perspective, the first steps are *opening to the unknown* and paying attention to how perspectives are naturally created through *automatic contrasts and associations*. The new perspective is automatically (non-consciously) created through comparison with previous experiences. Without learning perspective-taking flexibility, a complete letting go of the old perspective is impossible.

Opening to the unknown

This is a transformative adaptation, where a person begins to see that new perspectives are possible. People have described their experiences using words such as, 'everything is new', 'I see details I have never seen before', and 'I'm having thoughts that I didn't have before'. These new insights are blowing up the mind, and some people interpret them according to their fears or desires. For example, one may conclude that the new thoughts are from angels, demons, extraterrestrials, or disincarnated beings; this supposition could lead to delusional thinking. When the experience of 'openness' first occurs, usually during the earlier stages of inner development, people do not realize that this new perspective involves a way of life and that the perspective-taking process is fluid. Opening to the unknown looks simple for most people who are already involved in personal development, but this skill is a fantastic discovery for a person with a conformist self-identity. The end of this pattern is a permanent awareness of the present moment, when the person lives continuously in the ever-changing flow of 'now'.

Building perspectives through automatic contrasts and associations

Until our psyche can allow us to immerse ourselves fully in the new 'reality', the mind will use contrasts and associations with already known experiences. This new perspective is 'felt' through its association and comparison with previous feelings, not through an out-of-the-box interpretation. For example, we could go into the mountains and experience a magnificent landscape with forests and lakes, and we could enjoy a blissful 'here-now experience'. The content of the experience is new. However, the structure of the experience is not. Our emotions are generated not only by the actual landscape, but also through contrasts and associations with our past 'here-now' experiences. We have a built-in 'configuration for new landscapes', which unconsciously labels this experience according to our expectations, such as 'this is how the present moment is in nature'.

If we observe the configuration of the perspective, and how our mind creates the perspective through associations and contrasts, our action can relax the emotional structure. It is necessary to go beyond emotions, using the perspective-taking system, to connect fully with the here-now experience.

106. The transition from one perspective to multiple perspectives is catalyzed by *integrating the polarities,* by going from 'or/or' approaches, 'this or that', 'me or others', 'good or bad', to an inclusive view, integrating 'this and that', 'good and evil', 'me and others'. What is seen as the opposite/duality in a previous perspective must be seen as a whole in the new perspective.

———

Beena Sharma and Susanne Cook-Greuter, in 'Polarities and Ego Development: Polarity Thinking in Ego Development Theory and Developmental Coaching', write: "At each stage of development, we can again discern how human beings navigate the phenomenon of polarities and their dynamic. Whatever the stage we are at, we might consciously or unconsciously hold on to one pole, unaware of what we exclude. The current perspective provides us with a sense of self and certainty and with a set of clear values. When we grow beyond the confines of the current stage, we can begin to sense the value of a pole that becomes salient at the next stage of development. Once we have entered a new stage, we often consciously reject the pole we embraced at the previous stage because we are now aware of its limits and downsides. We are naturally drawn to the benefits of exploring the newly discovered perspective, and to privilege the new insights into what is important.[...] As human beings, we are always subject to blind spots, areas where we don't even realize there is a 'there' there. Subtler and subtler pole-preferences show up even at ego[/self] transcendent stages."[106]

Some other examples of polarities could be 'order vs. disorder', 'autonomy vs. connection', 'masculine vs. feminine', 'doing vs. thinking', 'discernment vs. intuition', 'being vs. doing', 'appreciative vs. evaluative', 'knowing vs. mystery', and 'seeking vs. non-seeking'. Working with polarities may also include subpersonalities, as in some cases, a preferred pole might give birth to a subpersonality.

107. Moving to a new perspective requires *prioritizing* the chosen qualities and configuration, among the variety of possible options, and fixating the quality by using it intentionally, until it habituates and becomes automatic.

————

In 'Stages: Growing Up is Waking Up — Interpenetrating Quadrants, States and Structures', Terri O'Fallon explains:

"In the early stage of a person perspective, the new person perspective quality is apprehended. Those moving into any new person perspective [...] are so naive to the unique quality arising at this new level that they cannot prioritize it easily. They tend to spend time familiarizing themselves with this new person perspective and its quality, rocking back to a more interior exploration of the quality. The incapacity to be able to prioritize with the new quality sometimes represents itself by shying away from categories, including developmental categories. When individuals mature and are in the later person perspective stage, they are then able to prioritize the quality, thus the rocking back and forth between the inability to prioritize, and the ability to prioritize the quality at successive person perspectives."[107]

108. When learning a new perspective, a *linguistic bias* may interfere: using old language to describe new perspectives. This is a natural phenomenon during the early stages of transitioning to a new perspective, when the 'feel' of the perspective is different from one's previous experiences. One of the tasks when transitioning to a new configuration is learning to use words in a new way.

Kaissa Puhakka, in 'Nonduality: A Spontaneous Movement To and Fro', writes: "Speech that spontaneously comes from 'nothing' and is the expression of a self arising afresh is creative in this literal sense that it comes from nothing. It is very different from the far more common speech that comes from notions of a fixated self and expresses the reactions of a fixated self. 'Original speech', as I call the former, has nothing to do with having high novelty value or shock value. The content of what is being said is often not important, but the qualities of saying it always are. Original speech is simple, spacious, and usually sparse. No words are said that are not meant, and nothing that is meant is left unsaid. It is simple because there is no hidden agenda to preserve or validate the existence or esteem of the self.[...]

Original speech has the qualities of extraordinary clarity and vividness as well. These, and the simplicity, and most of all, the truth of it, that seems to directly touch itself."[108]

109. While learning new perspectives, one can use a process called *anchoring*. An anchor is a stimulus that can serve to retrieve from memory a desired perspective or emotional state. Anchoring involves using and cultivating triggers in a deliberate way, to support the habituation of a new perspective. To do this, select a key object or element from the perspective you want to acquire (such as a ring, a flower, an idea, or an object) and keep the anchor around you in daily life, so that when you see the anchor, you can remember the perspective. Then—when you see the anchor—dive into its perspective and try to keep the perspective active as long as possible.

110. During inner evolution, there are some patterns of transformation that are relatively common to people of all cultures: the automatic life review, symbolic journey, and healing of transgenerational patterns. These transformative processes require many years to be completed, but the result is a more harmonic inner organization that facilitates the next steps in evolution.

111. *Automatic life review* is an automated process that offers new perspectives on past events, by reframing and reinterpreting our memories, thus providing new meanings for past experiences. Its outcome is an automatic *memory reconsolidation*. The life review unfolds in progressive steps, until the content of memory has been reorganized and allowed to participate easily in conscious experience.

——

During this process, our past experiences are re-loaded and revealed to the self via conscious awareness or in dreams. There may be gestures, images, actions, feelings, or elements of perspectives that were not considered when the memory imprint was first stored or analyzed in the past. This process does not select or discriminate between positive or negative life situations; it just allows everything from the past to be included in the current inner configuration, thus aiming at a better integration.

To support the life review process, you could periodically create visual life maps. Use small paper notes. Lay them down on a table, ensuring that all the essential systems and flows of your life are there. Then, look for the connections among them, and arrange them into groups, based on how they have emerged throughout your life. Contemplate them, both the groups and pieces, and notice how they are connected, and consider whether the connections are coherent. Then, rearrange them in more harmonic ways. Work for some months (or years) with yourself to adjust the flow. Then create a new life map, contemplate it, and see what needs to be rearranged again.

112. *The explosion of meaning: symbolic journey and theory of everything* – This associative mental process indicates the start of a profound transformation, generated by the emergence of systems thinking, by a traumatic life event, or by other causes. During this process, meanings begin to connect in various symbolic ways. The logical connections create the feeling of being an explorer, who is journeying continuously through a miraculous, uncharted territory. It is a natural process that will eventually lead journeyers to their own 'theory of everything'.

––––

When the symbolic process is active, the person is in a state of cognitive amazement most of the time. Many people start to talk about resonance, symmetry, Fibonacci sequences, fractals, etc. They begin to see how everything relates to everything, and every part is simultaneously contained in every other part and in the whole. This is a journey through never-ending circles of connections, by seeing how the parts form a whole, and then seeing this whole become a new part of a bigger whole. In this process, a person may see that a cup of tea is the primary vortex of the universe. While the systems begin to interrelate, the mind is continuously in a state of cognitive seduction. It is like a continuous flow of 'aha!', which may go on for years.

During the symbolic journey, 'hyper-priming' is active, allowing individuals to *easily relate distant concepts* by conceptual or spatial-visual connections, on many levels of abstraction. Hyper-priming is amplified if the person uses ganja frequently.[112a]

The symbolic journey is the natural way for the mind to re-balance itself and connect with deep meanings. A smooth navigation through the symbolic journey depends on the capacity to allow the interconnectedness of meanings to unfold, while maintaining at least some ability to carry out daily activities. To facilitate this process and keep the self-identity in a relatively stable state, activities involving the body are necessary, such as art, dance, massage, running, walking, climbing, or sports.

A side effect of this symbolic journey is that people tend to become stuck in their minds, during this process, hypnotized by the infinite numbers of connections among various and proliferating meanings. When this symbolic configuration interferes too much with usual activities, many people are hospitalized and labeled as psychotic, schizophrenic, or with related diagnoses.[112b]

A suggestion for therapists and transformational counselors who work with people in a symbolic process: supporting clients to create a visual map of their 'theory of everything' is helpful.

After the symbolic journey is completed, and a personal 'theory of everything' has emerged, a vertical shift occurs: the entire mind can become the 'object of awareness', and this shift activates a larger perspective, generating a more inclusive experience of being here-now.

113. *Healing the transgenerational patterns* – This process is about awakening from the spiral of continuous patterns that persist

from generation to generation. It requires an understanding of transgenerational schemes of thinking, feeling, sensing, and behaving. Growing up is not just for ourselves; we grow up as a part of a collective evolutionary process. To become fully free, a person has to notice these transgenerational patterns, do what can be done to harmonize them, and then extract oneself from their transgenerational flow, while connecting to the larger family of humankind.

114. What does it feel like when I change? What does it feel like when other people change? Deep change involves participating in a process that we do not yet understand. It involves changing physical, emotional, and intellectual patterns, and this growth process unfolds continuously during a transformative wave, day and night, until the evolutionary drive is satisfied.

Alison Crosthwait in 'What it Feels Like to Change' says: "Change is an interaction with something new. Over time, I have come to recognize change as it is happening—sometimes. Sometimes my brain goes fuzzy or suddenly empty. Sometimes I feel depleted. And thirsty. Like my psyche just had an intense massage. Sometimes I feel jacked up and manic. Sometimes I feel butterflies. Sometimes my shame is activated and past regrets, mistakes, and vulnerabilities take over with an insatiable vengeance. When I can catch this I call it backlash. Sometimes someone says something unexpected and I consciously try to take it in. To let it change my cells. Sometimes I cry about something I have never cried about before. Sometimes I have a dream or a fantasy, and part of its meaning hits home and I know this is a marker of an incremental shift.

Sometimes someone in my life puts words to a change and I recognize it as true but previously unarticulated. In talking, the change takes shape. Sometimes I have an extra glass of wine that I don't need or want. Later, I can identify this extra glass as a response to new feelings that seemed unmanageable even though unworded. Some of these changes are about my conscious self. Some are about unconscious shifts that I cannot fully articulate. And sometimes there is no perceptible sign of anything.

These are some of the ways that my particular body, mind, and soul respond to transformational work. By transformational work I mean intentional interactions with the new—in other people, in nature, in ideas, in the body. When we seek out the new, we change in response.

What does it feel like when other people change?

I hear something new in their voice. A little more strength. Or less questioning of their right to speak. They express emotion just a little (or a lot) more forcefully—anger, love, sadness, joy—it has more color and texture. My heart skips a beat with excitement and possibility as I realize that I am not trapped in one way of being with this person but that together, not just me but together, we are always creating something new. Together we are healing. I feel wildly angry, irritated, or annoyed at a limit, boundary or observation the person makes. I feel afraid and insecure at a limit, boundary, or new expression from the other person. I feel nervous or agitated around them or when thinking about them. I wonder about them. They say something that startles me. Something I haven't heard before from them. They make a big change that they have been struggling with for a long time. I feel loved in a new way—perhaps more directly or openheartedly.

This isn't a prescriptive list. Sometimes irritation or agitation are responses to other things. But sometimes they are our response to change. What I noticed as I wrote this list is that it is a combination of my own emotional experiences and my noticing of the other person. This is a live example of how our own growth changes the world. When others change it evokes feelings in us. This gives us the opportunity to change. When I feel wild with anger at my friend's new assertions I have the opportunity to explore that, express it, reflect on it—to live on the edge of it. This is my chance to evolve in response to my friend's growth.

Change has a ripple effect. Our change into the world. And the change of others into us and the world. The work that we do in healing and growing and exploring and reflecting: this work matters. It is not navel-gazing (a common critique) unless we make it so. The work of change is the work of healing what is wrong here. Each person's work matters. Every day."[114]

Chapter Five

Developmental Challenges

115. During inner evolution, a series of transformative challenges have been observed by psychologists and practitioners. They may not appear in all individuals, but it's helpful to know that they *could* emerge. If these challenges are not identified and recognized, their automatic unfolding may lead to unnecessary suffering.

116. *Depersonalization* — In the inner evolution journey, depersonalization may accompany the emergence of witnessing awareness. When witnessing first appears, there is a shift in the locus of identity: people see themselves as if from outside, and their entire life could look like a dream. Depersonalization can also occur as a natural post-traumatic response, due to drug addictions (such as ketamine), or as a side effect while learning the 'observing' point-of-view and 'non-dual' inner configurations.

The type of attention that is associated with depersonalization is the diffuse-objective type. In 'Attention to Attention', Les Fehmi explains: "The diffuse focus-objective mode of attention is one in which multisensory experience is simultaneously and objectively present, a potentially vast multidimensional objective awareness. An array of objective sensations hang suspended in the midst of a more general diffuse awareness of space. Playing in a band, appreciating a panoramic sunset, going for a walk or driving a car—these are among the activities for which an appropriate relational strategy may emphasize diffuse focus-objective attention."[116a]

Depersonalization disorder consists of persistent or recurrent feelings of being detached from one's body or mental processes, usually with a feeling of being an outside observer of one's life. In The Diagnostic and Statistical Manual of Mental Disorders (DSM), published by the American Psychiatric Association, depersonalization is often categorized as a reaction to severe stress. The DSM conceptualizes depersonalization as a dissociative disorder and also lists depersonalization as a coping mechanism of posttraumatic stress disorder.[116b]

In the inner evolution process, temporary experiences of depersonalization are just glimpses of the non-conceptual mode of being. 'Depersonalization' can begin as an external observation, and gradually, the experience of being an observer can trigger the activation of the witnessing awareness mode.

117. *Mara's daughters: the chosen one* – This is the tendency to think that 'I am the chosen one', that 'I am the only one that has awakened', or 'I am the next Jesus/Buddha/you name it', and 'there are no others like me'. Just say 'no thanks' to this proposal when it begins to unfold.

———

Māra is the Buddhist 'Lord of the Senses', the god of desire, who tempted Prince Siddhartha (Gautama Buddha) with various offerings. When Mara's direct attempts failed, he sent forth his three daughters, to seduce Gautama, but to no avail. In Buddhism, Mara's daughters are personified by sensual craving (taṇhā), aversion (arati), and passion-desire-attachment (rāga). Using a broader perspective, Mara's daughters are inertial tendencies of life, which could interfere with inner evolution and individuation, if their existence is not acknowledged and their true nature is not recognized.

118. *Mara's daughters: self/ego hijacking* – This is a pattern of experience whereby, after an awakening or transformative experience, or moment of pure awareness, the resulting energy is captured by self/ego-related desires and consumed by fulfilling them. Just say

'not yet' to the 'start-now-this-project' drive, while you are in the post-awakening high. Think about big plans, but don't start anything; wait until the high passes and then check with yourself again to see if you still feel like doing it. Or, create anything you like, but double-check to see if it's coming from your center.

————

In 'Sri Aurobindo or The Adventure of Consciousness', Satprem explains: "The first signs of psychic opening are love and joy; a joy that may be extremely intense and powerful, but without any exaltation and without object, as calm and deep as the sea. Psychic joy does not need anything in order to be; it just is. Even in a prison it cannot help being, for it is not a feeling but a state, like a river sparkling wherever it flows, whether over mud or rocks, across plains or mountains. It is a love that is not the opposite of hate, and it needs nothing to sustain itself. It simply is, burning steadily regardless of what it encounters, in all it sees and all it touches, simply because it cannot help loving, for that is its nature.[...]

The moment it appears, it is instantly snatched up by the vital, which uses it for its own brilliant flights of exaltation, its own 'divine' and tumultuous emotions, its possessive loves, its calculated generosities or gaudy aesthetics; or it is corralled by the mind, which uses it for its own exclusive ideas, its infallible philanthropic schemes, its straitjacketed moralities—not to mention churches, countless churches, which systematize it in articles of faith and dogma. Where is the psychic being in all that? It is there, nonetheless, divine, patient, striving to pierce through each and every crust and actually making use of everything that is given to it or imposed upon it. It 'makes do' with what it has, so to speak. Yet that is precisely the problem: when it comes out of hiding, if even for a second, it casts such a glory upon everything it touches that we tend to mistake the circumstances of the revelations for its luminous truth."[118]

119. Self/ego hijacking may be a cause of the *bipolar cycle* during inner evolution. After a moment of inspiration, the available energy is consumed by various activities (either everyday activities or 'divine missions' or 'change the world missions'). During the 'consumption' phase, the high activation of energy looks like a manic episode; after it is consumed, depression ensues. The solution for this challenge is to use the energy internally and allow it to transform internal mechanisms of being. In other words, the energy should be interiorized and processed similarly to how erotic energy can be converted into enstatic energy.

120. *Mara's daughters: when the self thinks there is no self* – The 'self' never disappears; it just fluidifies, becoming more flexible and adapted to moment-to-moment flows. The patterns of the body's adaptive processing are always in us, and they do have a preferred way of functioning that translates into our conscious experience as a self-identity. This challenge seems to be related to certain spiritual teachings and some spiritual or philosophical communities that promote a dominant perspective that 'I just am', 'there is no self here while I am talking', or 'the self doesn't exist'.

121. *Dark nights and regaining connection* – After the blissful high of the awakening, the energy level and creativity may decrease, and some people think that they have lost their 'gifts', or God has abandoned them, or related thoughts. If this challenge presents itself, instead of searching for ways to return to the awakening/connected state, know that most awakenings are new ways of flowing, not fixed states; they emerge by abandoning oneself continuously into the layers of the present moment and not through remembering.

———

> When a pause in the conscious connection between the individual and the collective is experienced, the individual may experience this disconnection as a 'dark night'. Various dark nights have been observed and described: the dark night of the soul, senses, or dark night of the self. In the

Christian tradition, 'kenosis' is a concept worth exploring, as it relates directly to this challenge of lacking an active connection with life, at least for a while. Kenosis refers to the act of self-emptying oneself to allow a later flow of divine energies.[121]

122. *Maya pattern* – When an individual first realizes the amplitude of the automatic collective patterns, or the collective cultural hypnosis, it may be dramatic from the social-relational perspective. After observing that many people live in an 'internal movie', the individual comes to realize that all humans are living primarily on automatic pilot. In this situation, the only one you can really 'save' is yourself. The collective awakening from illusion is at its earliest stage, and it will take many millennia to advance. Just do your part as well as you can.

123. *Premature transcendence* – The inner evolution journey can lead to openings that need to be 'framed' somehow. Sometimes, a spiritual framework may be the only way of coping with this positive increase in one's overall experience, and the individual can suppose that 'this is it—my search has reached its destination'. Still, the use of spiritual ideas and practices *outside their original context* can give rise to a weak self-identity, compulsive goodness, whitewashing, the repression of undesirable or painful emotions, spiritual narcissism, spiritual obsession or addiction, blind faith in charismatic leaders, the abdication of personal responsibility, and social isolation.

John Welwood, in 'Human Nature. Buddha Nature. On Spiritual Bypassing, Relationship, and the Dharma', comments: "When we are spiritually bypassing, we often use the goal of awakening or liberation to rationalize what I call premature transcendence: trying to rise above the raw and messy side of our humanness before we have fully faced and made peace with it. And then we tend to use absolute truth to disparage or dismiss relative human needs, feelings, psychological problems, relational difficulties, and developmental deficits.[...] Trying to move beyond our psychological and emotional issues by sidestepping them is dangerous. It sets up a debilitating split between the buddha and the human within us. And it leads to a conceptual, one-sided kind of spirituality where one pole of life is elevated at the expense of its opposite: absolute truth is favored over relative truth, the impersonal over the personal, emptiness over form, transcendence over embodiment, and detachment over feeling."[123]

An example of a perspective bias is the idea that 'thoughts are just thoughts; observe them, but don't pay attention to them', when the meditation perspective is used outside the context of meditation practice. In fact, our emotions and thoughts are helpful in our everyday life, as they direct our attention to the topics we need to connect to.

124. *Channeling* is a way of discovering an 'unusual' perspective and allowing information to flow from within, using that specific perspective. Some people misinterpret this process by thinking that the information source is an entity, a spirit, an angel, or an extraterrestrial, outside their psyche. The challenge in this situation is recognizing that *the channeling source is always internal*, while allowing the 'unusual' perspective to be integrated with the other perspectives, in a healthy self-identity. To do this, one has to modify the attentional structure, by allowing the 'channeled' configuration to participate in the conscious experience on a daily basis.

125. *Information overload* may happen during intense waves of transformation. In this situation, it is better to reconnect with nature and use visual methods for organizing the information (such as drawing or painting). A method that has proven helpful is to gather the information in categories and systems using visual 'life maps' or 'journey maps', and to repeat this process until the information has been organized.

When a person is highly social and conversational, or has energy openings (e.g., unconditional love, passion for being, or high levels of aliveness), there may be a lot of non-patterned information infusing the conscious experience. In these situations, when the mind remains 'auditory-verbal', the speed of processing is relatively low, and they may experience the 'hearing voices' phenomenon. In these cases, it could be useful to develop visual-spatial thinking, practice creative arts, and learn perspective-taking skills, so that the information flows may be 'patterned' and the non-conscious information flows integrated. Also, reducing or stopping 'subvocalization' could be helpful (subvocalization is the habit of semi-articulating speech using the throat and tongue, without making audible sounds).[125]

126. Echoes of information from the collective may populate personal inner experience, when there is a personal resonance pattern actively connected to external sources. This connection can happen, for example, through loving someone or something, or as a result of social interactions, reading books, or watching TV.

127. Differentiating between 'my' contents (my emotions, my thoughts) and externally induced contents (imprints from interactions with others' emotions and thoughts) is vital for inner exploration. After connecting with someone, notice if your mind tends to 'talk' with that person. If this is the case, switch the inner talk to self-reflection using a 3rd person perspective (talk with yourself *about* that person and the interactions with that person).

————

Identifying the source may sometimes be possible during inner art sessions, just by asking 'who started this?', 'where is it from?', 'what is the source of this?' or something similar; then listen/watch the possible answers that are formed. Still, this method of interrogating inner experience by asking and listening does not produce 100% correct knowledge. So the results should be interpreted with caution and not be considered the final truth.

128. Integrating a *spiritually transformative experience* includes challenges such as processing a radical shift in one's reality, sharing the experience, integrating new spiritual values and knowledge with worldly expectations, adjusting to hypersensitivities and psychic aftereffects, or finding purpose.

____

The American Center for the Integration of Spiritually Transformative Experiences has issued a white paper on this topic, titled 'Cultural Competency Guidelines for Professionals Working with Clients Who Report Issues Related to Their Spiritually Transformative Experience'. In the guidelines, the authors explain:

"An experience is spiritually transformative when it causes people to perceive themselves and the world profoundly differently: by expanding the individual's identity, augmenting their sensitivities, and thereby altering their values, priorities, and appreciation of the purpose of life.[...] Not all spiritual experiences are 'transformative'. Whether or not an experience is transformative depends on the nature of the experience, one's age at the time of the experience, the experiencer's culture and personal spiritual beliefs, and whether the experience(s) have been integrated into one's personality and everyday life. Not all paranormal, psychic, out-of-body, alien or other 'otherworldly' experiences are spiritually transformative.[...]

These experiences can happen to anyone, at any time, spontaneously or through intention, for any length of time and under any circumstance—including during clinical death as with near-death experiences. Induced spiritual experiences can happen through meditation, breathwork, drug intake, sensory deprivation, prayer, ceremonial or religious rituals, shamanic drumming, ritual dancing, in sweat lodges, in natural settings, during sex or sleep, or after extended periods of physical exertion, fasting, pain or silence, etc. They can also occur while conducting ordinary activities such as while conversing or driving a car. A person who has had—or is having—a spiritually transformative or emergent experience—with its subsequent changes or differences in values, beliefs, and identity, can become part of a larger shared culture or part of distinctive individual culture(s). Transformation following a spiritual experience can involve positive, negative, or mixed effects on feelings and/or functioning. The effects or challenges can be temporary or enduring."[128]

129. Inner evolution dynamics, related to the transition to a more fluid self-identity, are rarely approached successfully by traditional psychotherapeutic methods. They require therapists with experience in *non-dual psychotherapy* and knowledge of inner growth stages. The counselor must 'abandon' their regular self-identity, as the client experiences a self-identity/ego death or an identity change. Otherwise, the counselor will unconsciously 'fixate' the client's self-identity, stopping the transformation process. An appropriate therapeutic approach could be an unconditional presence, which doesn't require *establishing a rapport* between the counselor and the client.

——

In 'Nonduality: A Spontaneous Movement To and Fro', Kaissa Puhakka writes: "Nothing is required of the other in nondual presence, not even that the other be present. The last point is very subtle and its significance is easy to miss. I had missed it for many years without, of course, realizing that I had missed it. As a therapist, I felt my job was to help my clients to be present with me. I tried to use the relationship with my clients therapeutically, to bring them into presence through relationship with me. Then one day, I realized that I had been working on an assumption all along. This assumption was that I could not be in contact with my clients unless they were in contact with me. That contact is mutual and reciprocal seemed intuitively compelling, and so I had never questioned it, never even realized that I had accepted it as a premise to 'come from' into the therapy work.

But one day I realized it, and the realization freed me up to be present and connected unconditionally, regardless of whether my client was present 'with me'. My fixation around reciprocal presence was unraveled and my self was free to 'go into' nonduality in the presence of another, to be in full contact with her even when she was not with me. Nondual presence has no requirement for reciprocity. It did not require me to withdraw from it because my client did. It did not require me to be or do anything. And just as important, it did not require anything [from] my client."[129]

130. Sometimes the transition to a new inner configuration happens dramatically, leading to *psycho-spiritual crises*. Therapeutic approaches such as 'open dialogue', 'healing homes', and nature retreats have been proven effective in supporting individuals through these types of transformations.

————

Spiritual crises are natural responses to unusual life circumstances, occurring during the inner evolution process. Christina and Stanislav Grof have introduced the concept of 'spiritual emergency' or psycho-spiritual crises to describe moments of dramatic transformations. They have identified various types of spiritual emergencies, such as shamanic crisis; awakening of kundalini; episodes of unitive consciousness; psychological renewal through returning to the center; crisis of psychic opening; past-life experiences; communication with spirit guides and 'channeling'; near-death experiences; close encounters with ufos and alien abduction experiences; possession states; alcoholism and drug addiction.

In 'Psychology of the Future: Lessons from Modern Consciousness Research', Stanislav Grof explains: "Many of the conditions, which are currently diagnosed as psychotic and indiscriminately treated by suppressive medication, are actually difficult stages of a radical personality transformation and of spiritual opening. If they are correctly under-stood and supported, these psychospiritual crises can re-sult in emotional and psychosomatic healing, remarkable psychological transformation, and consciousness evolu-tion."[130a]

Since the introduction of the 'Religious or Spiritual Prob-lem' in DSM-IV, this perspective is expanding slowly into mainstream psychiatry, and training programs for spiritual competencies are available for therapists and coun-selors[130b]. The Open Dialogue approach was pioneered in Finland, and it focuses on early therapeutic interventions that include the individual, their family, and their social networks (early intervention means intervention within twenty-four hours of the initial contact with the person in crisis).[130c]

In the 'Healing Homes' approach, individuals are relocated to a host family and they live together for up to a year or two. This approach was developed by the Family Care Foundation in Gothenburg, Sweden, where staff members offer psychotherapy sessions and provide host families with intensive supervision.[130d]

Other approaches, with centers such as Diabasis, devel-oped by John Weir Perry, have shown that schizophrenia and bipolar disorder can be 'treated', if the transformation process is carried on. People can get un-stuck from their symbolic world, if the symbolic journey is completed and the reconstruction of the new self-identity begins. 'Schizophrenia' is a self-healing process. The reason we have 'chronic schizophrenia' diagnostics is in fact a cultural issue; it is society's negative response to what is a perfectly natural and healthy process, sometimes including visionary experiences.[130e]

131. To reach a global inner harmony, all components of conscious experience (such as witnessing, cognition, perspective, attention, emotions, pulsional energy, perceptual connection to the physical

body, and self-identity) must be transformed and allowed to function simultaneously. All systems need upgrades to create a harmonic conscious experience. For instance, shutting down the development of rational thinking to favor emotional connection ('all is love, nothing else matters', 'feel, don't think'), or shutting down self-identity to favor non-dual awareness ('all is awareness, universe is awareness') may be helpful for a while. Still, overall, these *unilateral trajectories* lead to unbalanced development.

———

Jeff Warren in 'The Promise and Peril of Spiritual Belief' says: "I know a man, a Buddhist vipassana teacher, who lives in emptiness. When he walks down the street, the world gushes like a fountain, emerging from and disappearing into emptiness, which for him is everywhere and nowhere. It is the great reassurance of his life. I know another man, an Advaita non-dual teacher, who lives in awareness. From moment to moment he is connected to the unshakable sense that everything is awareness and only awareness—solid, undying, unchanging. It is the great reassurance of his life. I know a woman, a lapsed Catholic, who lives with God. As she goes about her day there is a continual and vivid sense of presence, of being in relationship with an alive and loving Other. It is the great reassurance of her life.

The strange thing is, I kind of know what they mean. When I go on long vipassana retreats, my sensory experience of the world begins to thin. Everything pixelates; the whole sensorium seems increasingly dreamlike. I get a taste for emptiness then—but only a taste. I can understand how this is a direction I might take.

When I immerse myself in nondual teachings, my own awareness becomes vivid and spacious. I begin to see how there are no problems with awareness, only in awareness. I realize that even my desire to change the world is, in its way, complete. I get a taste for awareness then—but only a taste. I can understand how this is a direction I might take.

When I participate in plant medicine ceremonies, I get the sense that the whole world is alive and secretly winking to me. Everything is meaningful—the crow flying across the sky, the shadows in the trees, that person's voice, right there, at that exact moment. I get a taste for God then— but only a taste. I can understand how this is a direction I might take."[131]

Chapter Six

Discovery Journeys

132. There are three main types of inner configurations ('states of consciousness') that unfold naturally or that can be accessed through various transformative methods:
– Low arousal configurations, when the physical, energy, and information layers of the body have the same pattern of slow activity. These configurations are active in relaxation, yoga asanas, meditation, and deep sleep.
– High arousal configuration, when the body layers are hyper-activated. Some examples are dance, mystical rapture, ecstatic trance, and kundalini experiences.
– Mixed configurations, when the layers are not following the same pattern of activation. In these mixed configurations, a body layer could be aroused while others are relaxed, and there are various combinations of low to high arousals of the body layers. This category includes experiences such as night dreams, lucid dreaming, certain entheogenic experiences, or enstatic flowing.

133. On the low arousal continuum, a typical *inner art session* using relaxation has these stages: after closing the eyes and calming the body-mind, the inner experience shifts to relaxation, and the mind content is usually composed of the adaptive processing of daily activities. After a while, *pratyahara* occurs (i.e., isolation from external stimuli), and the body layers can either enter a dream state, or transition directly to deep sleep, depending on how tired the physical body is. For inner art sessions, it is better to allow a short journey into deep sleep (or practice yoga nidra), so that the body may replenish and reharmonize naturally. Then, after refreshing the energy resources, the person should be able to start the inner explorations with a clear mind.

134. On the high arousal continuum, during inner art sessions with an *energetic* component, the inner world has a specific quality when kundalini is activated (by itself or intentionally). *High-energy kundalini spikes* tend to energize *visual spatio-temporal thinking*, manifested as 'visions', as compared to audio-sequential thinking, mediated by words. The speed of thinking is higher through images, and the rich causal content of the high-energy experiences makes the perceived speed even faster, because *causal events enter awareness faster* than non-causal events.

____

The perceived *high-speed* of kundalini-spike experiences is due to these three factors: visual-spatial thinking (happening fast), the preference toward causal thinking (increasing the speed even further), and the fact that causal events enter conscious awareness experience faster[134a]. The extraordinary *intensity/density* of the kundalini-spike experiences comes from these elements: a denser content due to increased receptivity, increased synesthesia providing additional multidimensional connections, a higher speed of processing due to visual-causal thinking, and a faster entrance of causal content into awareness.[134b]

135. It is possible to *add spatial awareness and depth perception* to the workspace of inner experience. This is done through enhancing awareness of the physical space and the size of the perceived body layers. Try this sequence: maintain *pratyahara* with closed eyes, reach a stable isolation from external stimuli, and then use spatial awareness to *expand the attention* to include external space, not just the inner space, while maintaining *both external and internal space* as 'one'. In other words, use a deep connection with the inner space, specific to *pratyahara* style, but refine the perspective to perceive inner space and external space as one, while allowing information from outside the body to enter the experience. When external awareness is merged with internal awareness, and the physical 3D space is experienced as a common framework, the state is referred to as a *unitive experience* (or unitary mystical state).

____

In my inner explorations, one of my favorite styles of contemplation is to just watch the scenery, in front of me, and notice how stimuli in the environment modulate the attentional structure. I use a unitary configuration, combining the inner and outer worlds. I was practicing this exercise for a while, when the following experience occurred. I was near a fire, the day after an ayahuasca session, in the Santo Daime community. On my right, there was a friend, and on her right, there was another person I didn't know well. I couldn't see him, as we were in a line. The fire was near a forest, and so we were oriented towards the fire; beyond the fire the forest's rim was visible. As usual, I was contemplating the scenery, and for a while, I felt like I was the only observer paying attention to the landscape, using my own 'configuration'. But I had a surprise. While watching the trees at the edge of the forest, for the first time, I felt that someone else was looking at the scenery also. We were two observers witnessing, and I felt that the other person was just there, but not aware of my presence. She/he was there, scanning, but this person's attentional stream didn't have a collective self-reflection quality active.

Then I was curious, and I asked the collective, 'Who is watching?'. Instantly, the attention 'locked' upon the 'foreign' attentional stream, and the eyes searched the source. And I turned to my right, and guess what? It was the person sitting to the right of my friend. He was enjoying the contemplative experience. The attentional flux was coming from him. I leaned forward a bit, looking into his eyes, and there it was, the source of the 'foreign' attentional stream. We seemed to have a similar attentional configuration. But to him, my action of watching his flow was not in his conscious awareness bubble. In other words, this thread of information was unconscious for him; he interpreted my scans as a natural movement of the scenery.

I talked to him (he was a French guy, very relaxed), and I felt inside him the similarity of our perceptual styles, adapted to contemplative experiences. He told me that a possible explanation was that, perhaps, there is a limited number of inner configurations in human beings. I think this is true, but I also think that experiencing ayahuasca together, that night, had created a good sync between us.

The next step happened while I was at Waha, a transformational festival in the Carpathian Mountains of Romania. I was watching the trees at a distance, and in front of me there was a small path for people to move uphill, from the river below. I thought, 'Hmm, let's try something'. Some people were walking in a contemplative attitude, and after some tunings using samyama, I was able to enter their experience by noticing the difference: the scenery without a person or with a person. I detected that there were differences in my perception. So, while connecting to another person and the scenery simultaneously, I isolated their 'personal information' and—bing!—I participated in the person's contemplative experience, without interfering. For the other person, I was just a part of the scenery. During this connection, new information was available to me, usually information about various stimuli from other people's experiences. Some seemed to be in their local self-identity bubble, some were in a broader frame, including the event area, others were more connected to the trees, the Earth, or various other elements. I was able to feel some qualities of their energy, as new emotions entered my field (without being mine), while having the person in front of me as a resonance source.

The amazing part was how the perception of trees and the environment was changing while I was connected to the person's bubble. Some inner configurations were so new to me that I was amazed to feel how they were 'looking at' (and feeling about) the trees and the environment.

136. *The localization of the inner experiences in the physical 3D space,* using divided attention, could clarify some confusion in the interpretation of inner experiences. For instance, dreaming and dreamlike experiences, such as 'out-of-body experiences', take place in the inner space while *pratyahara* is active.

———

> An exploration of perceptual depths and various types of expansions are described in the case study no. 3—'Depth perception, space awareness, and other visual explorations'.

137. The *night dream* is a partial reflection of the automatic adaptive processing in the body layers (physical, energy, and information). The night dream may provide useful information about one's inner life dynamics, especially if the *dreamwork psychology* methodologies for exploration and interpretation are used. The books with dream symbols and their symbolic interpretation have no relevance or value for inner evolution, because each dream symbol has a personal significance to the dreamer. Moreover, the same symbol can have a different meaning in each dream, depending on the context. When analyzing dreams, the relationship of the dream self/ego with the symbol is more relevant than the symbol itself.

———

> Some relevant questions for exploring your dreams could be: What are you doing and not doing in your dream? Are you active or passive in this dream, and why? What kind of situation or issue is the dream trying to train you about? Are you resisting or in tune with what the dream is doing? What issues need resolving in this dream? Are you trying to control life or let go into a wisdom source such as the dream? Are you choosing in dreams and life, aware of what you are really doing? Who makes your ultimate choices for you? Your self/ego? Are you dealing with your nightmares and other scary situations?
>
> For additional reading, see: 'Dreamwork online course in 9 steps', available at www.dreamwork-psychology.com. The

course is a simplified and easy-to-use version of the dream-work methodology developed by Strephon Kaplan-Williams, the founding father of dreamwork psychology. The nine lessons are structured as an exploratory flow in an ever-increasing depth. The dreamwork methods selected for this course help you understand the functional meaning of the dream, not just the symbolic connections. *Objectifying the Dream* details the structures and units of meaning inherent to the dream itself as shown in the dream report. *Following the Dream Self/Ego* focuses on behaviors, actions, non-actions, and motivating attitudes and patterns of the dreamer in the dream. These discoveries can then be applied to life actions and attitudes, so as to evaluate and make changes according to the reality principle. *Dream Dialogue* releases unconscious contents associated with a dream symbol. *Dream Reentry* helps the dreamer re-experience dream contents by going back into the dream through the meditative state and through the door of the dream's imagery and actions. Dream reentry also works to help resolve dream issues and scenes. *Dream Enactments* are mini-dramas enacted from simplified dream scenes to help the dreamer re-experience dream contents and resolve issues. *Dream Tasks* are specific choices to be practiced, which come out of the dream and its dreamwork.

138. By *accessing a dream-like configuration*, in self-induced experiences during inner art sessions, it is possible to intervene in the automatic adaptive processing and modify or 'align' some patterns. While working with dream-like experiences, an active witnessing awareness mode is necessary, especially during the transitions through dream states and deep sleep states. It is healthy to do these dreamwork explorations separately from the natural night dreaming process; the night dreaming should be allowed to happen automatically, outside of self-identity control.

139. The automatic adaptive processing, which becomes available to conscious awareness during inner explorations in visual dream-like states, is grouped in *patterns* that have specific styles of unfolding (or flowing). As pieces of information can contribute to more than one pattern, the meanings would shift dynamically, while the visual-spatial thinking creates various visual landscapes and actions, based on non-conscious automatic processing.

140. When working with the visual-spatial content and patterns during inner explorations, the *pattern of flowing* is most relevant, not the interpretation of the symbolic content. In other words, pay attention to how the dream-like scenes unfold, explore why and how they transform from one into another, and notice how their flowing pattern is generated by your mental and emotional preferences. Then, work with yourself to adjust your life through harmonic actions, while watching again, in the inner art sessions, whether the unfolding pattern has changed.

141. *Lucid dreaming* or *visualizations* may alter some flowing patterns. Still, these methods require frequent actions on the same pattern to induce a real change in the pattern, as these methods do not usually impact the physical and energy correlate of the pattern. Visualization and lucid dreaming usually explore the *content of the patterns*, not their causal structure, nor their specific way of unfolding.

142. During visual dream-like states, all body layers are in a continuous state of flux, and they flow based on patterns that were developed through past experiences. Some of their relevant past configurations could be partially revealed to conscious awareness, when *samyama* is performed on a specific scene or pattern of flowing, during the visual dream-like state, while monitoring the inner workspace using witnessing awareness.

———

For inner evolution, it is more appropriate to just watch the inner visual workspace, allow all the contents, and use visuals as a feedback tool. The dream-like flows show you where you are in your inner development. Don't try to dress the messenger the way you prefer, using lucid dreaming or other controlling methods. Instead, use samyama to get more information and learn about your non-conscious patterns and flows. Still, lucid dreaming is a fantastic method if you just want to play with the visuals and enhance your ability to intervene in the flows, as a preliminary practice for learning samyama.

Some detailed explanations on how to use samyama are included in the case study no. 4, 'How to activate and navigate intentional visionary experiences', available in the Case Studies section of this book.

143. In dream-like visual configurations, it is possible to access the *H-band*, the pre-conscious adaptive processing. The H-layer contains information at the brink of associations that may further develop (or not) as patterns, which later enter the conscious experience. The attentional configuration that is useful for attending to the H-band is the global-objective style.

——

Robert Monroe explains: "The peak of uncontrolled thought emanating from all living forms on Earth, particularly humans, is found in the H-Band. If you consider it as truly all, even in the current time frame, you get a better idea of the magnitude of this disorganised cacophonous mass of noisy energy.[...] Passing through it quickly is advisable, just as one would try to work through a screaming angry mob—for that is what it sounds like, in a multitude of accents and tongues."[143]

Although it has no specific relevance for inner evolution, the H-band processing can be observed through visuals and can be fun.

144. Other layers that can be accessed during visual explorations include the *archetypal layer*, containing highly symbolic and emo-

tional content from various cultures, or the *visionary layer*, which includes densely packed information in higher resolution, with powerful insights and energetic effects when kundalini is involved.

145. Visionary experiences are available through exogenous entheogens, music, dance, or natural kundalini activations, but also intentionally, through practice, during inner arts sessions. *Intentional visionary experiences* are facilitated by previous experiences of kundalini activation, or kundalini peaks during experiences with entheogenic medicine such as ayahuasca, changa, or LSD, mescaline, psilocybin, or other plants or substances.

146. Navigating the inner world during intentional visionary experiences requires a *conscious transition* through the layers of experience and skills for diving into various contents (through samyama), without becoming fully absorbed in the content of the experience.

147. The densely packed information, accessed during high-energy kundalini peaks, can be perceived as *downloads* of information. This is a natural property of the *high-resolution* visual-perceptual style of thinking, as compared to the everyday low-resolution style. Because of its multidimensionality, even a simple high-resolution scene can have an intense meaning-making message, which can be later *unzipped* and re-encoded into everyday life as usable information.

148. During high-energy kundalini peaks, the perceptual visual flows, including visual-spatial thinking and perceptual visuals related to the eye retina, can be used as a *feedback tool* for navigating through visionary experiences, in an intentional and interactive way. When visual-spatial thinking is active (as in a dreamy state), visions can be similar to a lucid dream but with an intense meaning-making structure.

149. Learning the transition from *ecstatic* to *enstatic* configurations provides additional awareness during high-energy experiences and opens up new gates for exploration. Enstatic flowing is generated

when attention is divided to incorporate two configurations: *high-energy experience* of the moving body and the *silent-static experience* of 'center/space', simultaneously. Enstatic dance is one method that allows the management of high-energy kundalini spikes during visionary experiences, which sometimes feel overwhelming if the person is static.

150. The *enstatic skills*, allowing low and high arousal simultaneously, broaden the variety of inner experiences and enhance their multidimensionality. Developing enstatic skills and *practicing enstatic dance* is also helpful for individuals who experience sudden, uncontrollable body tremors or spasms, while going through the *pranotthana* stage of kundalini awakening. The practice of enstatic flowing enhances the fluidity of the energy body patterns.

———

The enstatic configuration in dance can be learned by using high-energy music, and moving the hands or the physical body very slowly, while keeping the high-level energy inside the energy body. During enstatic flowing, there is no 'static center' to lock the attention to, the entire body schema is the center (the flowing-through-the-body is 'the center'). The divided-attention style for enstatic flowing could be visually described as slow-flowing 'structure' (defined by static vibrations), plus high-flowing content (inside the 'structure').

Through enstatic flowing, the attentional configuration can be influenced even more: it is also possible to transition from an inner-oriented awareness toward a mixed configuration. Internal and external awareness (as in a unitary mystical state) allows a more expanded depth perception, influencing the spaciousness of experience and allowing even more energetic intensities, which can be managed by expanding/contracting the size of the expansion, consciously. Sufi whirling is one spiritual methodology, among others, that has successfully incorporated the enstatic configuration into its high-energy movements.

151. During intentional visionary experiences, a direct method that produces an *instant reconsolidation* is to enter the dream-like state, watch the unfolding automatic perception through dream-like visuals, and when a scene from the visual experience needs to be modified, intervene by activating the retina perception (i.e., inner eye vision). Then, focus on that specific flow/pattern, and dive-into/absorb that pattern (or visual scene), in a way similar to *samyama*, while allowing the automatic activation of kundalini. Then allow the pattern to be harmonized by itself within the body layers. When using this method of fully merging with a visual scene, *it is unnecessary to control* the pattern by directing it to a 'correct' flow. Instead, the *full acceptance* of whatever comes generates an automatic homeostatic integration process.

Inner eye vision is described as an awakening journey, titled 'Inner eye vision: merging of the inner mental space with the real physical space', found in the Appendix. Various techniques to merge with a pattern or scene are described in the case study no. 4, 'How to activate and navigate intentional visionary experiences', available in the Case Studies section.

152. The *high-pitched sound* that appears during high-energy DMT-like experiences, usually called 'carrier wave', comes from the self-tuning energy, due to the 'pressure' of the hyper-synchronizing process. This *inner sound* becomes noticeable not only in high-energy experiences, but also when people begin their transformational journeys in life, or go through transformative times. Sometimes, the inner sound is misdiagnosed as tinnitus.

In 'The Brain: Ringing in the Ears Actually Goes Much Deeper Than That', Carl Zimmer writes: "Winfried Schlee of the University of Konstanz in Germany and his colleagues have been making some of the most detailed studies of tinnitus ever, using a method called magnetoencephalography (MEG, for short). They take advantage of the fact that every time neurons send each other signals, their electric current creates a tiny magnetic field. MEG allows scientists to detect such changing patterns of activity in the brain 100 times per second. Schlee and his colleagues find widespread differences in the brains of people with tinnitus and those without it. A network of regions in the brains of people with tinnitus tend to fire their neurons in sync. Schlee has determined that his tinnitus-stricken subjects have a more synchronized pattern of signals coming out of regions in the front and the back of the brain. (For brain anatomy junkies, they are the dorsolateral prefrontal cortex, orbitofrontal cortex, and anterior cingulate cortex in the front; in the back, they are the precuneus and posterior cingulate cortex.) Schlee and his colleagues also discovered a more strongly synchronized flow of signals coming into the temporal cortex—a region that includes the auditory cortex—in people with tinnitus."[152]

153. Using *inner sound as a feedback tool*, while navigating visionary experiences, is a simple and effective tool for diving deeper into inner experiences, creating the inner workspace for intentional visionary experiences.

————

This is what I tried in my inner explorations. Lying relaxed on a couch, eyes closed, while the entire body goes into deep sleep, using earplugs, I move the inner observer, slowly, consciously, layer through layer, as described by Timothy Leary, Ralph Metzner, and Richard Alpert, in 'The Psychedelic Experience. A Manual Based on the Tibetan Book of the Dead'[153]. Previously, I practiced what they advised, in a few entheogenic sessions, and it worked; then I learned the process and applied it to my inner experiences. After internalizing the perception, I go through the emotional layer, the cognitive, the visual dreamy state, and finally, I approach the deep sleep stage, without active thinking, while witnessing is 'on'. It is like arriving in the inner spacious space-void, which is in fact the physical space occupied by my body-bubble of energy and information. In this inner space, I use the inner sound to create a sync in the audible vibrations, creating a single coherent wave in the entire energy body, by using the inner sound as feedback for micro-managing the transitions. It feels like taming the carrier wave, the same sound that appears strongly in DMT experiences, and the result is that, when the global sync is activated, I transition with my awareness to the energy layer, while remaining visually active, thus creating an inner workspace for intentional visionary experiences.

I noticed that smoking natural tobacco intensifies the pitch of the inner sound, and it is easier to work with the inner sound after I smoke a hand-rolled cigarette. Also, micro-doses of both ganja and tobacco work well, as ganja is a very intelligent navigator. Sometimes I use earplugs and over-the-ear headphones, listening to music with high 3D effects. The earplugs isolate the high frequencies, allowing a focus on inner sound, while the music provides the energy. The surrounding effect triggers a natural synchronization of the brainwaves, facilitating a smooth transition to high-energy experiences. In this way, centering is very strong, and it is possible to manage even the most powerful, high-resolution visionary spikes, or the high-energy experiences generated by diving into un-harmonized contents.

154. Engaging in frequent transformative experiences without allowing time for their *integration* may be partially helpful. For instance, an intense entheogenic experience needs at least half a year or one year to integrate, due to its cascading effects, from easy-to-observe changes, in the first weeks, to deep and subtle changes in the months and years following the experience.

———

It may happen that for some individuals, the entheogenic experiences could lead afterward to self/ego trips, ego hijacking, spiritual-framework absorption (spiritual bypass), or 'aliens/energy-beings' interpretations. Or side effects such as psychotic-like disintegration or ego inflation. If the person doesn't have a good grip on their self-identity structure, and the entheogenic experience brings in a lot of repressed or ignored information, chances are that the self-identity will be overwhelmed by the flux and collapse, or react with an ego trip.

155. During collective experiences with ayahuasca, such as the dancing ceremonies at Santo Daime, the synchronizing process is facilitated by the collective. Sometimes, a person would process a collective blockage, helping all the others. Or a person might cry, without having a personal reason, because it helps another person in the group who is energy-stuck.

I was amazed to experience and observe this collective healing in Santo Daime ceremonies. This intelligent redistribution of tasks, when each individual is a part of the One and is being taken care of by the One, is based on resonance. When, during a collective high sync, a participant has a release, a letting go of something, the release may be felt by the entire group. The profound eye contact during the intense waves of high-resolution spikes—well, that is another amazing experience worth trying.[155]

156. Practicing shared awareness consciously together, in groups, we awaken to who and what we all truly are, an *enlightening* universal intelligence, appearing as uniquely individuating minds and bodies. Awakeness has no image, yet—like a mirror—it unites, reflects, and transforms our imaginations, inspiring love and awe. By sharing awakeness, the delusions of separation dissolve, awakening and enlightening our selves and all of humankind.

In 'Sharing Awareness Consciously Together', Sperry Andrews comments: "We all understand what it means to give our undivided attention when we are listening carefully to someone. Instead of meditating on our breath or on a candle flame, we begin a process of zeroing-in on sharing undivided attention. By focusing moment to moment on sharing a sense of rapport with everyone in the group, we get better at it. This alters our experience of what it means to be conscious with at least one other person. The more we share a sense of undivided attention with everyone in the group, the more we share a sense of breathing together, of feeling together. This is a subtle process, and allows for a deepening sense of relaxation and the gradual development of effortless concentration. When collective attention is undivided and aware of itself, people can recognize its quality and presence. Participants experience the breath entering and leaving one another's bodies as well as a profound altruistic way of being together. Our minds and bodies serve as a lens—as do our eyes and ears—for attending to whatever we choose to notice. Clearly, we seem designed to receive, reflect, and be—whatever we attend to."[156]

To ignite deep conversations and facilitate co-evolution in interpersonal relationships and groups, you can use *Awake!—The Evolutionary Self-Discovery Test*, a reciprocal learning tool available at www.consciousness-quotient.com. The test is composed of 177 stems, designed to explore conscious and non-conscious patterns of thinking, feeling, acting and reacting, perspectives, attitudes, beliefs, and other facets of your inner world. Complete the test yourself, and ask your partner, your friends, or your clients to do the test, exchange the results, and then discuss together the deep meanings of life.

157. Conscious evolution in intimate relationships means transitioning from psychological and emotional co-dependency, or re-

lationships based on practical-psychological needs, to *conscious re-lationships*, either as a couple or in a marriage. In a conscious relationship, both partners have a growth mindset, oriented toward mutual co-evolution. The partners seek to empower each other, providing a space for their partner to evolve, while also enjoying the shared space. They appreciate what each partner provides, without forcing or manipulating the partner into desired behaviors or attitudes.

158. In this type of transformative connection, the relationship is primarily a space to share and practice deep connection, mutual awakening, growth, unconditional love, and caring. Fulfilling other needs comes as a secondary benefit. In a conscious relationship, *each partner is responsible for their own emotions and feelings* and committed to doing inner work to harmonize with their partner, without projecting self-oriented needs and desires on the other person. Working with the shadow and developing emotional intelligence are vital for a conscious relationship.

> A common we-space based on unconditional love and truthful communication can nourish the inner life of both partners, providing a safe container that supports the inner growth and awakening of each partner. Reciprocal learning, unconditional care, and support for the partner's inner process are essential.

159. Some conscious relationships are experienced by partners as 'soul-mate' connections, where there is a total openness to the connection, and the partners can 'see' and 'feel' each other in extraordinarily deep and interconnected ways. However, once it is developed, this harmonic profoundness can become a *conscious interconnectivity skill* and be used for interacting with other people from the larger 'soul-family', or with anyone open to this type of 'soul-level' connection.

160. The conscious skills learned during the developmental journeys can be used by couples and individuals who become parents to develop a *conscious parenting* style. Conscious parenting includes a positive parenting approach, as opposed to power-based approaches such as authoritarian, permissive, or uninvolved. Conscious parenting promotes an empathic and open communication based on emotional intelligence, respect, authenticity, unconditional love and support, especially in the early years when the brain patterns are developing their mainframes. The conscious parenting approach has roots in educational styles such as Montessori or Waldorf, proven to have positive effects on children's inner development.

————

Heather Lonczak, in 'What is Positive Parenting? A Look at the Research and Benefits', writes: "The Committee of Ministers of the Council of Europe defined positive parenting as 'nurturing, empowering, nonviolent', and 'provides recognition and guidance which involves setting of boundaries to enable the full development of the child'. These definitions, combined with the positive parenting literature, suggest the following about positive parenting:
  - it involves guiding
  - it involves leading
  - it involves teaching
  - it is caring
  - it is empowering
  - it is nurturing
  - it is sensitive to the child's needs
  - it is consistent
  - it is always non-violent
  - it provides regular open communication
  - it provides affection
  - it provides emotional security
  - it provides emotional warmth

- it provides unconditional love
- it recognizes the positive
- it respects the child's developmental stage
- it rewards accomplishments
- it sets boundaries
- it shows empathy for the child's feelings
- it supports the child's best interests."[160]

161. The conscious parenting style is highly intentional and deliberate about increasing the we-space and the presence-awareness in the parental relationship, thus supporting the inner growth of children. *Conscious parents are aware* that their non-conscious processes are easily transferred to their kids through imitation and resonance. Thus, they become interested in doing personal work to harmonize the *unhealthy transgenerational patterns* in themselves, so that these patterns won't be transferred to their children.

———

The conscious approach to parenting includes learning about the psychological processes and transfers between parents and their kids, including the effects that some parental actions and attitudes can have on children's personalities. If the parents' personal roads and values diverge, it may be better to separate and provide the children with a healthy parenting style, instead of feeding them with unconscious frustrations and dysfunctional family imprints. This is difficult in some cultures when divorce or separation is given a stigma, but there are always solutions if one looks for them.

162. Conscious skills can also be used for developing *conscious organizations* and for learning conscious leadership skills. A conscious organization is described in the following ways: it has a world-centric or planet-centric perspective, a collective evolutionary purpose, and a culture based on cooperation-collaboration; further, the employees are regarded as valuable human beings with complex personalities (they are not merely human tools). In a con-

scious organization, the relationships between hierarchical levels are based on reciprocal leadership (instead of power-based hierarchical structures), and the managers empower the individuals in their teams to develop and evolve as human beings.

In 'Discovering Your Company's Higher Purpose', Tara Jenkins states: "Your employees are looking for meaningful work. Purposeful, meaningful work is the top factor people consider when deciding to work or stay at a company. We all want to feel like we are contributing to something bigger. It's not enough to put in our hours and go home. Employees want to make a difference and contribute to their company's success. But too often there is no avenue for their input or they are criticized for deviating from the norm. All that potential is lost in minutiae and company policy (and often, employer ego). You can't afford not to pay attention to this for a number of crucial reasons.

When we hire employees, we are making an investment in them, not just for our business, but in their lives. Considering that your employees will spend most of their time and energy at work, those in the Conscious Business Movement believe we have a responsibility to them, fostering their prosperity, health, happiness, and wellbeing. When investing the time to discover your business's Higher Purpose, you create the opportunity for all those touching your organization to live a life filled with more purpose and meaning. What better gift is there?

To some, investing so deeply in determining the Higher Purpose of their company might seem like a frivolity, something that takes away from the focus of the bottom line. But in long-term gains, the potential is staggering. Purpose leads to higher employee and customer retention. Keeping your talent and your customers is paramount to long-term stability and future success. When employees and customers align with your Purpose, they will form a bond of loyalty that will not be broken and they will bring others to you. It's a virtuous cycle. It's that simple."[162a]

The Conscious Capitalism movement outlines the following principles of a conscious business, in 'Conscious Capitalism Philosophy':

"Higher Purpose – Elevating humanity through business begins with knowing Why your company exists. Without this, you have no compass to find and stay focused on your True North. Businesses should exist for reasons beyond just making a profit. We see profit as a necessary means to achieving your purpose—not as an end in and of itself.

Stakeholder Orientation – Recognizing that the interdependent nature of life and the human foundations of business, a business needs to create value with and for its various stakeholders (customers, employees, vendors, investors, communities, etc.).

Conscious Leadership – Human social organizations are created and guided by leaders—people who see a path and inspire others to travel along the path. Conscious Leaders understand and embrace the Higher Purpose of business and focus on creating value for and harmonizing the interests of the business stakeholders. They recognize the integral role of culture and purposefully cultivate Conscious Culture.

Conscious Culture – This is the ethos—the values, principles, practices—underlying the social fabric of a business, which permeates the atmosphere of a business and connects the stakeholders to each other and to the purpose, people and processes that comprise the company. All companies have a culture, but not all companies intentionally develop a culture that promotes their values and purpose."[162b]

163. *Conscious leaders* are aware, cooperative, and collaborative. Instead of following the hierarchical power-based paradigm, the

conscious leader is a facilitator who catalyzes group decisions and problem solving. Conscious leadership is grounded in the socio-cultural knowledge of reciprocity, allowing leaders to perceive patterns in their environment, recognize the interconnectivity of multiple problems, and subscribe to a participatory leadership style, which incorporates shared responsibility and problem solving. A conscious leader knows that communication is essential, while 'ghosting' someone (i.e., not replying to their initial message, or cutting off communication after an exchange) is an unacceptable behavior, which damages the organization and the human interconnectivity.

———

Valita Jones, in a research article titled 'In Search of Conscious Leadership: A Qualitative Study of Postsecondary Educational Leadership', writes: "Conscious leadership is a reciprocal connected practice. Conscious leaders are better at developing healthy authentic relationships with their employees and other leaders, especially as they are now more than ever able to work collaboratively and in partnership with other employees outside of their departments.

Conscious leaders are willing to approach and practice leadership in a diverse and unique way. A conscious leadership practice is a sustainable leadership practice and can assist in creating organizational practices where leaders embrace the chaos, and by observing the patterns and the themes in the environment, create order through the use of relational ways of being. Conscious leaders become responsible and create communities of practice, which serve as viable models of practice for others to follow. Conscious leaders use dialogical inquiry where strategic questions are posed to gather collective insight, in an effort to provide viable solutions to real-life challenges, all through collective activity and sharing their leadership practice."[163a]

The conscious leader is responsible for allocating resources and implementing proper communication procedures (including training for all employees at all levels). As part of this job, the leader should ensure that 'ghosting' does not occur within the organization. The 'ghosting' epidemic is a severe and dramatic communication problem, generated by the evolution of email exchanges. 'Ghosting' has two forms: not replying to an initial communication; and cutting off the communication, at any stage, after an exchange is underway. This unacceptable behavior is a form of emotional cruelty; it comes from a lack of social empathy, no doubt exacerbated by the perception of email interactions as 'virtual' and 'not real'. Usually, people who go through collective awakenings realize that every interaction is 'real', and they have adapted their lifestyle so as to reply to properly signed emails they receive, either personally or through another means, as a form of respect for their brothers and sisters.

In 'What Business Ghosting Says About Your Leadership, and Why Real Leaders Don't Ghost', Simma Lieberman explains: "If you are a leader, then show that you care about your word, your work and other people. Think about the damage and impact you have on that job seeker, supplier or consultant. When you don't respond because you don't want to be uncomfortable, you're keeping the job seeker from immediately looking for something else, that supplier from contacting another company or preventing that consultant from filling their schedule with another project. In addition, people talk to other people in their business and to your potential customers. Do you want to be known for ghosting and mistreating others? Can you and your business afford that? The next great candidate may pass you by because they choose to work in an organization known for caring, empathy and respect. It is hard to tell someone no, after saying yes, but it's much worse to say nothing. Be a leader, think about the impact your actions have on others, and say no to cowardice. That's good business."[163b]

164. Similar to personal growth through developmental stages, an organization can be viewed as having stages of development, depending on their leaders' stages of maturity. Each stage is an increasing step toward a more conscious leadership structure. Developing an *awareness of organizational stages* can be helpful for organizational consultants and trainers.

————

Frederic Laloux in 'Reinventing Organizations' describes how personal development stages can translate into organizational styles: "What determines which stage an organization operates from? It is the stage through which its leadership tends to look at the world. Consciously or unconsciously, leaders put in place organizational structures, practices, and cultures that make sense to them, that correspond to their way of dealing with the world."[164]

These are the main stages of organizational development, viewed from this vertical development perspective:

"**Conformist-amber organizations (metaphor: army)**

Characteristics: highly formal roles within a hierarchical pyramid; top-down command and control (what and how); stability valued above all through rigorous processes; future is repetition of the past.

Leadership style: paternalistic-authoritative.

Key breakthroughs: formal roles (stable and scalable hierarchies); processes (long-term perspectives).

Achiever-orange organizations (metaphor: machine)

Characteristics: the goal is to beat competition, achieve profit and growth; innovation is the key to staying ahead; management by objectives (command and control on what; freedom on the how).

Leadership style: goal- and task-oriented, decisive.

Key breakthroughs: innovation, accountability, meritocracy.

Pluralistic-green organizations (metaphor: family)

Characteristics: within the classic pyramid structure, focus on culture and empowerment to achieve extraordinary employee motivation.

Leadership style: consensus-oriented, participative, service.

Key breakthroughs: empowerment, values-driven culture, stakeholder model.

**Evolutionary-teal organizations
(metaphor: living organism)**

Characteristics: self-management replaces hierarchical pyramid; organization is seen as a living entity, with its own creative potential and evolutionary purpose.

Leadership style: distributed leadership, with inner rightness and purpose as primary motivator and yardstick.

Key breakthroughs: self-management, wholeness, evolutionary purpose."[164]

Chapter Seven

Conscious Evolution

165. The inner evolution of humans toward a more conscious experience is part of a larger evolution of life on Earth, and the evolution of the universe through the Stelliferous/Galaxies Era, providing the necessary ingredients for life, and the energy to sustain it.

___

The evolution of our universe has five stages: Primordial era, Stelliferous era, Degenerate era, Black Hole Era, Dark era. "The Stelliferous Era stretches from the time the universe was 1 million years old to the time when the universe will be 100 trillion years old. In the following list, each cosmological decade represents a tenfold increase in the number of years which have elapsed since the beginning of time: the Stelliferous or Star-Filled Era: 6-14; the Degenerate Era: 15-37; the Black Hole Era: 38-100; the Dark Era: 100 and beyond."[165]

166. In the cosmological timeline, we are positioned at the *midpoint of the Stelliferous Era*. Many stars and planets are yet to be born, long after cellular life on Earth is no longer possible. The universe may produce other types of life, not necessarily carbon-based, and the tendency to self-organization will also generate some self-reflective consciousness in these species, but their 'consciousness' may have other evolutionary purposes than for life on Earth.

___

Instead of providing feedback through self-reflection, the alien consciousness could be hive-based, focused on providing openings and more connectivity with the environment, resulting in 'connectivity-adaptation flows' instead of 'conscious experience'. Other life forms could develop entirely outside the physical layer, developing a self-identity based on patterns of energy flows. If such life forms can adapt to be animated by fundamental 'forces' such as gravity and electromagnetism and maintain a self-identity as some sort of 'musical pattern', then possibly such life forms will live up to the end of the Stelliferous Era, as long as there is energy moving through our universe.[166]

167. Although at the global scale of the universe, the potential for life, intelligence, and consciousness is immense, in our local timeline on events, life on Earth has a big survivability issue: it is at the end of its journey. It started approximately 4,000 million years ago, and it only has approximately 500 million years left until C3 photosynthesis becomes no longer possible due to the sun's increased radiation, leading to a global extinction of multicellular life, which will take place up to 1 billion years in the future.

Using the average age expectancy on Earth nowadays—72 years—as a metaphor for the entire lifespan on Earth, earthly life, at this point, is 64 years old and has only eight more years to live. But the human species has a more urgent survivability issue, due to the high possibility of another mass extinction triggered by humans themselves.

168. Organic life on Earth is the only known process that systematically records the information about its past dynamics in a self-reflecting and local way, through various recording systems, including DNA and books, and uses this knowledge for adaptation and creative evolution. Individuals from various life species use previously-stored experience in creative ways. Self-consciousness is not necessarily needed for reacting creatively to an inertial tendency; a high intelligence may be enough in some situations.

To explain the dynamics of life, there is no need for a 'planetary morphogenetic field'. Life dynamics itself, through all its local processes, interconnected as systems of systems, is the 'morphogenetic field'. The dynamics of life are integrated with the universal-wave harmonics, as various types of resonance fields. Life-less reality doesn't need to keep track of 'previous' positions in 'time'; it just resonates continuously, and it moves based on inertial movements, updated in each moment with resonance-provided information.

169. It may be that conscious experience itself is just *a layer of life's intelligence*, which uses sophisticated feedback loops and adds an additional layer of processing to the adaptive processing already taking place in all life on Earth. *Conscious intelligence* is evolving throughout all species, at various rates.

———

The various openings and awakenings, occurring throughout the human species, may be the beginning of a collective shift toward the habituation of all conscious skills and patterns, leading to a time in the future when conscious experience is so habitual that all newborns will have an expanded, hardwired 'conscious intelligence' configuration, that nowadays is partly attainable, through hard inner work and many years of transformation.

170. The inner evolution is a reflection of the collective evolution. Although some humans may develop themselves to incredible levels of inner harmony, this personal 'achievement' was only possible because of the collective, and it is essential to feed back the 'personal achievement' to the collective. Although life's evolution is supported by interdependence and cooperation, it is likely that not all the 'personal achievements' are later integrated by the intelligence of collective life. Some individuals or groups may be living using *highly unique conscious configurations*.

———

Life has experimented with 'human paradise' in many ways. One of the ways was the Pirahã tribe in Amazon. They were hunter-gatherers, living in harmony, only in the present moment, with a simple causal language—they had no past and future words. They slept only when needed, and lived without coercion. Sadly, this evolutionary branch is now fading away due to technological colonization.[170]

171. These unique personal configurations may have a source not only in psychological and social aspects. They can also be related to specific configurations of the physical body, such as high quantities of *unique codes in the microbiome's DNA*. For example, the human genome has about 20-25,000 genes, and there are barely 1% genetic differences between individuals, while the microbiome has millions of genes, half of them unique. The extraordinary variety of information in the microbiome impacts the qualities and nuances of the conscious experience.

172. In these collective frames of reference, some questions can hardly find answers. How conscious can someone become? How awake and alive? Where is humanity heading to? Finding purpose in these complex perspectives may be difficult, but what has proven useful is the development of *evolutionary awareness* and the 'intentional evolutionary' path.

————

John Stewart, in 'Evolution's Arrow: The Direction of Evolution and The Future of Humanity', explains: "Evolutionary awareness enables us to see the direction of evolution, and what we have to do to achieve future evolutionary success. We can use our mental models of future evolution to test whether we will be successful if we continue to be organized by our existing motivations and needs. But, it is not easy to escape the control exercised over us by our own self-identity. It is one thing to notice the patterns, and another thing entirely to change them. This is because any decision we make about changing our behavior will be influenced strongly by our existing motivations, beliefs and values. We will tend to use our existing characteristics to decide what we want to do with our lives. And if we have little evolutionary awareness, the evolutionary needs of far-distant generations will not count for much against our more immediate needs for food, sex, money, power and social status.

But evolutionary awareness can change this. It tends to produce individuals who place more value on the evolutionary success of future generations, and less on the gratification of their own immediate urges and needs. Individuals can see that it is the on-going and evolving population of organisms that are important to evolution, not any particular individual."[172]

173. The *intentional evolutionary path* has already been opened by the vows of boddhisattvas, millennia ago. Across the planet, there is an emergence of individuals who are choosing to dedicate their lives to consciously advance the evolutionary process. They recognize that their lives are an essential part of the global evolutionary process, and they realize that they have a significant role in its future evolution.

In 'The Emergence of Intentional Evolutionaries', John Stewart writes: "Redefining themselves within a wider evolutionary perspective is providing meaning and direction to their lives. Intentional evolutionaries no longer see themselves as isolated, self-concerned individuals who live for a short time, then die irrelevantly in a meaningless universe. They know that if evolution is to continue to fulfil its potential, it must be driven intentionally, and it is their responsibility, their destiny to contribute to this. For human individuals on Earth, key realizations that will contribute to this shift in perspective could be:

The insight that a life dedicated to the pursuit of narrow desires and pleasures is not worthwhile. Our basic instincts and desires programmed us to be adaptive and successful in past environments, but not in future environments.

We have the opportunity to be conscious participants in the evolutionary processes that will shape the future of life on Earth. We can play an important role in the actualization of the next great steps in evolution.

The successful future evolution of life depends on our conscious participation. Unlike past great evolutionary transformations, the steps to a unified and sustainable planetary society are too complex to be discovered by trial and error. We need to envision the planetary society and design strategies to get there.

Our actions can have meaning and purpose insofar as they are relevant to the wider evolutionary process. To the extent that our actions can contribute positively to evolution, they are meaningful in the context of a larger process. This larger process has been unfolding long before we were born, and will continue long after we die. The evolutionary perspective therefore provides us with an answer to the great existential question that confronts all conscious organisms: What can I do with my life?"[173]

174. The *intentional evolutionaries* are living answers to life's most challenging self-inquiries: Why am I here? What is my purpose? What can I do with my life? Since I am aware of the *cooperative direction of evolution*, can I use this knowledge to do what I can to ensure that humanity achieves future evolutionary success? What contribution can I make to the evolution of humanity?

———

In 'The Evolutionary Awareness in a Planetary Society Based on Cooperation', John Stewart discusses these questions: "What human individuals could do to contribute to the future evolutionary success of life on this planet?

First, we could work on ourselves to improve our adaptability and evolvability. Our objective could be to develop the self-knowledge and psychological skills needed to transcend our biological and cultural past. We could develop a psychology that is no longer controlled by the needs and motivations we inherit biologically and culturally. This psychology will enable us to be self-evolving. It will equip us with the capacity to find motivation and satisfaction in whatever we need to do to contribute to evolutionary objectives.

Second, we will promote in others a deeper understanding of the evolutionary process, and will encourage and assist them to develop the psychological capacity to use this understanding to guide and manage their own behavior. Humanity cannot make significant progress in evolutionary terms until the majority of us embrace evolutionary objectives. Future evolutionary success can only be achieved collectively and cooperatively. And if human society as a whole is to be an evolutionary warrior that transcends its biological and cultural past, its members could first become evolutionary warriors.

Finally, we could support the formation of a unified and self-actualized planetary society. We could do what we can to develop a society that uses its understanding of the direction of evolution to guide its own evolution. Critical steps along the way to achieving such a society will be the establishment of a system of global governance, and the implementation of new forms of governance and economic systems that are more evolvable and better at organizing cooperation."[174]

175. In our collective evolution, the next global shift, after conscious intelligence, may be the expansion of *harmonic intelligence*, which includes 'harmonic resonance' and 'synchronization' as essential skills. *Conscious harmonic resonance* skills are already emerging in humans.

176. What will happen when conscious harmonic resonance evolves to its full potential, in all three layers of our body: physical, energy, and information? There may already be a word for this vibrational harmony: *satcitānanda*—harmonic existence and truth,

harmonic conscious awareness, and harmonic enstatic bliss. And maybe the path is *spanda*—harmonic synchrony with the primordial vibration of the universe.

Imagine the life 'pulses' happening in simultaneity, in all 1,000+ ranges of life frequencies, and in various systemic combinations of these frequencies. When life pulsates, it 'forces' a synchronization between all the parts of the system. The parts that are not in synchrony tend to 'tune in' to the global synchrony by performing micro-adjustments. The micro-adjustments and their effects are what we perceive as thinking, feeling, or kundalini spikes. For instance, repetitive thoughts occur because some parts of us are not in synchrony with the whole, and the life pulse is trying to synchronize them, using conscious awareness. This oscillating-vibrational process is continuous, not just in life processes, but in the entire universe.

From this perspective, it seems technically impossible for any human being to achieve 'perfect' or complete harmony, now or in the future. The entire universe is looking for this perfect synchrony; but, the entire universe—life included—is on a continuous evolutionary-expansive cycle. And this expansion will continue until there is no more 'movement' potential left in the universe, and matter, energy, and information will reach their final destination: maximum entropy or stillness.

Then what?

A big collapse and a new big bang?

An eversion?

Or maybe, the primordial dancer will begin another dance?

Or maybe, that will be all; we are just an amazing blossoming in the cosmic spring.

Time will tell.

177. *Id est omnia.* Please filter these consciousness sutras through your own experience, and add your color to the rainbow.

——

A timeless blessing, inspired by Metta meditations

May I Be Peaceful.
May I Be Free.
May My Body Be Strong and Healthy.
May I Be Filled with Loving Kindness.
May I Be Happy.
May I Awaken to the Light of My True Nature.
May I Be Safe.
May I Have Simplicity and Prosperity in Life.
May I Be Well.
May I Have Equilibrium in Life.
May I Be Free from Suffering.
May I Live in Harmony with Life.
May I Be in Resonance and Intimacy with Life.
May I Be Free of Unhealthy Attachments.
May I Be in Harmony with the Life Force.
I Offer Compassion for Me.
I Offer Loving Kindness for Me.

May You Be Peaceful.
May You Be Free.
May Your Body Be Healthy.
May You Be Happy.
May You Awaken to the Light of Your True Nature.
May You Be Safe.
May You Have Simplicity and Prosperity in Life.
May You Be Well.
May You Have Equilibrium in Life.
May You Be Free from Suffering.
May You Be in Resonance and Intimacy with Life.
May You Be Free of Unhealthy Attachments.

May You Be in Harmony with the Life Force.
I Offer Compassion for You.
I Offer Loving Kindness for You.

May All Beings Be Peaceful.
May All Beings Be Free.
May All Beings Be Healthy.
May All Beings Be Happy.
May All Beings Awaken to The Light of Their True Nature.
May All Beings Be Safe.
May All Beings Have Simplicity and Prosperity In Life.
May All Beings Be Well.
May All Beings Have Equilibrium in Life.
May All Beings Be Free from Suffering.
May All Beings Be in Resonance and Intimacy with Life.
May All Beings Be Free of Unhealthy Attachments.
May All Beings Be in Harmony with the Life Force.
I Offer Compassion for All Beings.
I Offer Loving Kindness for All Beings.

Thank You.

Appendix

Overview of Awakening Journeys

Each of the transformative experiences described in this section has different degrees of depth and involves various unfolding ways. As some of them are quite rare and I could find no appropriate descriptions in Eastern or Western literature, I include here my subjective perspective and some of my field notes, to support future researchers in exploring these openings. Although this list covers a broad array of awakenings, this index presents only what I could experience and observe in other people during my researches. Further studies are necessary for making a complete inventory of emerging openings in humans.

Awakening from the collective culture-civilization hypnosis

This is a shift that occurs when people begin their journey toward autonomy and develop their personal system of values, instead of merely conforming to the group of which they are a part. This awakening begins with becoming aware of the consensual cultural reality and concludes by seeing how culture itself is the consensual reality.

However, I have met people who have switched from one cultural system (e.g., the corporate style) to an alternative community, without realizing per se how culture itself influences their inner experience. They just change from an unpleasant environment to one more suited for their preferences and way of life. Still, choosing a preferred way of living or a preferred cultural environment are steps that could ignite the awakening, as the person develops an increased awareness of group narratives.

Sometimes, this awakening may reinforce the self-identity by providing the 'I am special' energy, but this is a positive inflation that provides energy for further transformations.

The 'I am' experience:
Activation of the witnessing awareness mode

This experience is about disconnecting from absorption in the mind self/ego and discovering new ways of 'being awake'[1]. It is the experience generated by the activation of witnessing awareness (becoming aware of awareness itself). This type of non-conceptual opening is what people usually describe as 'enlightenment', providing the basic structure for various other types of non-conceptual experiences. The activation of the witnessing awareness is sometimes preceded by a dramatic experience of 'self-identity/ego death'. However, in time, this 'death' can be viewed as a 'relaxation'; what is dying is a rigid structure, and the lesson I learned after this awakening was to allow myself to be more fluid, more 'liquid'.

This experience is created by a shift in the attentional configuration, from being permanently immersed in experiences and using narrow focus, to a diffuse-wide attention, and then a combination of attention styles, wide and focused simultaneously. Mindfulness techniques provide good steps toward the habituation of the witnessing mode, by calming down the streams of recurrent thoughts and supporting an acceptance of all that is, in a non-judgmental way.[2]

Conscious embodiment—the reconnection
with the body energy and body perceptions

This experience is a natural part of inner evolution, experienced as an 'awakening' by individuals who previously haven't explored their physical body in a conscious way—although conscious embodiment is quite natural for massage therapists, dancers, or yoga practitioners.

For me, this opening was facilitated by Feldenkrais workshops and contact improvisation courses or jams. I discovered a world of impressive expressivity, and everything related to my body changed. As a result of these practices, my body awareness just opened up, and I became aware of how the psychological letting go emerges together with the relaxation of the body. This opening also gave me a new awareness of what food the body requires at different times, depending on inner experiences. It took me about two or three years to fluidify the body and develop a good body awareness.

I want to mention a few explorers of conscious embodiment who have amazing insights: Janet Adler[3] and Andrea Olsen[4]. Here is a description from Scott Kiloby: "An awakening experience itself is merely the first step. It takes a while for the body to catch up.[...] This exploration became so intimate, tender and gentle, like falling in love with every sensation and every thought about the body. A complete surrender to all of that as it arose. I would gently feel into the body all over all the time, throughout the day. It truly became a love affair. I started to see that all my life I had been looking for attention, love and everything else outside of myself. I was just looking for something to change how I felt, for someone to love my body, my experience. I realized that this is my job, not someone else's. Looking for that outside myself is next to impossible. And it's so indirect and inefficient to think that something outside of me will comfort and love my experience. It's up to me to do that."[5]

Awakening to the energy flows and kundalini awakening

Kundalini awakening is a psychosomatic process that seeks a fluidified way of being, and the most accurate description of the process that I have encountered is Jana Dixon's 'Biology of Kundalini'[6]. Over the years, I have met a few people in this process who have helped me to understand that the process of energy activation has at least three parts: the first part is pranotthana or the cleaning process; the second part is when the energy begins to flow; the third part is when the person can increase the energy without losing it by generating 'heat' (energy spikes that dissipate it).

Some people I've met have been at different points on this journey. Some decided that the pranotthana process was too hard to cope with; they began taking antipsychotics and got stuck in the process. Some people found other ways to ignore the drive, while others completed the pranotthana journey, entered the kundalini free flow, and transformed the energy into aliveness.

The damaging aspect of using antipsychotics, during energy awakening, is that the medicine doesn't actually stop the energetic process. Instead, it simply blocks some of its features. I discovered this accidentally while dancing with someone at a contact improvisation jam. She had a charming body-contact energy, and she was super-sensitive to touch. We melted our senses into an incredibly spontaneous and deep connection, even though we had never met or spoken to each other before. However, later I discovered that she was on antipsychotics. But wait, what? How could she be on antipsychotics? Weren't these drugs supposed to stop all such kinds of energy manifestation? But it looks like I was wrong in that respect. The antipsychotics just blocked her ability to consciously and cognitively manage the energy flow, but the energy still found ways to manifest. After some conversations with this person, I found out that she had an inability to manage and work with her sexual energy; this energy was manifesting itself in various forms, by radiating externally through an intense and over-the-top sensuality. But, in her case, the issues related to her increased sexuality were less important. The fear of 'losing her mind' was stronger, and so she decided to continue with the antipsychotic treatment.

Vibrational awakenings: from erotic to ecstatic, enstatic and beyond

Some experiences related to this awakening are available in the literature, described by devotional mystics such as Teresa of Avila, Francis of Assisi, the Indian mystic Ramakrishna, and Saraha (one of the founders of Tantra).

The first part of this awakening is the transition from erotic, externally-directed energy to ecstatic-internal energy. The next step is to allow all the energy to vibrate enstatically inside oneself without producing ecstatic explosions, by increasing the density of the energy body (or increasing the frequency, as some would say).

Allowing unconditional love seems to be an essential step here. When the energy body is configured in such a way that the high frequency habituates, it creates an enstatic-vibrating life most of the time, an increased aliveness that may look like a background 'silent ecstasy', not necessarily related to the sexual, emotional, or mental energy.

This is an excerpt from an interview by Jeff Warren with a Buddhist monk:

"What about the feelings of bliss and rapture? In the jhanas these are seen as part of a progression, aren't they?

He looked out the little window onto the muddy tracks behind the house, then chose his words carefully. 'This happens when an object becomes an aesthetic object for you, when it feels like the most beautiful thing—you're delighted, fascinated. You have a strong emotional interest, like being in love. You pass a threshold where experience becomes so beautiful that there is nothing else you would rather be doing. Everything else fades away, even pain if you're sitting uncomfortably. A lot of meditators get this. The object of your devotion can be anything—a vase, a piece of music. Once I was climbing up a hill and I entered an alpine garden of mosses and rock flowers and I got down on my knees and just gazed in wonderment'.

He stopped, a bit embarrassed. 'This is a kind of bliss'.

'So how often does that happen for you?'

'It's hard to say because it's all a matter of degree. Maybe once a week or so. It began many years ago. I would be meditating and once in a while I would feel joy and delight, at being so totally engaged in the one thing. It was a kind of concentration where all energies—emotional, physical, intellectual—are centered upon one pointedness and sustained attention. I used to wonder how far I had proceeded along the jhanas. Whether I had reached level one or two or three. I don't know how deep I've been, but to be honest I no longer concern myself with all that'. He waved his hands. 'None of that is the point of the practice'.

'So what is the point?'

He looked at me with great sympathy and patience. 'It's not

about the special effects, Jeff. Meditation is about increasing your awareness. I would say that after twenty-two years of practice the main 'effect' has been more presence of mind."[7]

It seems that some people can experience a high-density vibrational life, in the body, in relative silence and inner peace, without involving any significant energy explosions through ecstatic emotions, bliss, ecstasy, or enstasy. Like a multidimensional buzz in the energy body, this vibrational experience is about just enjoying life, without manifesting feelings or any desire to actively share something by actions, emotions, feelings, or thinking. The energy is active, but in a 'static' vibratory condition. This transformation to enstatic living could be related to endogenous DMT production, as the inner experiences seem similar to a mild-DMT experience (or active kundalini). When there are no blockages, the energy flows naturally; the layers vibrate altogether more quickly, and they are more responsive to each other. The human being bends quickly and adapts smoothly, and this ease is simultaneously in silence and high energy.

Interconnectedness awakening—the shift from individual to collective awareness

This shift from individual to collective experiences is an amazing awakening, and it can emerge in all layers. It can happen when people realize they are just a cell in a big planetary organism (as in the spiritual ecology movements), and they discover group emotions, 'hive mind', 'unconscious' group communication, and collective awareness.

During this opening, perhaps the conscious connection to other minds is the most frightening and hard to cope with. My way of adjusting was to realize that, to maintain personal integrity, it was necessary to find and continuously sustain my own 'vibrational style'. In other words, I had to remain centered in my own space while accessing bits of information from the social interactions.

Some years ago, I met someone with this type of super-sensitivity, who was able to detect when I thought about her. This type of bonding is usually experienced in couples with a good resonance exchange. Still, the shift from 'perceiving my partner' to 'perceiving everyone' is quite a step. There are only two ways to deal with it: by reducing the sensitivity, or by coping with it and finding a personal way of managing the information overflow from the collective.[8]

Awakening the heart and the experience of unconditional love as deep resonance

Some women I met told me that they experienced this shift after the birth of their first child. As heart opening is well described in psychology and spirituality, I only want to add that for me, love is a deep and silent resonance with life, and full empathy is a skill that is worth developing very early in one's inner evolution journey. The challenge of this opening is to keep a complete openness and deep connection in all types of interactions, positive or negative, familial or non-familial. Some of the preliminary steps for this opening require a mature emotional intelligence. Connecting through love feels to me like a deep resonance and intimacy with life. In 'technical' terminology, unconditional love maintains a continuous open perception of the connection between equals. There are no masters and disciples in love; we are all equals in this layer of emotional energy connection.

Awakening of the multidimensional awareness

This is about expanding witnessing awareness to reach a perspective from which witnessing is simultaneously experienced as a presence inside all body layers—physical, energy, information, and space. In my experience, this awakening was possible by splitting attention across multiple layers while keeping my global attention active. Still, keeping this multidimensionality was only possible after I had managed to center myself—I do not mean centering in the heart, but in the bubble-of-space, measuring approximately two meters in diameter, which includes everything from my body to my thoughts to the energy around me.

Consciously using automatic perspective mechanisms to create a framework for conscious awareness content

A high flexibility of perspective is usually found in people who are at a later stage of inner growth. Susanne Cook-Greuter describes the unitive stage in these terms: "Unitive perceivers can shift focus without effort and behold the whole simultaneously with its constituting variables. They operate within an expanded time frame which includes all of earth's history and its future. Life is seen as a form of temporary and sometimes voluntary separation (Bodhisattva vow) from the creative ground to which it will eventually return. Though adults at the Unitive stage are aware of themselves as separate and unique embodiments, they also identify with all other living beings. The separation of self from others is experienced as an illusion, an invention to safeguard the [self/]ego's need for permanence and self-importance, and to defend against the fear of its death."[9]

Usually, the mechanism that allows selection of information through perspective-taking is a non-conscious process, but it can become conscious, and we can interact with it in more creative ways than when it's automatic, by allowing a higher flexibility in information selection and a wide variety of experiences that wouldn't arise naturally.

To consciously access the perspective-taking mechanisms themselves, it is necessary to have a simultaneous awareness of their components: space length (the length of the space we decide to use for the perspective), time length, and various styles of paying attention. All three elements form a specific lens color through which we look at the world, and this color filters our conscious experience, by selecting the information that is introduced from non-conscious processing to conscious awareness. Inside the perspective mechanisms, space and time set the frame of reference, and attentional styles select the flows of information that reach conscious awareness.

Using this awakeness skill, we can instantly change the perspective filters with almost zero consumption of attentional energy. For example, inside the perspective, we can increase the space around us from two meters to an expanded space, e.g., by introducing the planet's size. This changes the global view, but we are still denser in our local two-meter area of space, occupied by our body, and lighter outside of it. So, we can set the perspective to a planet-size frame of reference, but the content is still coming through the localized space, measuring two meters in diameter, aka our body. The result is a global view with local content. If we see this information flow in real-time, we can see how pieces of information in the spatial two-meter bubble of our body become entangled in a new way with the planet-size information. The same effect occurs when a person watches a view of Earth from above and allows the images to generate shifts in conscious experience (e.g., using time-lapse videos from the International Space Station).

Flow awareness and the modulation of life events

This awakeness skill combines 'systems thinking', 'systems dynamics', and an attentional style focused on the dynamics of transformation. It is an awareness of life events that unfolds in a succession of small events, which intersect with other sets of events. In other words, this is about becoming aware that everything is connected, but that some things/events are more connected than others. We can participate in these unfolding events with patience. Or, sometimes, when action is needed, we can invest our energy and modify a flow, by altering its speed, direction, intensity, and other such properties.

Life has become much simpler since I have started to look at the world as an intersection of flows and intermixing groups of events. The preliminary stages of this opening begin with observing 'synchronicities', but usually positive things are noticed. The less positive things are not seen as being in sync. However, everything is in sync all the time, good and evil, and this sync is fractally expanding to every level, layer, and depth of life.

Each of us has some way of contributing to life flows, but the key is to select the flows in which we participate, carefully. Some flows are adjustable, some aren't.

Inner eye vision: merging of the inner mental space with the real physical space

This is a result of the perspective that everything emerging inside me happens in a region of space measuring perhaps two meters in diameter, which contains my thinking, my body, and my emotions. When I meditate with my eyes closed, I continue to use my eyes, but differently. I keep the visual perception activated and focused on the space. When the senses are internalized, and the point of viewing is this space, after a while, the eyes begin to work in sync, and the vision from both eyes transforms into a centered vision. This center is located in the middle, in the region between the eyes. The inner eye vision activates when the entire brain acts as a whole; I think this is the effect of the whole brain working in synchrony in certain frequencies.

In my view, inner eye vision has nothing to do with mystical realization; it is available through this simple training to interiorize one's vision. Then, when both eye-flows synchronize, people can experience the inner space in a 3D/360-degree perspective, and this space is where things can manifest. The inner eye vision seems to result from the synchronized perception of both eyes, which generates a central point of view in a region between the eyes, together with a body-anchored spatial awareness.

After the inner eye begins to see, a wide range of inner experiences become available during inner art sessions. In my experience, the content can be either inner projections/inner visions or physical perceptions. With time, I realized that inner visions are just a visual way of thinking, conscious or unconscious, nothing else. Sometimes they are incredible, sometimes not. However, the physical perceptions are quite impressive because the area we inhabit is vortexing through space. The planet is moving around the sun, the sun is moving around the center of the galaxy, and the galaxy is moving towards the Great Attractor. Our experience is static only because of our frame of reference. If I tune into the fundamental grid of reality, or use various frames of reference, I find myself flowing a lot. Relevant to this topic are Walter Russell's insights[10], cubic wave field theory[11], and Hannah van

Houcke's 3D graphics[12], which show how energy is vortexing through the cubic grid.

I have played around with inner eye vision a few times, by mixing the inner-outer perceptions with energy perceptions. With my eyes closed and in sync, looking from the center, I moved one hand in front of my body and tried to attune the inner vision to the energy flowing in the space occupied by my hand. After a few rounds of tunings and by opening and closing the eyes, I could adapt the inner vision to the actual 3D position of the hand. The inner vision 'locked' onto the energy of my hand by recognizing its qualities.

The adjustment of the inner vision took place this way. I was scanning through the almost-dark field in which these light-like particles were moving, and then I asked where the hand was, and I let the attention move by itself, until it arrived at my hand. After that moment, I recognized the hand as though it were a group of energy bubbles moving through space. After the 'locking', every time I tried to verify the 3D location of my fingers by opening the eyes, the 3D position of the fingers in both the inner and outer space was identical.

In this enhanced state of perception, with eyes open but eyelids closed, everything physical looks like a fine shower of particles, some of which are grouped within flexible boundaries. This exercise was easiest to perform in a dark setting, relaxed, but with an activated kundalini. People who live in dark environments for many days report similarly enhanced perceptions. So I guess the perceptions are related to melatonin and endogenous DMT production.

Entheogenic awakenings

I have listed these separately, as they seem to be part of a different world of openings than 'regular' awakenings. Each plant/substance has its own intelligence. The experiences I consider relevant for my inner evolution journeys were mediated by ayahuasca, changa or DMT, LSD, mescaline, and psilocybin. Moreover, the sacred use of ganja is also a good tool; she is like a navigator, taking us where we want to go.

Some people use the argument that awakenings are possible without entheogens. For sure they are possible. But some particular types of openings generated by entheogens have almost a zero chance of developing without them. The informational wisdom in these plants is an added value for any explorer wanting to dive deeper into reality.

In my opinion, there are two ways of using entheogens wisely: as a tool for insights, to support inner evolution journeys and to live a good life, and as friends and allies for inner explorations, for taking us to where nobody has ever gone before. It is a fact that in nature, we have plant friends who can open some doors. And it is a personal decision to step through those doors and to discover new ways of functioning. And, after coming back from that configuration, it is our choice to decide whether the discoveries are worth incorporating into our daily lives.

Other awakening journeys

Here are some other experiences and shifts that may be included as awakening journeys.

Awakening the voice – Connecting with the voice and using it to modulate the inner core of our beings and its relation to ourselves and others. This is very visible in some musicians and singers.

The overview effect – This is illustrated by seeing Earth from above, described by astronauts as a remarkable shift in perspective. The 'overview effect', as a term and concept, was coined in 1987 by Frank White.

Space awareness (spaciousness, spatial/depth perception) – This is a shift in perceiving the physical space inside and outside, a transition to being connected with space as a deep and intimate experience, while maintaining a connection with the inner (body space) and outer space at the same time; an example is the unitary mystical experience.

Awakening the passion of being (awakened aliveness) – This is the journey toward allowing life energy to flow unbounded, while the pure heart is the home, and having, as a result, highly coherent experiences of aliveness and love/joy. Along with this activation comes the feeling of beauty generated by all that is, and this is a significant shift in the energy body configuration.

Spiritual awakening – This seems to be a combination of awakening experiences already included in this research, but all of them have this common theme: the rigid previous structure has dissolved, resulting in a powerful surge of energy/freedom that reconfigures the layers in various ways. This experience usually unfolds as a dramatic way to get out of the conventional stages of inner growth (i.e., getting out of the collective cultural hypnosis), and individuals begin to see the beautiful interconnectivity of all life, beyond their previous frameworks.

Embracing the curiosity for life – Some people are curious, and if they embark on the journey toward understanding life, and pursue it diligently, the process brings unique insights about all that we are, opening the mind toward what is essential in life, and it adds awe as a coherent flow in the energy body.

Information awakening – This is an opening to an increased perception of the information flows that exist in all body layers—physical, energy, and information. This openness allows the nonconscious processing to be available through body sensations and perceptions, emotions, cognition, and perspectives. Although rare, this opening expands the content that runs at the edge of conscious awareness, as pre-conscious awareness, which is more readily available to conscious access.

Harmonic resonance awakening – This opening refers to an increased awareness of the resonance processes, developing naturally in all body layers, in connection with life processes. This opening provides a complementary 'filter' for all experiences, through the lenses of 'synchrony', 'vibrational resonance', and 'harmonic resonance'.

References and notes

1 Brazdău, O. (2014). Witnessing awareness and modes of cognitive awareness. A terminology proposal for the psychological assessment of witnessing and (meta)cognitive experiences. In D. Chopra (Ed.), *Brain, Mind, Cosmos: The Nature of Our Existence and the Universe (Sages and Scientists Series Book 1). Kindle Edition (1st ed., chapter 4).* Chopra Foundation.

2 Further reading: James, M. (2014, April 25). *Scientific research on consciousness.* Happiness of Being: The Teachings of Bhagavan Sri Ramana Maharshi. Retrieved January 14, 2022, from https://happinessofbeing.blogspot.com/2014/04/scientific-research-on-consciousness.html

3 Adler, J. (2002). *Offering from the Conscious Body: The Discipline of Authentic Movement.* Inner Traditions.

4 Olsen, A., & McHose, C. (2015). *Body and Earth.* Retrieved January 14, 2022, from http://www.body-earth.org/work

5 Kiloby, S. (n.d.). *Conscious Embodiment.* Science and Nonduality. Retrieved January 14, 2022, from https://www.scienceandnonduality.com/article/conscious-embodiment

6 Dixon, J. E. (2020). *Biology of Kundalini: Exploring the Fire of Life.* Emancipation Unlimited LLC.

7 Warren, J. (2007). *The Head Trip: Adventures on the Wheel of Consciousness* (First Edition). Random House.

8 Further reading: Gunnlaugson, O., & Brabant, M. (2016). *Cohering the Integral We Space: Engaging Collective Emergence, Wisdom and Healing in Groups.* Integral Publishing House.

9 Cook-Greuter, S. (2013). *Nine Levels of Increasing Embrace in Ego Development: A Full-Spectrum Theory of Vertical Growth and Meaning Making.* Retrieved March 01, 2021, from http://www.cook-greuter.com

10 Russell, W. (1994). *The Secret of Light* (3rd ed.). University of Science and Philosophy.

11 B. [Ben]. (2013, August 3). *Mirror Cube demonstration of the Russell's Cubic Wave field.* [Video]. YouTube. https://www.youtube.com/watch?v=6NaDy4Kgtbo

12 H. [Van Houcke]. (2010, May 9). *HannaH Vh* [Video Channel]. YouTube. https://www.youtube.com/user/helenahannah

Case Studies

Case Study I

Psychological Explanations of Inner Growth Challenges that Could Develop into Psychiatric Conditions

The following explanations of 'delusions' are provided in the context of inner growth. Still, I would like to mention that these 'delusional' configurations may also emerge in other contexts, such as through traumatic events, substance abuse, or brain disorders. Many delusions are rooted in ideas that are not fundamentally 'wrong', but problems emerge because these ideas tend to loop in people's minds and to attract too much psychic energy, narrowing the attention and reducing the contextual overview. If these ideas are detected at an early stage of their development, and then rearranged in a larger collective perspective, usually they integrate naturally in the self-identity structure.

Persecutory delusions

The schizophrenic believes that he or she is being followed or is under surveillance, or that he or she is being made fun of, tricked, or treated very unfairly by others. When schizophrenics experience this type of delusion, they may feel very frightened or paranoid. As a result, they will often do things to protect themselves from the persecutor(s).

In the inner growth journey, an increased sense of interconnectedness may emerge due to various causes that dissolve or diminish the self-identity boundaries. Some of these causes include the activation of an observer perspective, the opening of the heart, and the resurfacing of a trauma. Smoking ganja, or an extraordinary event, either positive or negative, can also cause this sense of interconnectedness. If they are not accustomed to this type of information, some people may feel that they are under permanent surveillance. They begin to see the connections among all things but they fear this pervasive connectedness.

If the individual has activated 'the negative' as a primary filter, due to their fears, they will see 'the negative' in the people around them. Using these unconscious filters, the person's mind could develop imaginary stories or beliefs that other people are persecuting them, as a coping mechanism.

Grandiose delusions

These involve the belief that they have exceptional power, talent or worth, or they are someone famous. They may believe they are God or some other type of deity.

This could occur in the inner growth process, during the symbolic journey ('explosion of meaning'), or before the first 'self-identity/ego death'. When the person connects to a specific archetypal energy during the symbolic journey, the cultural stories of that archetype emerge from their memory. For example, if the person reconnects with the feminine or mother archetypes, they could think of the Virgin Mary, if they have a Christian background. They could spontaneously 'feel the thought' and feel they are the Virgin Mary. Then, one day later, they may think of the story of Cleopatra, and again fall into this thought, becoming Cleopatra for a few moments.

In these cases, an optimal therapeutic intervention would be to adapt the person's meaning-making system, phrasing the experience like 'the Virgin Mary is also in me' or 'Cleopatra is also in me'. These characters are cultural shapes and forms of the archetypes, and deeply connecting with them shows that the symbolic journey is ongoing.

Delusion of reference

The person falsely believes that insignificant remarks, events, or objects in one's environment have personal meaning or significance. For instance, some people may believe that they are receiving special messages from the news anchorperson on television. Usually, the meaning assigned to these events is negative, but the 'messages' can also have a grandiose quality.

This view is another result of the newly discovered interconnectedness that is unconsciously processed by the body-mind. From this perspective, we are all one collective organism, and we are all highly interconnected. Everything is in the right place at the right moment, for all of us. This 'delusion' is similar to the grandiose delusion mechanism. Indeed, these messages are 'exactly' for me. Everything that I experience in my environment is there for me; how else? However, a proper interpretation could be that 'it is there for me, also'.

In the initial stages of interconnectedness, some people tend to reduce everything to their self-identity, as the self overreacts to defend itself from 'dissolution'. The more interconnected people feel, the more their self-identity defenses activate, thus narrowing their range of attention. An intervention that may be useful is to work with wide-diffuse attention, as this approach could relax the self-identity grip over the experience. But 'specialness' is the main issue that needs a therapeutic intervention, not the idea of 'receiving messages' from the collective.

Erotomanic delusions

This type of delusion involves the belief that a particular person, usually a celebrity or someone especially important, is romantically or sexually involved with or in love with them.

This is a result of interconnectedness, seen through a relational filter. At our deepest levels, we are all in love with each other, as we are all interconnected humans. Usually, this delusion is due to a projection mechanism, layered over the interconnectedness.

Somatic delusions

This involves the belief that they have a medical condition or other physical problems or flaws.

This delusion can have multiple sources. When the self-identity begins to fluidify, a somatic delusion may appear as a coping or defense mechanism, 'fixating' the attention on the body. This fixation on the body may be the final solution for a self-identity that defends itself against change. Someone I met was so scared of getting cancer that her unconscious processing was locked onto this topic for almost a year. The idea that she might already have cancer, though undetected, led her to frequent medical check-ups and investigations.

Delusion of control

This is a false belief that another person, group of people, or external force controls one's thoughts, feelings, impulses, or behavior. A person may describe, for instance, the experience that aliens actually make them move in certain ways and that the person affected has no control over the bodily movements. Thought broadcasting (the false belief that the affected person's thoughts are heard aloud), thought insertion, and thought withdrawal (the belief that an outside force, person, or group of people is removing or extracting a person's thoughts) are also examples of delusions of control.

This could also happen when the self-identity begins to fluidify, and the person feels (non-consciously) that we are all connected to a 'hive' mind. Actually, this is mostly true: we are a collective organism, with a collective cultural 'mind'. When the self-identity grip relaxes, the body-mind moves according to collective movements and individual programming, received through education. 'Thought insertion' is the unconscious recognition that some of our thoughts could develop in our mind because of an empathic connection to someone else or the collective, while having no identifiable source.

Nihilistic delusion

A delusion whose theme centers on the nonexistence of self or parts of self, others, or the world. A person with this type of delusion may have the false belief that the world is ending.

Yes, our world will end, but a more appropriate wording is 'my world' will end. This idea could be a sign that the self is about to pass through a 'dark night'. During this challenge, the nonexistence feels as real as possible, and eventually, this could lead to the emergence of non-conceptual facets of the self-identity. As we evolve, the self-identity will be rebuilt many times, with increasingly flexible boundaries, and an increased capacity to allow the 'void-nature' of ourselves to participate in the conscious experience.

Delusion of guilt or sin (or delusion of self-accusation)

This is a false feeling of remorse or guilt of delusional intensity. For example, a person may believe that he or she has committed some horrible crime and should be punished severely. Another example is a person who is convinced of his or her responsibility for some disaster (such as fire, flood, or earthquake) with which there can be no possible connection.

This is another effect of an unconscious connection to the global human organism, where personal responsibility is emphasized. A flood, killing hundreds of people, could occur because of my imperfection, even if my contribution is 0.00000001%. The lesson of this challenge is to learn the value of our existence and to do what we can in our individual lives to improve collective harmony.

Delusion of mind being read

The false belief that other people can know one's thoughts. This is different from thought broadcasting, where the person does not believe that thoughts can be heard aloud.

It could happen that some people can sometimes hear some of our thoughts; spontaneous telepathy just happens. We all have a connection to the collective field; otherwise we would die. However, this is not under our voluntary control, and the idea that people can read one's thoughts is just an exaggeration of a real fact. Still, even if individual thoughts are being broadcast to the minds of the people with whom we resonate, the evolution of our species is not currently allowing a direct conscious exploration of this complex connectedness.

This challenge can be solved if the individual learns to accept that spontaneous exchanges could occur, and that being transparent and authentic is a better way to live.

Religious delusion

Any delusion with a religious or spiritual content. These may be combined with other delusions, such as grandiose delusions (the belief that the affected person was chosen by God, for example), delusions of control, or delusions of guilt. Beliefs that would be considered normal for an individual's religious or cultural background are not delusions.

Archetypal symbols from religions are very powerful, as they are culturally fed throughout many generations. Suppose a person undergoing inner transformation has a personal or transgenerational religious background. In that case, specific symbols will activate in their minds in various situations, especially when trying to get out of that particular religious framework. For example, if the transformation process has reached 'the source' archetype, the person could feel and think that he or she is Jesus, Buddha, or another symbolic source archetype. That is why in hesychasm, they say, 'Do you see Jesus? Ignore him'.

Thought disorder

It describes an underlying disturbance to conscious thought and is classified largely by its effects on speech and writing. Affected persons show loosening of associations, that is, a disconnection and disorganization of the semantic content of speech and writing. In its severe form, speech becomes incomprehensible and is known as 'word salad'.

First, it's good to know there is a phenomenon called 'hyper-priming', whereby people can easily relate distant groups of concepts, on many levels of abstraction, by conceptual or spatial-visual connections. This is amplified by ganja, and it is the source of many creativity spikes. As a downside, many young adults smoking ganja are not prepared for a fluid association style, and they could reach a point when they lose the coherence.

Second, I have observed that the activation of the witnessing awareness changes something in the way we think, by activating a visual style in some individuals. If a person is unfamiliar with the visual-spatial thinking style, the amount of information involved is so vast that the mind gets blocked, and the only thing to do is to catch up by loosening associations, which can look like a word salad. I would instead consider this delusion a temporary stage, which occurs when people's thinking evolves from auditory-verbal to visual-spatial thinking. This is why art is a perfect tool to facilitate profound changes in the way we experience inner life.

Sources for delusions description

* Encyclopedia of Mental Disorders. (n.d.). *Delusions – Functioning, Withdrawal, Examples, Person, People, Brain, Mood, Description.* Advameg, Inc. Retrieved January 14, 2022, from http://www.minddisorders.com/Br-Del/Delusions.html

* American Psychiatric Association. (2013). *Diagnostic and Statistical Manual of Mental Disorders, Fifth Edition (DSM-5)* (5th ed.). American Psychiatric Publishing.

Case Study 2

A Perspective on Autism, Deep Connection, and Pre-Conscious Awareness

This research was developed in partnership with Raluca Ciobanu[1], an art therapist who works with children on the autism spectrum, using various methods for developing a better adult-child relationship and finding new ways to improve the acquisitions sustainably.

We hope that the perspectives described here will be helpful for any adult interested in new ways to connect deeply with an individual on the autism spectrum. Our observations show that a deep connection style is already used by some therapists and family members of individuals on the autism spectrum, and those who seem to use this method, along with the classical approach, consistently produce excellent results. That has encouraged us to advance on this path and study the underlying mechanisms.

Field observations and hypotheses

1. The autism spectrum includes individuals with a dense synchrony of their body layers, generating a denser than average pre-conscious awareness, perhaps as a mutation in our species, resulting in neurodiverse individuals.

Due to the dense synchrony in their body layers (physical, energy, information), life's adaptive processing is still learning how to build higher-order structures such as self-identity, systems thinking, conceptual thinking, meta-cognition, meta-attention, meta-emotions. Also, due to the initial lack of second-order organization of systems, the conscious experience tends to remain in a nascent stage of complexity, resulting in a dominance of the pre-conscious awareness ('something is there, but I cannot figure out what it is').

2. As an adaptation to the denser perception, nature has adapted the attentional styles and seems to have enhanced contextual and visual functioning in these individuals (as compared to the neurotypical person), as a way of meaning-making.

We are not implying that this inner configuration would always generate better performance at visual-spatial assessments; instead, we want to emphasize that the visual-spatial approach generates meanings more rapidly, as an adaptation to the sensory data overload.

3. Sometimes, the density of the autistic inner experience is very similar to the high-density energy experiences known as kundalini activations, or to the experiences generated by the DMT molecule (as experienced in high-energy spikes during ayahuasca experiences).

For individuals on the autism spectrum, with this dense high-synced information configuration, to learn perceptual patterns and their function/meaning is more difficult when using standard learning methods, as compared to the neurotypical population. The majority of humans have a 'lighter' inner environment, and they only experience high densities occasionally, in situations such as natural childbirth, manic episodes, kundalini awakening experiences, altered states of consciousness induced by hyper-ventilation or entheogens, or after staying in the dark for at least a week.

During group experiences with ayahuasca, participants experience a very intimate connection and information-energy transfers among them, as moments of 'deep connection', technically described as spontaneous samyama (merging, full absorption). Samyama is a process of perfect and continuous fusion with the object of attention. Or, in other words, knowing an object by completely merging with it. The interconnections and reciprocal learning, observed during ayahuasca experiences, provoked us to test whether the information transfer and mutual learning also emerge in the connection between the individual on the autism spectrum and their closest relationships (such as their family or therapist).

4. We observed that if the therapist/parent opens up to the dense con-figurations using approaches such as mindfulness, or increased present moment awareness and witnessing awareness, the child on the autism spectrum may 'click' and connect with the adult, and unconsciously 'learn' how the information is organized in the adult nearby, and nat-urally 'absorb'—through resonance-based information exchanges—the patterns necessary to organize the pre-conscious information.

Initially, we tested this hypothesis with some kids on the autism spectrum, and our observations showed that just by being present in the same space with the child, as a witness, and using a 'unitive consciousness' approach, the child naturally clicked with the adult, getting a sense of safety and becoming more creative. In time, this helps with the acquisition of meaning and self-iden-tity structures.

In 'Presence: From Autism to the Discipline of Authentic Movement', Janet Adler says: "Forty years ago, autistic children were described as those beings who never had an experience of re-lationship with another human being. In such a child there is no hint of an internalized other, a mother, an inner witness. There is no internalized presence. For a decade I worked in big and empty rooms where autistic children, one by one, filled the space with their absence until, because of a momentary presence, we experi-enced a connection. Such moments of grace created resonance within our relationship, revealing a glimpse of light."[2]

How is this deep connection/transfer generated? As the adult al-ready has a meta-organization of information, the child uncon-sciously 'absorbs' various patterns and begins to use them unconsciously, thus contributing to the inner development of their self-identity, as the self-identity is composed of habituated patterns.

In 'A Future for Neuroscience', Mike Johnson explains: "I sug-gest breaking EQ (emotional intelligent quotient) into entrain-ment quotient (EnQ) and metronome quotient (MQ). In short, entrainment quotient indicates how easily you can reach entrain-ment with another person. And by 'reach entrainment', I mean how rapidly and deeply your connectome harmonic dynamics can fall into alignment with another's. Metronome quotient, on the other hand, indicates how strongly you can create, maintain, and project an emotional frame. In other words, how robustly can you signal your internal connectome harmonic state, and how effectively can you cause others to be entrained to it. Autism might be reconceptualized along two dimensions: first, most forms of autism would entail less general ability to reach interpersonal entrainment with another's connectome harmonics—a lower EnQ. Second, most forms of autism would also entail a non-standard set of connectome harmonics. I.e., the underlying substructure of core harmonic frequencies may be different in people on the autism spectrum, and thus they can't effectively reach social entrainment with 'normal' people, but some can with other systems (e.g., video games, specific genres of music), and some can with others whose substructure is non-standard in the same way."[3]

What can parents and therapists do to maximize this effect? Connect deeply with the child, habituate the connection, and stay around, purposefully, to allow the transfer to unfold over time. After the connection is there, if the adult has access to post-autonomous stages mechanisms (as described by Susanne Cook-Greuter in inner growth theory), the adult can consciously feed the child with patterns and systems. If the adult is in the conventional stages, the feeding still happens, but it requires an emotional connection, such as an unconditional love flow. Some post-autonomous features are real time self-identity awareness and perspective skills, witnessing awareness (or developing an inner observer), and the ability to have meta-experiences (e.g., emotions about emotions, reflections about the thinking process).

5. Gazing into each other's eyes is a powerful connection method, but it may temporarily destabilize the inner configuration of both participants.

That's why some individuals on the autism spectrum avoid eye contact. Collective experiences with ayahuasca show that looking into each other's eyes during high-density kundalini peaks facilitates a massive information transfer.

6. In individuals on the autism spectrum, the dense high-sync sometimes leads to an increased self-stimulation drive.

In this situation, an option would be learning to self-adapt to the denser interconnections in the energy and information body layers[4]. In other words, learning to manage low-level kundalini-like experiences as everyday habits. We have noticed that the repetitive inner and outer movements of the individuals on the autism spectrum support their inner experience by 'patterning' certain content, let's say about 30% of it, so that the individual can access and process the other 70%.

7. We hypothesize that individuals on the autism spectrum may have a higher natural (endogenous) DMT production in the body, as compared to neurotypical individuals, or they may have a different rhythmic patterning similar to synesthetic individuals.

Simon Baron-Cohen and collaborators in 'Is Synaesthesia More Common in Autism?' explain: "Synaesthesia is a neurodevelopmental condition in which a sensation in one modality triggers a perception in a second modality. Autism (shorthand for Autism Spectrum Conditions) is a neurodevelopmental condition involving social-communication disability alongside resistance to change and unusually narrow interests or activities. Whilst on the surface they appear distinct, they have been suggested to share common atypical neural connectivity. In the present study, we carried out the first prevalence study of synaesthesia in autism to formally test whether these conditions are independent. After exclusions, 164 adults with autism and 97 controls completed a synaesthesia questionnaire, Autism Spectrum Quotient, and Test of Genuineness-Revised (ToG-R) online. The rate of synaesthesia in adults with autism was 18.9% (31 out of 164), almost three times greater than in controls (7.22%, 7 out of 97, P <0.05). The significant increase in synaesthesia prevalence in autism suggests that the two conditions may share some common underlying mechanisms. Future research is needed to develop more feasible validation methods of synaesthesia in autism."[5]

The autistic tantrums involve a spontaneous reconfiguration of energy, as in kundalini spikes during ayahuasca experiences. The notable difference is that the child is entirely overwhelmed by the peak, cannot manage the overload, and fades out. This is a natural coping mechanism, also observed when people who participate in entheogenic ceremonies go beyond their processing capacity and fade out, or dissolve their identity into a temporary psychotic-like experience.

Some methods for developing a deeper connection with individuals on the autism spectrum

1. Develop better body awareness: contact improvisation and any form of authentic dance would help.

We recommend watching 'Body and Earth. Seven Web-Based Somatic Excursions', proposed by Andrea Olsen and Caryn McHose, available at www.body-earth.org:

"This series of short films offers resources for ease in the body by restoring inherent flow, our birthright. They are for anyone with curiosity about living more consciously.

Two underlying concepts inform this work: Body is Earth. Our bones, breath and blood are the minerals, air and water inside us. When you arrive in a new place, in just a few days the 70% of your body that is water is now from that watershed. The local eggs, milk, and greens that you eat shape your muscles and bones. Humans are nature too, not separate but same.

The second concept is that dance—and movement—are essential ways to experience this interconnectedness. Rather than superficial, peripheral, or extraneous, movement is central, essential, and core to what it means to be human in this time. Bodies have intrinsic intelligence formed from over three billion years of evolutionary history—since the origins of the first cell. Rather than seeking control over the body and the places we inhabit, we develop practices for deep attending. To explore these concepts experientially, we begin with our feet. In Day 1, we orient to weight and space and practice arriving. In Day 2 we refresh fluidity, followed by Day 3—investigating breath and voice. In session 4 we remap verticality, and in Day 5, we explore the process of perception, remembering how orientation and perception underlie every movement we make. In Day 6 we focus on balancing the nervous system. And finally, in Day 7, we apply all these resources to embracing mystery, meeting the uncertainty and challenges of our days more consciously and with more spontaneous joy.

These seven movement explorations can be done individually, part-by-part, or linked for an hour-long practice. The verbal cues are meant as invitations, not commands. Follow what captures your imagination, finding your own inroad to embodied awareness. You'll need a space to move in, that feels private enough for focused concentration, a yoga mat or other clean surface, and comfortable clothing. It's helpful if you have a writing journal to reflect on the process. You can work alone or with a group, as we enter this journey together."[6]

2. Learn meta-attention styles (monitoring attention to attention); learn to divide attention and practice wide attention, mindfulness, and witnessing awareness.

Attention is the 'scanner' that connects us with various sources (internal and external), making the information available for our awareness and the conscious experience. To connect with individuals on the autism spectrum, use a type of attention called 'diffuse/wide' attention, or attention to the big picture, and combine 'objective' and 'immersed' styles.

Les Fehmi in 'Attention to Attention' explains: "How we pay attention determines significantly and immediately our experience, physiology, and behavior. How we pay attention determines our subjective experience of our own identity and our objective experience of internal and external sensation and perception. Also, we can learn to flexibly choose and determine how we attend. Certainly most of us have the ability to choose the direction of our narrow attention, in order to choose to experience any subset of available stimuli at any given time. With training, we can also choose to broaden the scope of our attention to include a more diffuse and integrated background awareness of available stimuli, even in multiple sense modalities simultaneously. Moreover, we can choose to flexibly pay attention in other ways which help us function more or less well in specific conditions."[7,8]

In 'The Head Trip: Adventures on the Wheel of Consciousness', Jeff Warren writes: "We must learn, said Smritiratna, to treat our thoughts the way we treat sounds or sights or smells. They are temporary bits of content that flit across the mind. They don't own us.[...] There are four foundations to mindfulness. The first is mindfulness of body, both the senses, and the physical feeling of the body, the pressure of the seat against our backsides, the pressure in our bellies. The second is mindfulness of pleasure and pain—the two extremes we flit through on a daily basis. The third is mindfulness of mood. And the last is mindfulness of our mental patterns and thoughts. Try to identify all of these things, even if some of them may be unpleasant. Remember: every experience is bearable one breath at a time."[9]

3. Develop the ability to connect with space, stay present, and witness the individual on the autism spectrum, using the techniques from authentic movement developed by Janet Adler.

In 'Witness Consciousness in the Development of the Individual', Paula C. Sager explains: "What makes Authentic Movement unique as a practice is that the mover is in relationship to a non-moving external witness. The primary intention of the external witness is to pay attention to her own internal experience while tracking the spatial, temporal, and physical journey of the mover. A seasoned witness, evolving from practice as a mover, typically has a well-developed inner witness, capable of separating her own experience from the mover's and of discerning any tendency to judge, interpret, or project her own experience onto that of the mover.

The external witness, who typically sits on the periphery of the space, plays a vital role in supporting the development of the mover's inner witness. For the mover, the process of becoming conscious of one's experience while 'in movement' (stillness can be a form of movement) is the ongoing practice of developing and strengthening the 'inner witness'. After the movement portion of an Authentic Movement session, time is usually given to a transitional activity, such as writing, drawing, or working with clay or other art material, followed by a set time for verbal processing between the mover(s) and witness(es). The mover is considered to be 'the expert of her own experience' and is therefore invited to speak first.

The witness is careful to be conscious of how she talks about her experience of witnessing the mover, often deliberately acknowledging her own experience as distinct from that of the mover. For some movers the experience of being witnessed is a relief. For others, especially at first, being witnessed can bring up feelings of ambivalence and discomfort. If the witness can convey a sense of 'compassionate-enough presence', the mover will likely, over time, develop greater trust and security."[10]

While working with children on the autism spectrum, we observed that using narrow-focused attention exclusively may inhibit their activities and reduce the connection between the adult and the child. Although their attention is very dynamic, many children on the autism spectrum notice the attentional style of the therapist/adult. After they learn to be in the same space, while acknowledging that they are being witnessed, they relax, allowing the adult into their inner space (which is usually merged with the outer environment). We tested this idea, in therapy sessions, and we noticed that after the mutual attentional recognition had been established, the child learned that the therapist's attention is not dangerous; so it was possible to watch the child for over an hour, without being disconnected from the shared space.

Other resources: 'Looking for me' and 'Still Looking' by Janet Adler.[11]

4. Develop the mechanisms to connect deeply with the child as a whole and learn to access an expanded presence, specific to the 'unitary mystical state' or unitive/nondual consciousness.

Jeff Warren, in 'The Head Trip: Adventures on the Wheel of Consciousness', says: "Robert Forman is a former professor of religion, and the author of some excellent articles in the Journal of Consciousness Studies. I think of him as a kind of mystical action figure. He transitioned into nondual consciousness a few years ago, neural tubes 'unzipping' along the back of his neck with a long tearing sound, in his memorable description. It's fascinating to think about how the various mystical states all relate to one another.[...] For Forman, there is a clear progression: first you tap into the Pure Conscious Experience (PCE), then the PCE expands so it exists alongside the normal run of mental content and you get the Dual Mystical State, and finally that 'interior silence' balloons out beyond the confines of the body to include everything, so that, in the words of German idealist Malwida von Meysenburg, who describes one such Unitary Mystical State experience, 'Earth, heaven, and sea resounded as in one vast world encircling harmony... I felt myself one with them'. When we hear about 'becoming one with the universe' we tend to roll our eyes, or turn down the volume on the Final Fantasy DVD. But it's only a cliché because so many people have reported the experience, and not just New Agers. No one knows what's behind these episodes—is it some oddball bit of brain activity, indigestion, or, as Forman himself puts it, 'an encounter with Ultimate Truth?' But their very commonness—the fact that they happen both spontaneously and as a result of deliberate practice—suggests that they may have implications for the study of consciousness itself."[12]

While studying the family environment of the children on the autism spectrum, we observed that some adults tend to have many unconscious anxieties, worries, or disappointments with regard to the child, and these tensions become a part of the child's experience. They are unable to discriminate between their tension and the adult's tension. So the child may reason that they are the cause of the stress they feel from the adults. The unconscious transfer has to be very carefully managed, as the children may have moments when they experience an external tension as their own.

In the art therapy sessions, we observed that if the therapist's emotional life was too heavy, that quality was reflected in the child's behavior and interfered with the interconnectivity with the adult. Some children managed to communicate with the therapist that they felt discomfort due to the therapist's emotional overdrive. The solution in this situation was to acknowledge, 'Yes, what you feel in me is correct. I feel like this, thank you', to communicate that 'It's my responsibility to manage my emotions', and then to correct the energy flow, so that the child can learn that managing tensed or unpleasant emotional states is possible.

5. Learn about subpersonalities and observe them manifesting in the child's actions and attitudes, as flows of behaviors.

Due to the intense sensory experience, in an individual on the autism spectrum, the subpersonalities are 'sequenced', and they interfere with each other and follow one after another in rapid succession (as compared to the neurotypical population, where they are more stable and tend to be integrated into a habituated self-identity). In a few minutes, more than one subpersonality may become active.

For instance, let's assume that a child on the autism spectrum has 20 subpersonalities (mini-identities). Let's use a chronology by 'minutes' as a metaphor. In the 1st minute, due to the sensory input, subpersonalities no. 1, 7, 9, 10, 15 may become active and fade away quickly. In the 2nd minute, the subpersonalities no. 2, 8, 11, 16 may be rolled in. So if we analyze only these two minutes, it may seem that there is no coherent organization. But then comes the next minute, when maybe subpersonality 7 gets triggered and activates again. In the inner experience of the child as seen from subpersonality 7, there are no gaps; the 1st-minute events and the 3rd-minute events are in succession (flow). For an adult observing the child, it may look as if there is no coherency because of the 2nd-minute gap. If an adult asks a question about something in the 1st minute, waiting for the answer in the 2nd minute, and there is no answer, the adult may conclude that the child didn't receive the message (or didn't understand it). Yet, in the 3rd minute, here it is, the feedback. However, due to the interference of the 2nd minute, it may be mixed with other stuff.

Now, expand this example to a day, and the behavior of the child on the autism spectrum may become more familiar. It's as if, to connect with the child, the adult needs to learn delayed gratification (delayed feedback), while still keeping an ongoing connection with the child as deeply as possible, to provide the necessary patterning for developing their own sense of self and their own patterns of adaptive processing.

In art therapy sessions, we observed that the children tend to start up to ten projects in the first sessions if they are allowed to do what they want. In the following sessions, as the connection between the child and the therapist began to emerge, the number of art projects generated in a session became significantly lower. After the body tension gets fluidified, and the self-identity fragmentation reduces, the child becomes more attentive to the connection and provides more feedback on what they are doing.

References and notes

1 Contact information: https://www.facebook.com/kaRAmearttherapy

2 Adler, J. (2006). Presence: From Autism to the Discipline of Authentic Movement. *Contact Quaterly*, Summer/Fall 2006, 11–17.

3 Johnson, M. E. (2018, August 13). *A Future for Neuroscience.* Opentheory.Net. Retrieved January 14, 2022, from https://opentheory.net/2018/08/a-future-for-neuroscience

4 Brazdău, O. (2019, February 27). *Entheogenic Insights I: Psychology of DMT/Ayahuasca Experience.* Consciousness Quotient Institute. Retrieved January 14, 2022, from https://www.consciousness-quotient.com/psychology-of-dmt-ayahuasca-experience

5 Baron-Cohen, S., Johnson, D., Asher, J., Wheelwright, S., Fisher, S. E., Gregersen, P. K., & Allison, C. (2013). *Is synaesthesia more common in autism? Molecular Autism*, 4(1). https://doi.org/10.1186/2040-2392-4-40

6 Olsen, A. (2015). *Body and Earth. Seven Web-Based Somatic Excursions – Introduction.* Body and Earth. Retrieved January 14, 2022, from http://www.body-earth.org/introduction

7 Fehmi, L. (2003). Attention to Attention. In J. Kamiya (Ed.). *Applied Neurophysiology and EEG Biofeedback*. Future Health.

8 Bahrami, B., Carmel, D., Walsh, V., Rees, G., & Lavie, N. (2008). Spatial Attention Can Modulate Unconscious Orientation Processing. *Perception*, 37(10), 1520–1528. https://doi.org/10.1068/p5999

9 Warren, J. (2007). *The Head Trip: Adventures on the Wheel of Consciousness* (First Edition). Random House.

10 Sager, P. C. (2008). *Witness Consciousness in the Development of the Individual* (Master's thesis). Faculty of The Owen Barfield School of Sunbridge College. https://www.academia.edu/1102112/Witness_Consciousness_in_the_Development_of_the_Individual

11 Additional resources: Expressive Media Inc. (2010, July 4). *Looking For Me by Janet Adler* [Video]. YouTube. https://www.youtube.com/watch?v=FsRfMm7DCww; Expressive Media Inc. (2010, November 11). Still Looking by Janet Adler [Video]. YouTube. https://www.youtube.com/watch?v=fcZGUTy5wYk

12 Warren, J. (2007). The Head Trip: *Adventures on the Wheel of Consciousness* (First Edition). Random House.

Case Study 3

Depth Perception, Space Awareness, and Other Visual Explorations

These explorations were inspired by the Vibhuti Pada chapter in Patanjali's 'Yoga Sutras'[1], and previous entheogenic experiences, which showed me new perceptual ways of connecting with reality[2]. Through practice, I trained the perceptual mechanisms so that entheogenic-induced modifications could become available without the use of powerful entheogens. I used only micro-dosed ganja, from time to time, to enhance specific awareness flows.

Depth perception and the quest for 'expansion' mechanisms

Training depth perception was a challenge for me. Since high school, I have been practicing with energy expansion visualizations, using mental visualizations of expansion and then letting the perceptual expansions unfold. And there have also been ecstatic sexual experiences, where boundaries seemed to be melting. But with time, many questions arose: What is happening when the boundaries seem to disappear? Am I really becoming a larger energy body, or is that just the subjective experience? What is the trick with these perceptions? What is arising inside me when I have this inner sense of 'spaciousness'? There are so many techniques related to 'expanding' our energy body, but do we really expand the energy? Which energies? Because subjectively, it feels as if we expand something of ourselves. And what about 'explosions' of energy? Or 'dissolving into infinity'. What infinity? Am I really becoming infinite? How large is the infinite, perceptually? How large is the expansion?

Visualizing the expansion has always been a puzzle because I felt something was missing about how these expansions took place. Could I expand the energy with the mental 'visualizing techniques'? I felt like I was lying to myself, although something was happening. But what?

After I began my conscious inner evolution in my 30's, I tried to answer these questions and looked into the processes regulating the expansion experience. I needed a model that would rationally explain these subjective experiences. But I was unable to get any satisfactory answers until I started to explore with LSD and DMT and to build a bridge among different domains of knowledge, including physics, cosmology, and inner experiences of energy expansion.

In my view, depth perception is the crucial element for understanding the subjective qualities of the expansion experiences. I am using 'depth' as a physical concept, as it is used in eye-vision studies, meaning the visual ability to perceive distances from an object and to make sense of the three-dimensional positioning[3]. Whatever is expanding, the expansion has a radius, or a length. But, from a subjective perspective, I think that the term 'depth' instead of 'length' is better. So, in this research, depth means a physical, spatial wideness.

Thinking provides a notable spaciousness, but it is not felt as 'expansion in cognition'; it is rather interpreted as a 'bigger picture' or a larger frame of reference. Using Earth as a frame of reference (akin to 'one life on a big rock traveling through space'), we can allow our cognitive and emotional world to be filled with informational systems with a larger size. As thinking and emotions are two layers in continuous resonance, a larger cognitive overview brings in 'expanded' emotions.

Still, until Yuri Gagarin's journey, we could imagine Earth as One, but the mental representation was just that, an exercise of imagination, not a connection with a perceptual fact. Life didn't know what it was like to be on Earth. With time, this perception was shared collectively. Now there are people in the International Space Station, reinforcing this viewpoint and this overview. As a result, our inner sensitivity as a species is adjusting its functioning. Nowadays, it seems quite easy to 'imagine' and sense a bit that we are one life on Earth, as the information from the astronauts' journeys expands into our collective culture. The astronauts share their perceptions with us, all the time, through interviews and live broadcasts. We have books and movies that include facets of the planetary overview. As a result, the new global perceptions are spreading, through resonance, or emotional-perceptual imitation. And, this perception is spreading quite fast, I would say.

In the vibrational energy world, what is important for the subjective experience of expansion seems to be the wavelength and the resonance process. As we have many body layers, there are different types of depths, all happening in space, on various scales. Expansion experiences usually occur in the basic energy layers: vital, sexual, emotional, and within/around the size of our body, as a result of inner physical processes. It seems that the quality of openness (or fluid energy structures), not expansion, is responsible for many inner experiences of being a 'larger energy body'. But our energy is not expanding anywhere. We just connect more, resonate more with larger systems, allow more, and as a result, we tend to feel that we are more than our local body.

The boundary observer and the Moon's overview

Infinity was the first clue that something was not right in my understanding of the so-called 'expanded states of consciousness'. I began to question the 'perceptual' infinite after I noticed that the word 'infinite' from people's descriptions of mystical states was rather an emotional label, not a technical one. I've had many moments in life when, during yoga, I've felt like I was larger or vast, but this never felt like infinity. Yet, some people have talked about their subjective infinity experiences, and it seemed they must sense something I was not sensing. I understood later that they were referring to their no-boundaries flowing style.

In 2013-2014, when the witnessing awareness activated and habituated, I explored a lot with divided attention, to simultaneously access various aspects in me. In 2014, the first LSD experience in nature brought me a new configuration, a felt sense of distances. But it was still a fog in my mind, as I didn't have the proper concepts to describe the expanded perceptual experiences. Then,

I began dividing attention in a new way, allocating a percentage of the attentional resources to the boundaries of my vision. So, I created a 'boundary observer' in my attentional structure, placed at the boundary of the personal perceived bubble-field.

Then, I began gazing at the Moon, the night sky, the stars and planets, and the Milky Way structure. I tried to compare my perceptual experience with scientific information about their position and distances. And to try and see if I could adjust the depth perception to sense, and to perceive and feel the distance to them.

I used the Moon, first, and I practiced samyama with it. I put the boundary observer on the Moon, as if I were looking back, from Moon to Earth, to see if I could get an overview perception or not. At that time, I was familiar with these exchanges during samyama. They occurred before with some birds, when spontaneously I was merging with them through my gaze, and I felt as if I could see myself on Earth with a different quality, a quality more like a bird's gaze. So I thought, Why not? Let's try it with the Moon. And it worked. Using the Moon as a reflective layer witness, my perspective changed, the inner experience was becoming larger, and I could easily feel the Earth as one. As months passed, I became more aware of the changes that developed when the boundary observer was locked to the Moon, while I was on Earth. The boundary observer provided an excellent overview quality to my perceptions of distances. It was not like, 'I am expanded to the Moon' but like, 'I am here on Earth, with my perspective larger'. The Moon was altering the self-reflection mechanism, embedded in the perspective, which influenced my perceptions.

Sometimes I wondered: If the Moon had not been there in the sky, for us to stare at, throughout our evolution as a species, would the development of self-consciousness in mammals have been slower? The Moon provides an excellent self-reflective framework, and we see the Moon because the sunlight reflects upon the Moon's surface—and so it already has a 'physical-witnessing-reflecting' quality.

The boundary observer begins to travel through expansion

In 2015, when I began to explore using ayahuasca and changa, my practice of dividing attention turned into something unexpected. During the first ayahuasca session at Santo Daime, while in a break, I experienced the entire visual scenery as a high-resolution field (HD), in a way I had never experienced before. The visual field was ultra-mega HD, and inside the focal attention, I had an extra HD area. It was as if visual acuity became 100 times more powerful. So, later I thought: OK, the vision can adapt. Let's see if I can reproduce it without ayahuasca.

I discovered that if I gazed into a ray of light, coming from a star, and tuned into the HD resolution by re-activating the DMT-sync style configuration, while isolating the attention to the inner part of the ray, I could see-by-sensing through the ray, and I could use the light ray to expand the limits of the perceptual field, step by step, by moving the boundary observer through the light. In this way, the inner experience was similar to an expansion experience. But, as I was adapting to these advances through light and allowing myself to go deeper and deeper into the light-ray, the expansion-perception quality seemed to fade away. I felt more like a traveler with the boundary observer. At this point, after months or practice, the purpose of this boundary observer changed. I was now more interested in providing myself feedback about its spatial position ('how far is it?') or improving the larger perspective qualities.

One day, I began to wonder: What if I could expand/send the boundary observer all the way to the emitter-star? Could this be possible? I mean, doing this exercise to connect with the Moon was OK. I felt the finite distance to its position when the boundary observer reached the Moon. But with the stars, there was another scale necessary. I soon noticed that the distances are perceptually immense. Any strategy that I used to speed up the boundary observer to the emitter star was not fast enough to reach the emitter. The only technique that seemed to produce any results was the ayahuasca style of flowing continuously: paying attention to the 'increase' of the increase in speed (and not the physical distances).

But even so, I was unable to sense that I was making progress. The speed of light was not enough. I needed a higher wavelength, or another way of propagation, to make more significant steps through the light ray. A faster speed was necessary.

At that time, I began to study the size of the Milky Way, how large it is, how far away are the stars in the sky. To my surprise, all the stars I was seeing were in a small bubble of space (small—compared to the size of the Milky Way as a whole). I began to research the distances within the galaxy and between galaxies, up to the limits of the observable universe.[4]

This was the context in 2015 when an experience shifted my overview. I was with a friend, under the sky, on a wooden terrace of a summer house somewhere in a small village near the mountains. We both experienced with changa, one after the other. After the experiences, which lasted half an hour each, we were relaxing and gazing at the night sky. It was a very clear sky, and the Milky Way was beautiful. I was trying to figure out its 3D position in the sky, in relation to the Earth, and the position of the spiral arms. Then I started the exercise by focusing attention inside a ray of light, emanating from a star, and I began to practice the expansion-traveling of the boundary observer. I was practicing with increases of increases in the speed, to see if I could reach the emitter star. So, I had the eyes wide open and focused on a star-light, when something unexpected emerged.

The boundary observer was pulled through the ray. Then, my primary attention moved from the body to the boundary observer, and I jumped to a speed I could not imagine before, and then I reached the emitter star. I know this because the samyama was still active, but somehow, the perspective had been reversed, my sensing center-of-gravity shifted to the boundary observer, and the new center was in the light ray.

Then, after I reached the emitter star, the journey continued, and I was pulled through another ray of light, this time at about a 90-degree angle from the previous journey. But, at a distance, something happened: I began decelerating until I stopped. Then I was rotated, and during rotation, the attention shifted from narrow focus to global vision, and then I saw the Milky Way from above and laterally; it was not exactly as it is represented by graphic descriptions, but rather a clear HD image of white lights and clouds. I stayed like this for a few seconds in awe. Then, the ray of light I came through isolated again in my attentional configuration, and I lost the global view. I was pulled back through the light to the star and then I bounced back to Earth into my physical body, and I rotated again. And there I was, back in the initial attentional setup, with the focus inside the ray of light, but this time the boundary observer was in the body.

I was back! In space. And also, back in the present, because I was back at the exact moment before I had been pulled through the light, maybe just a second later or so. I was perplexed; this took place instantly, while I was gazing with open eyes. Even the breath was in the same position as it had been where I left it. But wait, what? I mean, what? Approximately 50-100,000 light years in less than a second? I was not in a dreaming state, so the visual-thinking mechanisms were not active. I was just perceptual. But how was it generated? How hard had I been 'hallucinating' to create this experience? Or rather, could it be that I had not been hallucinating?

I paused the 'boundary observer through light' experiment after this experience, as I no longer felt the need to explore this line of research. For me, this had been enough for a while. It seemed an impossible action. This occurred in a state of enhanced perceptual presence, without symbolic visuals or fractals; there was nothing related to the usual retinal DMT images[5]. With time, as the research on DMT experience advanced, I remembered that the boundary observer is just information-on-a-wave, not a wave, not a particle, and in theory, something without mass or energy can travel at any speed, just by switching the wavelength used as a carrier.

A possible explanation: millions of years ago, when a satellite galaxy crossed our galactic plane, it created ripples, and it seems that the entire Orion arm is located in one of these ripples. From a 'topological information' perspective, during the crossing, a star from a satellite galaxy could become entangled with our Sun and Earth, or a star nearby; thus, my journey could have been possible due to this energy-information entanglement.

Maybe in the future I will start again these travels with the boundary observer, but for the moment, I am not ready to advance more. I have more questions than answers, related to this topic. But perhaps when my body is almost at the point of losing its synchrony and it is about to die, I can try again, although I would have a 99% chance of failure. When I reflect on the possibilities for life, we look naive, thinking that we are alone while looking for other intelligent life forms that would communicate their messages through electromagnetic waves—these waves are, after all, forms for polluting space. Instead we could be looking for messages and melodies encoded as sequences through light or space.

In the meantime, let's get back to the here and now and continue my field notes from the experiments with depth perception.

Inside the eye: depth perception and one-eye sensitivity

Once, while I was contemplating the night sky from the balcony, there was a building under construction, approximately 2 km away, and the crane had a very powerful light, with blueish nuances, and I was able to see it clearly. I decided to try a new way of looking into the ray of light by covering one eye and adjusting myself to see the intermediary objects in the visual field, with just one eye. I wanted to see if I could detect the ray as it was touching the retina.

These were the elements that I could see in this micro-macro visual experiment, using the light from the crane:

• On the retina, the most intense was the light center itself. This was not a point of light, or a shape like a circle, such as light from the stars. Instead, it was spread into an irregular shape, with blue, red, and green filaments, grouped in an unusual way, like the rim of a butterfly. This butterfly shape stayed constant whatever I was doing with the eye. It became larger or smaller depending on the eye focus. So, I suppose this is what the retina sees.

• The reflections/refractions around the main shape were fantastic RGB filaments, 30-40% the size of the butterfly, located around the main shape, like a tiny, super HD psychedelic filament.

• Something was acting as a filter—perhaps the cornea, aqueous humor—so that I could see tiny bubbles of liquid moving onto it from time to time. This filter was transparent but had a consistency, like a glass that was not perfectly translucent.

• The crystalline lens was not visible per se; but when I changed the style, it seemed that something was moving; it was producing different results based on my actions upon the eye muscle, as it changed the size of the opening (the iris perhaps). I am not sure that I identified the eye structure correctly, but this was not the point.

• The distance from the retina to the lens and cornea system was perceivable; there was more or less depth, depending on the resolution used to observe the butterfly shape.

• Sometimes, the eyebrow reflections were visible.

• And there were other elements, various things that existed in the environment around me.

What actions were available to me in this type of experience, while doing samyama with the light and observing the effects?

• I could use all types of attention: focused, diffuse, immersed, objective, and combinations of them, through dividing the attention. The combinations are so diverse that in time, I could integrate the depth vision easily within the experience, as a natural part of the mix (e.g., diffuse immersed attention on the butterfly shape, focused-objective attention on the space between the retina and iris).

• Zoom in and zoom out to make the butterfly shape larger or smaller.

• Changing the resolution of the butterfly shape: I could focus on an RGB filament emanating from the butterfly shape, and after a few seconds, it became possible to dive into the filament and get a high-resolution of it (when zooming in, the butterfly shape size of light increased, sometimes to the point that it was 60-70% of the entire visual field). I never reached the maximum resolution, but there seemed to be more to see whenever I zoomed in.

• Control of the micro-movements of the eye: This involved using one-pointedness and locking the size of the image or allowing some micro-movement. As a side fact, micro-movements allowed me to detect the elements and their positions more clearly. During the experiment, when I was discovering a new configuration, I explored it deeply by blocking the eye through one-pointedness. This locks all the micro-movements of the eye and the lensing system (the crystalline system).

In the HD configuration, deep inside the retina image, it is nice to see what happens when I use the finger or an object in very close proximity to the main ray of light. The light bends, and the surrounding filaments of the main butterfly seem to increase in length. I see textures on the object very clearly. When I use the finger, the fingerprints are so HD that the distance between two skin waves seems like 3-4 meters (subjectively speaking).

In the HD position inside the eye, I sometimes like to let the mind play its games and form shapes that have meaning (similar to how it is to gaze at ourselves in the mirror for a while). The brain seems to tend to compensate for the lack of movement by creating perceptual interpretations. It is like a dialogue: 'Is this a butterfly or a castle?' Then a buzzing appears inside me, followed by a conclusion. 'Here it is, a castle'. Then, after some moments, it changes again; 'Nope, it's not a castle. Now it seems more like X, maybe. Let's see, yes, this resembles X'. It is a funny game, to watch the information being processed into a representation, without any reference point except my memory.

What I cannot hack, though, is the main shape of the light. No matter what I do, the brain keeps that image intact. Even if I rotate the head, after the vision locks in a one-pointedness schema on the ray of light, nothing changes. The adaptive processing highways are so large that I cannot detect any visible change in the continuity of the butterfly shape. The continuity of shape perception is perfect.[6]

What I want to add about the experiences inside the eye is that in order to dive deeper into an HD zoom, at a certain point I need a higher vibrational sync. I need the vibrational DMT-like configuration and the carrier wave sound to be active, in a very high-pitched and loud configuration, to be able to zoom in deeper. I noticed that the carrier wave also appears naturally when I try a new attentional setup for the first time. I can try and try, but the attentional styles just won't 'lock' as I want, until a wave of reconfiguration develops in my vibrations. Then, all of a sudden, the carrier wave appears throughout the entire energy body (and static-vibrational kundalini activates, in other words). And voilà, the attentional mechanisms adjust, and I get what I want.

Advances in depth perception: exploring the environment and hacking the perceptual mechanisms

The next step was to apply the inside-eye attentional mechanisms to the visual field outside the eye. To do this, I used what I had, the balcony and the balustrade. So, while looking at the sky, with stars, Moon or clouds, I discovered that it is possible to hack into the depth-representational mechanisms, like this: I set narrow attention on a high distance, looking at the sky, and then I use the global-diffuse attention to lock my vision into space in between the arms of the balustrade. In other words, the global field elements are arranged as if each inner rectangle, formed of the space between the arms of the balustrade, is a 2D screen. I will use clouds to describe the effect. It is as if there is a printed banner, with clouds displayed in each rectangle, between the horizontal-vertical arms of the balustrade. To get this, I need to attend, in a diffuse-wide way, to the entire balustrade. When the effect emerges, the balustrade transforms into a 2D wall with crossings, and a 2D sky image is on each rectangle, forming a big picture, similar to a video wall composed of multiple screens.

If I kept this style, the 2D balustrade wall created a nice luminance inside the balcony. I see the balcony as if the air is luminous, with a uniform light available at all points of space. I liked to lock this attention style, watching the diffuse city light inside the balcony. After the global attention locking was set to the balustrade, I could easily move the eyes around to explore the balustrade and the air, without losing the wall schema—2D wall and 3D sky with depth perception at the same time.

An interesting experience unfolded when I moved the focus to the sky, above the temporary 2D balustrade wall. I needed to be very silent and still; otherwise, the 3D depth information from the sky would destabilize the 2D wall schema. But when I managed to keep the 2D wall schema, and the 3D sky, the stars above the balustrade looked to be in their position as in the standard vision, but they had new information available. The visual tends to be HD, clean, with a lovely nuance of tactile resolution. This is hard to say in words.

After months of practice, I figured out a key to induce the 2D wall configuration. I just need to interfere with cognition a bit, when looking through a rectangle of the balustrade as if looking far ahead, and then set a percentage of attention on the close-range distance, where the empty rectangle is located. Then, I need to repeat a few times, 'This is full'. As a result, the inner configuration buzzes, and the 2D wall appears, and then I expand the focused attention, from one rectangle to 3D global attention to the entire balustrade-wall, without losing the 2D wall quality.

I want to mention that in all these experiences, I am very relaxed, and the eyes are very relaxed. So, when the 2D wall-with-rectangle-cloud is locked, I can look around inside the balcony very easily, using regular 3D vision and depth perception. The 2D locking mechanism is not possible by putting pressure on the attentional mechanisms. I just flow and, from time to time, lock them in a configuration and keep them still in that position. The locking is, in fact, a stillness, as when we go to sleep. We find out the sleep position and then we stay there and relax.

The following experiments have derived naturally from the ones I've already presented, as I applied the inside-the-eye and balcony-wall depth sensitivity to the elements in the sky, the Moon, certain constellations, and the Milky Way.

The 3D Moon and the lunar eclipse

At this point in the explorations, I was aware of the following aspects: I could use various combinations of attentional styles to create a representation, including depth perception in the representation. I could cognitively interfere in the information-representation selection process, by prioritizing some information. I could add information-representation from my memory, referring to the actual physical distances to some objects—I mean, simple information, like 'this X is closer than Y', 'this X is farther than this Y', 'X is after Y' etc.; as a result, the visual perception of depths was adjusting itself, and I could perceptually sense the visual field, e.g., that X is in front of Y, or X is closer than Y.

I decided to try and see if I could extend these skills to the elements in the sky. I used the Moon first. I paid attention to its shape, how it reflects through the atmosphere, what happens if I look from inside my room, adding the window as a third layer. I began to study astronomy to understand the position of the Moon, its trajectory, how the Earth moves, where the light comes from, the location of the Sun, what the 3D configuration is (Earth and Moon orbits), how far the visible stars/planets are, how large the atmosphere is. And I tried to translate the abstract distances in km, into perceptual-recognizable information, such as 'the distance to the Moon is 'n' times the width of the Earth's atmosphere'.

I also tried a direct method by focusing inside the Moon light (actually, the Sun light reflected by the Moon), to see if I could perceive the scale of the distance by diving-expanding the boundary observer through the ray and, after I hit the Moon surface, to see how long the journey would be. This didn't work. I was only able to estimate in scales, e.g., hundreds/thousands of times the width of the atmosphere.

But what came unexpectedly in these explorations with the Moon was that the Sun light, reflecting on the edges of the Moon, was providing extra information, and I managed to configure my perception to see the Moon like a 3D movie. I also had the chance to witness a total Moon eclipse, which was amazing; the 3D quality of the Moon was impressive. It was as if someone had removed a cloud from perception, and there it was, my own private 3D cinema, running the 3D Moon movie while being at home. I guess this was possible because previously, I was used to compiling the 3D image of the Moon with less information about depths, and when the eclipse took place, I got additional information about the position because of Earth interference.

I understood later that the experiences with the Moon used all my sensitivities, the low-scale inside-the-eye skills, the nearby balcony-wall mechanisms, and the far-away environmental depth sensitivity. When looking at the rim of the Moon, especially when it is full and just arises from below the horizon, in the days when it rises after midnight, the information from the rim is enough to create a 3D representation. I want to mention that this 3D quality is better achieved with one eye. If I use both eyes, there are too many variables, and the depth perception is not so clear.

3D Milky Way

This is the last exploration I want to describe here, and it is the most complex of all. It developed without my intention. So I would say that someone gave me a gift. I was at a psytrance festival, and in one night, I went to the periphery, where I could see the sky perfectly, and I used micro-dosed ganja. I was on a hill, and the last stage/source of light was 200-300 meters away, and some 30 meters above my level. The sky was very clear, and the Milky Way was up above. I could see the center of the Milky Way area and most of the left side. There was a bit of the right side but not too much. I lay down on my back, and the Cygnus constellation was directly in front of me. And lovely music was feeding the vibrational sync.

So that was the setting. I was trying to figure out the 3D position of the elements I saw in the sky. I was aware of the distance scales, e.g., all the stars were in close proximity, as compared to the cloudy light coming from the galaxy arms[7]. I allowed all my perceptual skills to attune themselves for some minutes, to let all the information configure itself in perceptual representation. I didn't know how to mix them consciously, so I let the automatic patterns do the job if possible. And—bing!—I got the carrier wave, really intensely, a full vibrational buzz, and then I got a new perceptual-attentional configuration. Usually, this carrier wave is just a pulse, but now, something more profound was unfolding, a new re-arrangement that required a higher sync in me. The increase of the synchronizing process lasted a few seconds, and it was as intense as in my first changa experience, but in this experience at the festival, it remained active for many minutes.

As a result, the inner configuration molded in a totally new way, and a perceptual-visual formed. I saw the light from the stage in the atmosphere, and the next layer was with the stars, then far away the Milky Way clouds, in a 3D perceptual shape, with arms. The attentional structure was locked (as in the experiment with the balustrade). So, I started to move around with narrow attention through these layers. And guess what? In the layer with the stars (clearly closer to me than the light from the Milky Way), I was able to sense-feel-know whether a star was closer or farther than other stars. It was as if, all of a sudden, someone had poured in me all the information about their positions. I didn't have one boundary observer, but instead, I had multiple boundary observers in each point of the depth, and in each star light, and they were all exchanging information about what was in that layer.

That lasted for 10 minutes or so, and during this time, I was able to sense-perceive the depth positioning of all the stars in the star layer. I mean, I could select one star, and the perception was 'ok, this one is in front of that one', and 'that one is in front of that one'. I was able to perceive all their positions without any cognitive-reasoning interference. I was connected to the information about their close or far positions. The difference from my previous experiences was huge. It was as if I were looking at Orion, and suddenly, someone rotated the view[8] and transferred into me all the necessary 3D information[9], about the distances and relative positions between the stars.[10]

It took me half a year to understand the experience. I figured it out, partially, and I was able to reproduce some parts of it by using constellations[11], and it partially works. It seems that to access this configuration, the perception needs to lock into all the elements together. All the micro-HD and macro-HD skills were intermixed to provide the experience. The trick is to have a layer of light in the atmosphere, so that the depth perception may lock onto it as a whole, as a sort of depth regulator, similar to the balustrade wall experiment. Or something like that. This full-depth perception locking in all points provided information about all the positionings.

And for me, it only works perceptually, not cognitively. I can 'feel' the distance, I perceive their 3D positions (closer/farther), but I cannot 'know' the distance, and if I ask cognitively, 'How far is this from that?', cognition interferes, and I lose the global lock. It only works pre-consciously, meaning... when all elements are locked and transmit information about their position, as a whole, and the brain manages to mix this into one representation, similar to the diffuse-wide perception of the body during relaxation.

A possible explanation is that my perception used the luminosity filter only ('the bright stars are closer'). Still, my subjective experience was more complex: high- and low-luminosity stars seemed spread across the 3D depth field, and stars with the same luminosity were not in the same depth layer.

Or, perhaps my perception has become complex/sensitive enough to feel the differences in amounts of light/energy radiating from stars, and somehow to calculate position (closer/farther), including the star energy (or 'hot-ness') and the physical distance (using depth perception).

Afterword

The perceptual explorations were amazing for me, and I felt it would be a good idea to write them down, just in case future scientists may want to advance and develop these experiential experiments. These experiences may also be helpful for advanced psychonauts who wish to dive deeper into human biology. I noticed that ganja can facilitate the relaxation in the eyeball when I am practicing with inside-the-eye perception. She may create agitation in muscles, and micro-movements in the eye, but she can also deepen the one-pointedness. I think it's a matter of personal choice, and it all depends on the personal relation of the journeyer with the plant.

I like to think of these explorations as a tribute to Patanjali and the wisdom of the 'Yoga Sutras'. It looks like he was right in these sutras from Vibhuti Pada:

pravritty-aloka-nyasat sukshma-vyavahita-viprakrishta-jnanam

'Through samyama on the shining, effulgent light, one gains knowledge of the small and subtle, the hidden and veiled, and the remote'.

bhavana-jnanam surye sanyamat

'Through samyama on the Sun, there comes knowledge of the solar system, cosmic evolution and involution'.

chandre tara-vyuha-jnanam

'Through samyama on the Moon, there comes knowledge concerning the arrangement of stars'.

dhruve tad-gati-jnanam

'Through samyama on the Pole-Star comes knowledge of the relative motions and positions of the stars'.[12]

References and notes

1 Satchidananda, S. S. (2012). *The Yoga Sutras of Patanjali* (Revised ed.). Integral Yoga Publications.

2 Brazdău, O. (2019, February 27). *Entheogenic Insights I: Psychology of DMT/Ayahuasca Experience.* Consciousness Quotient Institute. Retrieved January 14, 2022, from https://www.consciousness-quotient.com/psychology-of-dmt-ayahuasca-experience

3 For an overview of mathematical and physics' infinity, take a tour through PBS Infinity Series:
PBS Infinite Series. (2016, September 6). PBS Infinite Series [Video]. YouTube .
https://www.youtube.com/channel/UCs4aHmggTfFrpkPcWSaBN9g

4 Additional resources: Butler, D. (2013, February 5). *David Butler - Video Channel* [Video]. YouTube. https://www.youtube.com/channel/UCNwSxyl2KmhdAjHLR6xGR0A; Kurzgesagt – In a Nutshell. (2020, September 22). *The Largest Star in the Universe – Size Comparison* [Video]. YouTube. https://www.youtube.com/watch?v=3mnSDifDSxQ

5 Later, I found this image, that resembles the journey through the light ray: Moskowitz, C. (2013, January 15). *Warp Speed: What Hyperspace Would Really Look Like.* Space.Com. Retrieved January 14, 2022, from
https://www.space.com/19268-star-wars-hyperspace-physics-reality.html

6 Further reading: Cherry, K. (2021, May 2). *Monocular Cues for Depth Perception.* Verywell Mind. Retrieved January 14, 2022, from
https://www.verywellmind.com/what-are-monocular-cues-2795829

7 I also knew this information: Fizixfan, F. (2021, October 10). *Orientation of the Earth, Sun and Solar System in the Milky Way*. Physics Forums | Science Articles, Homework Help, Discussion. Retrieved January 14, 2022, from https://www.physicsforums.com/threads/orientation-of-the-earth-sun-and-solar-system-in-the-milky-way.888643

8 Additional resource: Frank Summers. (2013, January 29). *The Orion Constellation in 3D* [Video]. YouTube. https://www.youtube.com/watch?v=lD-5ZOipE48

9 I described some parts of this experience in these posts on a Physics Forum (see from post #87): Fizixfan, F. (2021, October 10). *Orientation of the Earth, Sun and Solar System in the Milky Way*. Physics Forums | Science Articles, Homework Help, Discussion. Retrieved January 14, 2022, from https://www.physicsforums.com/threads/orientation-of-the-earth-sun-and-solar-system-in-the-milky-way.888643

10 Additional resource: Niffelheim Frya. (2013, October 22). *Universe Sandbox - Simulation of the Milky Way in 3D* [Video]. YouTube. https://www.youtube.com/watch?v=kr9JINBXooo

11 Additional resource: Steven Sanders. (2014, March 17). 3D Tour of Constellations [Video]. YouTube. https://www.youtube.com/watch?v=Bom3jubAaNY

12 Patanjali. (n.d.). *Vibhuti Pada: Yoga Sutras Book III*. Theosophy Trust. Retrieved January 14, 2022, from https://theosophytrust.org/920-vibhuti-pada-yoga-sutras-book-iii-patanjali

Case Study 4

How to Activate and Navigate Intentional Visionary Experiences

Introduction

Before using these methods, practice and learn pratyahara, internalization of perception, and samyama, complete and continuous connection to the object of attention, by flowing into it. Previous experiences with energy flowing, such as authentic dance, enstatic dance, Tai-Chi, or entheogens are helpful. Before practicing these methods, please read the consciousness sutras to understand better what is happening. When you use music as an entrainment technology, choose new music you have never heard before; it keeps the attention in the present moment. Novelty is essential.

These exercises are mostly experiential, and to understand the methods and observations, one needs to practice beforehand and re-read and review these methods after a while. For exploring visionary experiences and diving deeper, I couldn't find a straightforward method that works all the time, as if going from A to B to C. In all points, A mixes with C and B, and sometimes when A appears, BC run in the background together. So, these descriptions may appear fuzzy if analyzed through the lens of semantic logic. The techniques described here definitely work, but treat them as options, and use them to expand your own skills, so that, in each stage of the visionary experience, you may have some available tools to influence the flow, and dive deeper or get out of the experience (if you want to).

Please consider this when you begin the practice: the visionary experiences happen while we are in the body. We are not moving anywhere. Instead, we use awareness to attend to the body layers (physical, energy, information) and space. Visionary experiences are not out-of-body experiences, but in-the-body experiences. We just dive into ourselves while staying where we are, in the area of space occupied by the body. We can work with the body-schema structure, expand or delete it. But the witnessing, the awareness that it is I who is doing this action, happens through the body, all the time, even if the 'I am' presence is lighter, denser, flowing-journeying toward the edge of the universe, or without any content except empty space.

These experiences can sometimes be related to 'lucid dreaming', but they are not the same. In visionary experiences, we do not interfere with the flow by changing the course of the flows too much; or by introducing our self-identity/ego desires, to control the flows to the desired outcome. Instead, we dive into the content that we don't like, to deeply connect with its causal structure, harmonizing ourselves so that the specific flow that we don't like never appears again. We do this by allowing ourselves to change instantly through the experience, while we accept the processing and integration in the moment. The correlate of this psychological experience in the neuronal patterns would be 'instant reconsolidation', or 'updating consolidation', or 'allowing brain-body rhythms to coalesce in new ways'.

Many of the field notes were written while I took small breaks during an intentional visionary experience. I paused to write them down, and then I went back to the experience, or sometimes left the experience entirely. I compiled this text after a few years of practice, and so I don't remember exactly how I was when I started, or how I progressed through this process. Each visionary experience produced structural changes in me, each time. Later on, I arranged them as logically as possible. Still, some of the methods were left intentionally unedited, as I wrote them down. I didn't align them with the perspective used for this introduction. And, I link words-like-this to provide visual images. My hope is that these observations will inspire you to develop your own methodologies and techniques.

The entrainment and a preliminary training for accessing visionary layers

Wait one or two hours after sunset, in a setting without artificial light, and give your eyes some time to adapt to night vision. Use red lighting, if necessary, as it will not spoil the rods' adaptation. Close your eyes, listen to some music on your headphones, or just go inside yourself using your own method. Perform a full pratyahara (internal absorption, as described in the 'Yoga Sutras'). Activate visual perception through the eye retina, to watch what is happening. In other words, activate the eyes as if with eyes open in a fully darkened room, but keep the eyelids closed. Relax deeply, witness yourself, and wait 20 minutes or until the dream state begins to emerge naturally; then watch the dream visuals. Keep witnessing awareness active, and just look at the visuals generated in the dream (the visual-spatial thinking layer). Then align the dreamy landscape with real body perceptions, and allow retina perception and dreamy landscapes to unfold simultaneously.

Another view: keep the witnessing active while the dreamy state is activated, providing visual-spatial thinking, and allowing the dreamy visuals to unfold, while maintaining body presence and an active meta-attention. Once the dreamy state is fully active, notice that the eyes seem to be looking in various directions, as if following the dream (this is natural in dreams). At this point, while keeping the energy body and the brainwaves in the dream mode, concentrate the attention onto one scene, in front of your visual field, and add the dream content to here-now retina perception, by adding spatial depth to the attention span. In other words, merge the eye visuals with dream visuals, while keeping pratyahara and the spatial perception active. Then, enter into the wave realm by allowing yourself to flow within the here-now experience constantly. Sense this change. And watch how the visuals tend to unfold in new ways.

At this point, a new category of actions is possible, e.g., through consciously interacting with the visual content. Notice the visuals. You could ask, 'Are they mine?' Or ask the collective, 'Are they mine?' Usually, the collective senses our presence. Let yourself connect. Watch how this collective feedback reflection modifies the field, while the reflection process unfolds. The collective adds information to the local field, and sometimes energetic visions appear.

Diving deeper, the images become archetypal. Archetypes are vibrational-information patterns translated into images. During this experience, it seems that the automatic selection criterion for visuals that appear is this: what is selected is the most powerful or quasi-harmonically visual form, which exists in the collective field (culture) or the personal field (personality), related to the specific topic that is active. Watch the visual flow and experience this layer as long as you want.

How to harmonize misalignments, connect with shadow roots, and ignite instant reconsolidation

This is what I tried, and it worked for me.

When the brain is in the dream state, and there are dreamy visuals, as if looking from a third-person perspective, I may happen to see myself from above, watching certain things developing as 'the dream'. One path of interaction is this: I wait for the 'dream visuals' and watch. When a scene intensifies, emotional energy appears, and usually I become aware of myself as a character. Depending on the flow, 'me-in-the-dream' (dream self) has various reactions to the images, while processing my 'unconscious' information. If 'I-as-observer' notice that 'me-in-the-dream' is not reacting harmonically, I interact with the flow, move 'I-as-observer' inside the dream position, and add perceptual vision to the dream, by adding retina perception, body perception with space awareness, and the present moment. Through this action, I collapse into a reduced-freedom configuration, transforming the 'cognitive' dream into an 'energetic' dream. While collapsing myself into the dream self, I give up the objective-overview attention and adapt to a new style of overviewing, which feels narrowed, less spacious but more intense, and I allow myself to experience the 'inside bubble' perspective.

Sometimes, it's not necessary to dive into my dream self, as the dreamlike content could be just a reorganization of information, without an active dream self. In this situation, I can merge with a scene or a character, using samyama and allowing the energy body to activate. Through this action, by entering a specific dream scene perceptually, it is possible to understand the nature of the scene or character, by allowing its roots to become conscious.

Usually, in the inner art sessions focused on harmonizing the daily content, I choose a dream scene or character with a 'misalignment'. Then, during samyama, I allow the energy body to activate if necessary. Sometimes kundalini spikes or vibrations may appear, if integration needs more synchrony, or the misaligned patterns have deep roots in the physical of energy body layers. After I figure it out and perform the right internal action, usually acceptance or integration, the misalignment harmonizes by itself, accompanied by an instant reconsolidation of memory engrams.

In the experience of diving into something, inside the dream, the flowing speed is simultaneously aligned with relaxation. I need to relax to go faster. But I can also simply increase the speed, by accelerating the diving, and accelerating the previous acceleration method, until I connect with the source of the scene/character. And when this diving through increase of increase of increase becomes fluid, the DMT-like kundalini spikes appear, sometimes accompanied by the carrier wave. But, in this experience, compared with exogenous DMT, I still have the gamemaster tools, which allow me to interact with the experience consciously and dive deeper, no matter what I encounter. I can adapt quickly from inside. In these intentional high-sync experiences, as compared with my first Santo Daime experiences, I can manage the intensity of the experience and process and understand everything as it shows up, without any aftereffects, such as the unzipping of information. The memory reconsolidation happens instantly, and its depth depends on how much I can dive into and how much I can maintain the simultaneous connection between my physical body layer, the energy body layers, and the 'misalignment' from the dream scene content.

But sometimes, samyama on a dream scene could happen instantly, and there is no need to flow and work with the speed of the flow. I just connect, after a few seconds of flowing, and merge with the information root of that scene, and allow it to diffuse into all my body layers. If I am flexible enough, the harmonization of the misalignment could happen in a few seconds.

In other situations, after I decide to merge with a scene or a character and until I can complete the samyama fusion, the scene has already changed, and I need to do samyama continuously, as a flow-of-samyama so that I can reach its roots. And in some situations, the dream unfolds quite fast and for some minutes. I flow along with the dream, until at one point, 'I-as-observer' and the dream scene can merge. In this situation, the diving skills described above are necessary, as the intensity or the speed of the unfolding dream may change, and this going-side-by-side transforms into a 'catch-me-if-you-can' game.

These are just examples, to illustrate that there are various dynamics possible during a merging-through-samyama action, and it takes practice to be able to really connect with certain scenes. Especially if the dream scene is rooted in our shadow, and we have ignored or rejected that content for many years, the 'catch-me-if-you-can' game can take some time, until we manage to find a way to connect. Remember that the dream is just our own adaptive processing; the more rejected some content has been, the harder it is to connect with it.

Another path to high-synchrony flowing: liquifying the liquifying

This is how it works for me: using headphones, and listening to some nice flowing music, beneath the sky (it is essential to have empty space in front of the closed eyes), I begin to look inside myself, relaxing or diving into thinking, but using visual-style thinking, by seeing and by being.

Sometimes, the mind tends to be verbal, so I transform the verbal process into visuals. This transmutation is possible by accessing the dream state configuration and then using the dream visual style to process the intended information, as 'interactive visions', or lucid dreaming, but adding the physical awareness from the body.

In this visual-thinking inner space, with perception activated, if I want to activate the vibrational flowing-in-hypersync high-energy state, I perform this action: I 'liquify' everything-that-is-inside-dreaming-including-me, and let the reality flow. But the action of 'liquifying' is not just a one-time action, and that's it. The liquifying is continuous; I liquify the liquifying, like jumping into a flowing dynamic condition. This feels like switching from my physical-particle self to my energy-wave self, and—bing!—the experience structure changes, and I usually find myself in a 3D surrounding experience of inner-space presence, with tunnels evolving in the visual perception, from the retina. It is as if I switch to a smaller wavelength, and I feel the body's energy vibrating in a static way, and the mind is no longer thinking in visuals-with-forms. The flowing style itself is the new way of thinking. And thinking is the same thing as perceiving; they are merged. The liquifying process is like returning home to the energy world, where all that is static becomes fluid. Like a breeze flowing through me, synchronizing all the layers into a pleasant vibrational experience, or like a gentle kundalini activation, or an ayahuasca aftereffect. Intense, but in a friendly way. The speed of the liquifying can also be modified through intention, by relaxing and allowing the experience to flow faster.

There is an interesting adaptive processing in the mind, in this configuration of continuous liquifying. When I add the Moon or a star by shortly opening the eyes and doing samyama with the Moon or the star, then close the eyes again, the configuration seems to facilitate the flow of information about the evolution of our species, the evolution of life on Earth, or various other topics, as seen from an evolutionary perspective. Evolutionary processes are so clear in this flowing of reality! If I stop to consider some aspect, decompression ensues, usually in the form of positive insight, and I write down some ideas. But I have to be careful about these 'detours', since I need to be brief and focused, when taking these notes, and to write just a few minutes, so that I can return to the flowing state from where the insight was 'ejected', without losing the connection. Sometimes, however, I prefer not to take any detour, and I simply enjoy the insight-in-the-moment, knowing I may never encounter it, while continuing the flowing experience. Sometimes, I exit the experience completely and enjoy the insight and the new configuration, until it fades, usually after a few minutes or hours.

It seems that there is no limit to how fast I can flow using the continuous liquifying method. The only limit is my own ability to accept and connect with the increasing frequency. Or, in other words, it depends on how capable my body layers are (the physical, energy, and information layers), to incorporate and maintain the higher and higher frequencies—or the smaller and smaller wavelengths. Through this method, it is possible to access configurations similar to DMT peaks, or other types of high-synchrony peaks. The action of 'liquifying the liquifying' is similar to the events that happen in our body layers when the carrier wave is active, and frequency increases from, say, 100 Hz to 1,000,000 Hz, or when the simultaneous processes increase from 10 to 1,000.

The liquifying sometimes ends in white light, as the body cannot discriminate anymore at that frequency layer, and the entire experience collapses into white light, abandoning the discrimination process due to overloading. But after doing some personal work, the second encounter may be more manageable, as we are able to process more connections. And there is no white light overload anymore. Progressively, while allowing this step-by-step habituation of even higher frequencies in our body layers, we can get insights about how reality functions at that wavelength, instead of just being blinded by the white light effect.

I don't know if this process has an end. Perhaps it ends when we reach the shortest wavelength possible, the quarks layers, or the Higgs boson wavelength. My limits are at the cell size, for the moment. What is amazing is that journeys in the opposite direction are also possible. We can access larger wavelengths, but instead of going faster and faster, we would have to go deeper into stillness, while tuning into larger and larger wavelengths. I sometimes wonder if I can attune myself to feel the ripples generated by the galaxies that have crossed through the Milky Way in the past. Could a human being develop this sensitivity? Where is the limit?

Using hyperventilation

Alternatively, here is a simple method to activate the high-energy synchronic configuration. I begin from the 360-degree vision and 3D inner space, while attention is focused on internal perceptions, pratyahara is active, and inner eyes are opened and locked onto the global inner ambient. In this space, I hyperventilate by breathing deeply and merge with the fresh energy that builds inside the energy body. I use samyama, fully absorbing myself to become one with this raising energy process. The key seems to be this: it is necessary to keep my body perfectly still and fully relaxed while the energy builds up. Further, I must keep the mind perfectly still, just watching the effects of the increasing energy, even if there are moments when the energy naturally tries to expand and generate ecstatic emotions. If the energy is not expanded, but maintained inside, in a static-vibrational form, the experience leads directly to high-energy experiences, and kundalini is aroused.

The path through ecstatic emotions is also usable if, just before the expansion begins, I rearrange the perspective from being inside focused, to being in a unitary mystical state—external awareness merged with internal awareness. So, when the expansion occurs, an increase in synchrony simultaneously happens, leading to a high-sync experience plus enstatic flowing in the energy body. But this method also activates the physical body, and I cannot remain still. In this configuration, I like to dance using a free-flow Tai Chi-like style, which comes naturally and allows me to interact with the flowing, rather than simply being ecstatically raptured with no control over the ecstatic expansion.

I need to say that, even if this method is simple, I think this works better for people already familiar with the high-energy spikes, due to previous entheogenic experiences with vibrational kundalini spikes.

Using 'let-go' keys for transitioning through layers of inner experience

Hint: choose your own method for transitioning through layers and anchor it in your psyche as a personal 'let-go key'. It can be a word, image, visual, process, previous experience, or something you like that reminds you that you can do it, or a method that you have done before. This privacy is necessary to ensure 100% effectiveness. And don't tell your key to anyone, until you feel the need to change it again. It is fine to share, but when shared, it expands with the next person and, temporarily, becomes harder to access when needed. So, find your key, transform it into an anchor, and use it when necessary.

After merging with the visionary flow, using the method described previously, watch, but when you feel you are curious or have a question about a scene, just dive into its stream by using your key, and get more information by watching the experience. If you need to know 'what is the cause of the experience?', 'why am I experiencing this?', you can go deeper using your keys. Or just ask politely to be allowed to dive further. It is possible to advance to the next depth of reality by developing another attitude as a key. After you learn to dive by flowing into the unknown, no further keys are needed. What you think or want-to-see is what you get.

In my explorations, I realized that there are so many ways to let go and allow the transition through layers of reality, that what matters most is the ability to use the appropriate tool for the situation. The availability and diversity of these tools are essential, not the keys/tools themselves. When we are flowing through visionary experiences, it may happen that some parts of our memory are not available easily, and so practice is essential.

When I use a tool, I select it intuitively. Sometimes it works, sometimes not; it is a matter of resilience. It is not like in the 'Matrix' movie, where there is one key for one door. Instead, a key can open many doors, with each new input generating a chain reaction in the experience.

In other words, the let-go key is an action, a transformational option available to witnessing awareness. For me, it is not that the witness is an observer who commands the change. It is more like this: I allow the attentional flows to change it, with me inside as 'the flow', allowing a new style of 'eversion' every time, never knowing what is on the other side.

Navigation tweaks

- For diving into a perspective (visionary flow) by seeing-being the visual landscape, one must use full samyama and develop the ability to perform full absorptions into the flows of events presented by the collective. To accept everything. Unconditionally.

- Multiples dives through visionary layers, inside a current vision, are possible by focusing fully the narrow attention into a point, a flower, or a shadow, and then diving again through that point, like a zooming journey through fractals. Watch a Mandelbrot Fractal Zoom video to see what I mean; they are available on the internet.

- In the visionary configuration, if we wonder: 'What is this, that I see?', the answer reveals itself. A complete letting go is needed. Ask 'What is this?' and then forget about the question, and just watch. Watch what new landscape is configured due to the previous action, whatever that was.

- Do not be brave when you see a 'demon'. Just let it in, experience it, dive into it or breathe it in. Allow its energy to enter and transform you. Feel it when it passes through you, while it passes. Use equanimity. But, sometimes, be brave. There are no general rules. I prefer to use a perspective based on curiosity, instead of courage-like attitudes, for these situations. For some time, I used to ask the adversity characters directly: 'What? Now what? What is this? Who's playing with me?' And usually, certain characters would smile at me, and then they faded away. However, sometimes it is hard to be so relaxed as a freezing response appears naturally, and only direct interaction tools are available, rather than the self-reflection tools. Now I see 'fear-generating characters' as dense packets of energy-information, too dense to be processed because of our limited flexibility. At this fundamental level, the adversity bubbles are just dense 'presence triggers'. They cause a shock to our system. We compress ourselves, and the visual is formed as an explanatory layer. And when an adversity character appears, we stop. One way to manage these events, learned from the Santo Daime community, is to let it flow, every time it appears, while singing and dancing continuously during the experience. So, if you see a 'demon', flow through it and connect with the energy and information that created it. Or do whatever you feel like to embrace the information; just don't stop too much. Unfreeze yourself, using any tool that is available at the moment; just don't run away. Interact. The mechanisms I described above also happen when the visionary visual is positive, and a character invites us, and we go with them, to connect and communicate. They usually transmit presence in a pleasant way.

• When I used music, I noticed that I could interfere in a positive way with the visionary flow, by modifying the energy source, the source from which the visionary flow feeds. I just picked another sound flow, like switching from bass to vocals. But, to do this, some previous practice with full let-go is needed.

Some reflections for advanced psychonauts

If you are a psychonaut and prefer to dive deeper into experience, using music and ganja as journey companions may densify the dives, by facilitating samyama processes. But using ganja is not an easy method, as the plant intelligence fluidifies the psyche. And, during high-energy experiences, if the psyche is not pure enough, inner tensions may appear, and the flow of experience may be hijacked by the self-identity/ego, resulting in dreamy-style self/ego trips which de-focus the experience for a while.

Sometimes, however, it is perfect to enjoy the self/ego's visions. If you detect any hijacking while it is happening, at least you can be creative: you can play and interact with the visionary self/ego contents, no matter whether it is a 'positive' or 'negative' or an 'explanatory' story. Practice equanimity and continue to use witnessing awareness actively. After all, any vision will end sooner or later, after the energy is consumed and information is rearranged.

For very deep explorations in the mind layers, sometimes I prefer to navigate with a micro-dosed ganja aboard. If it is too intense, the high activates the vibrational kundalini configuration, and the experience becomes enstatic. In addition, this high is energy-consuming, so it's a choice depending on what's happening in me. Micro-dosing fits in me better because it offers me a sort of control. If I choose to dive deeper, it is easier to add ganja little by little, and to monitor the effects, instead of jumping directly into a very intense experience where I would be blown out by the density. If I take this step-by-step path, the entire experience may last up to 5-6 hours. Of course, I don't just sit down during this time. I move, eat, dance, watch the sky, but, if I use music, I like to keep my headphones on and keep the flow of the experience through music. And all the activities that I do with my body, during the ceremony—well, they feel like a dance.

In my opinion, ganja/charas are highly skilled navigators, who can allow amazing transitions. We just need to behave appropriately with the plant and tell it where we want to go, and then be brave enough to navigate wildly, allowing ourselves to change the navigation style.

Stages of psychedelic-induced visionary experiences and how to choose the post-session personality

For a better understanding of the methodologies used to activate and navigate the intentional visionary experiences, without using psychedelics, or when using micro-dosing, it is helpful to take a look at how the psychedelic-induced experiences are unfolding. The most in-depth research was undertaken by Timothy Leary, Ralph Metzner, and Richard Alpert. What follows in this section are the stages of psychedelic experience, as described in 'The Psychedelic Experience. A Manual Based on the Tibetan Book of the Dead'. My suggestion is to consider these stages as layers of experience, as they don't necessarily activate in the order described below. Please remember that in the following quotes, 'ego' refers to self or self-identity, not to the 'selfish' aspects of self-identity.

"You must be ready to accept the possibility that there is a limitless range of awareness for which we now have no words; that awareness can expand beyond range of your ego, your self, your familiar identity, beyond everything you have learned, beyond your notions of space and time, beyond the differences which usually separate people from each other and from the world around them. You must remember that throughout human history, millions have made this voyage. A few (whom we call mystics, saints or buddhas) have made this experience endure and have communicated it to their fellow men. You must remember, too, that the experience is safe (at the very worst, you will end up the same person who entered the experience), and that all of the dangers which you have feared are unnecessary productions of your mind. Whether you experience heaven or hell, remember that it is your mind which creates them. Avoid grasping the one or fleeing the other. Avoid imposing the ego game on the experience. You must try to maintain faith and trust in the potentiality of your own brain and the billion-year-old life process. With your ego left behind you, the brain can't go wrong.[...]

Following the Tibetan model then, we distinguish three phases of the psychedelic experience.

First Bardo: The Period of Ego-Loss or Non-Game Ecstasy (Chikhai Bardo)

Part I: The Primary Clear Light Seen at the Moment of Ego-Loss.

The duration of this state varies with the individual. It depends upon experience, security, trust, preparation and the surroundings. In those who have had even a little practical experience of the tranquil state of non-game awareness, and in those who have happy games, this state can last from thirty minutes to several hours.[...] Here is a list of commonly reported physical sensations: Bodily pressure, which the Tibetans call earth-sinking-into-water; Clammy coldness, followed by feverish heat, which the Tibetans call water-sinking-into-fire; Body disintegrating or blown to atoms, called fire-sinking-into-air; Pressure on head and ears, which Americans call rocket-launching-into-space; Tingling in extremities; Feelings of body melting or flowing as if wax; Nausea; Trembling or shaking, beginning in pelvic regions and spreading up torso.

These physical reactions should be recognized as signs heralding transcendence. Avoid treating them as symptoms of illness, accept them, merge with them, enjoy them.[...]

Part II: The Secondary Clear Light Seen Immediately After Ego-Loss.

The preceding section describes how the Clear Light may be recognized and liberation maintained. But if it becomes apparent that the Primary Clear Light has not been recognized, then it can certainly be assumed there is dawning what is called the phase of the Secondary Clear Light. The first flash of experience usually produces a state of ecstasy of the greatest intensity. Every cell in the body is sensed as involved in orgastic creativity.

It may be helpful to describe in more detail some of the phenomena which often accompany the moment of ego-loss. One of these might be called 'wave energy flow'. The individual becomes aware that he is part of and surrounded by a charged field of energy, which seems almost electrical. In order to maintain the ego-loss state as long as possible, the prepared person will relax and allow the forces to flow through him. There are two dangers to avoid: the attempt to control or to rationalize this energy flow. Either of these reactions is indicative of ego-activity and the First Bardo transcendence is lost.

The second phenomenon might be called 'biological life-flow'. Here the person becomes aware of physiological and biochemical processes; rhythmic pulsing activity within the body. Often this may be sensed as powerful motors or generators continuously throbbing and radiating energy. An endless flow of cellular forms and colors flashes by. Internal biological processes may also be heard with characteristic swooshing, crackling, and pounding noises. Again the person must resist the temptation to label or control these processes. At this point you are tuned in to areas of the nervous system which are inaccessible to routine perception. You cannot drag your ego into the molecular processes of life. These processes are a billion years older than the learned conceptual mind.

Another typical and most rewarding phase of the First Bardo involves ecstatic energy movement felt in the spine. The base of the backbone seems to be melting or seems on fire. If the person can maintain quiet concentration the energy will be sensed as flowing upwards. Tantric adepts devote decades of concentrated meditation to the release of these ecstatic energies which they call Kundalini, the Serpent Power. One allows the energies to travel upwards through several ganglionic centers (chakras) to the brain, where they are sensed as a burning sensation in the top of the cranium. These sensations are not unpleasant to the prepared person, but, on the contrary, are accompanied by the most intense feelings of joy and illumination. Ill-prepared subjects may interpret the experience in pathological terms and attempt to control it, usually with unpleasant results.[...]

If the subjects fail to recognize the rushing flow of First Bardo phenomena, liberation from the ego is lost. The person finds himself slipping back into mental activities. At this point he should try to recall the instructions or be reminded of them, and a second contact with these processes can be made.

The second stage is less intense. A ball set bouncing reaches its greatest height at the first bounce; the second bounce is lower, and each succeeding bounce is still lower until the ball comes to rest. The consciousness at the loss of the ego is similar to this. Its first spiritual bound, directly upon leaving the body-ego, is the highest; the next is lower. Then the force of karma, (i.e., past game-playing), takes over and different forms of external reality are experienced. Finally, the force of karma having spent itself, consciousness returns to 'normal'. Routines are taken up again and thus rebirth occurs.

The first ecstasy usually ends with a momentary flashback to the ego condition. This return can be happy or sad, loving or suspicious, fearful or courageous, depending on the personality, the preparation, and the setting. This flashback to the ego-game is accompanied by a concern with identity. 'Who am I now? Am I dead or not dead? What is happening?' You cannot determine. You see the surroundings and your companions as you had been used to seeing them before. There is a penetrating sensitivity. But you are on a different level. Your ego grasp is not quite as sure as it was.

The karmic hallucinations and visions have not yet started. Neither the frightening apparitions nor the heavenly visions have begun. This is a most sensitive and pregnant period. The remainder of the experience can be pushed one way or another depending upon preparation and emotional climate.

If you are experienced in consciousness alteration, or if you are a naturally introverted person, remember the situation and the schedule. Stay calm and let the experience take you where it will. You will probably re-experience the ecstasy of illumination once again; or you may drift into aesthetic or philosophic or interpersonal enlightenments. Don't hold on: let the stream carry you along.[...]

Second Bardo: The Period of Hallucinations (Chonyid Bardo)

If the Primary Clear Light is not recognized, there remains the possibility of maintaining the Secondary Clear Light. If that is lost, then comes the Chonyid Bardo, the period of karmic illusions or intense hallucinatory mixtures of game reality. It is very important that the instructions be remembered—they can have great influence and effect.

During this period, the flow of consciousness, microscopically clear and intense, is interrupted by fleeting attempts to rationalize and interpret. But the normal game-playing ego is not functioning effectively. There exist, therefore, unlimited possibilities for, on the one hand, delightful sensuous, intellectual and emotional novelties if one floats with the current; and, on the other hand, fearful ambuscades of confusion and terror if one tries to impose his will on the experience.

The purpose of this part of the manual is to prepare the person for the choice points which arise during this stage. Strange sounds, weird sights and disturbed visions may occur. These can awe, frighten and terrify unless one is prepared.

The experienced person will be able to maintain the recognition that all perceptions come from within and will be able to sit quietly, controlling his expanded awareness like a phantasmagoric multi-dimensional television set: the most acute and sensitive hallucinations—visual, auditory, touch, smell, physical and bodily; the most exquisite reactions, compassionate insight into the self, the world. The key is inaction: passive integration with all that occurs around you. If you try to impose your will, use your mind, rationalize, seek explanations, you will get caught in hallucinatory whirlpools. The motto: peace, acceptance. It is all an ever-changing panorama. You are temporarily removed from the world of game. Enjoy it.

The inexperienced and those to who ego control is important may find this passivity impossible. If you cannot remain inactive and subdue your will, then the one certain activity which can reduce panic and pull you out of hallucinatory mind-games is physical contact with another person. Go to the guide or to another participant and put your head on his lap or chest; put your face next to his and concentrate on the movement and sound of his inspiration. Breathe deeply and feel the air rush in and the sighing release. This is the oldest form of living communication; the brotherhood of breath. The guide's hand on your forehead may add to the relaxation.

Contact with another participant may be misunderstood and provoke sexual hallucinations. For this reason, helping contact should be made explicit by prearrangement. Unprepared participants may impose sexual fears or fantasies on the contact. Turn them off; they are karmic illusory productions.

The tender, gentle, supportive huddling together of participants is a natural development during the second phase. Do not try to rationalize this contact. Human beings and, for that matter, most all mobile terrestrial creatures have been huddling together during long, dark confused nights for several hundred thousand years. Breathe in and breathe out with your companions. We are all one! That's what your breath is telling you.[...]

Following the Tibetan Thodo, we have classified Second Bardo visions into seven types: (1) The Source or Creator Vision; (2) The Internal Flow of Archetypal Processes; (3) The Fire-Flow of Internal Unity; (4) The Wave-Vibration Structure of External Forms; (5) The Vibratory Waves of External Unity; (6) 'The Retinal Circus'; (7) 'The Magic Theatre'.

Visions 2 and 3 involve closed eyes and no contact with external stimuli. In Vision 2 the internal imagery is primarily conceptual. The experience can range from revelation and insight to confusion and chaos, but the cognitive, intellectual meaning is paramount. In Vision 3 the internal imagery is primarily emotional. The experience can range from love and ecstatic unity to fear, distrust and isolation. Visions 4 and 5 involve open eyes and rapt attention to external stimuli, such as sounds, lights, touch, etc. In Vision 4 the external imagery is primarily conceptual and in Vision 5 emotional factors predominate. The sevenfold table just defined bears some similarity to the mandalic schema of the Peaceful Deities listed for the Second Bardo in The Tibetan Book of the Dead.[...]

Third Bardo: The Period of Re-Entry (Sidpa Bardo)

If, in the second Bardo, the voyager is incapable of holding on to the knowledge that the peaceful and wrathful visions were projections of his own mind, but became attracted to or frightened by one or more of them, he will enter the Third Bardo. In this period he struggles to regain routine reality and his ego; the Tibetans call it the Bardo of 'seeking rebirth'. It is the period in which the consciousness makes the transition from transcendent reality to the reality of ordinary waking life. The teachings of this manual are of the utmost importance if one wishes to make a peaceful and enlightened re-entry and avoid a violent or unpleasant one.

In the original Bardo Thodol the aim of the teachings is 'liberation', i.e., release from the cycle of birth and death. Interpreted esoterically, this means that the aim is to remain at the stage of perfect illumination and not to return to social game reality.

Only persons of extremely advanced spiritual development are able to accomplish this, by exercising the Transference Principle at the moment of ego-death. For average persons who undertake a psychedelic voyage, the return to game reality is inevitable. Such persons can and should use this part of the manual for the following purposes: (1) to free themselves from Third Bardo traps; (2) to prolong the session, thus assuring a maximum degree of illumination; (3) to select a favorable re-entry, i.e., to return to a wiser and more peaceful post-session personality.

Although no definite time estimates can be given, the Tibetans estimate that about 50% of the entire psychedelic experience is spent in the Third Bardo by most normal people. At times, as indicated in the Introduction, someone may move straight to the re-entry period if he is unprepared for or frightened by the ego-loss experiences of the first two Bardos.

The types of re-entry made can profoundly color the person's subsequent attitudes and feelings about himself and the world, for weeks or even months afterwards. A session which has been predominantly negative and fearful can still be turned to great advantage and much can be learned from it, provided the re-entry is positive and highly conscious. Conversely, a happy and revelatory experience can be made valueless by a fearful or negative re-entry.

The key instructions of the Third Bardo are: (1) do nothing, stay calm, passive and relaxed, no matter what happens; and (2) recognize where you are. If you do not recognize you will be driven by fear to make a premature and unfavorable re-entry. Only by recognizing can you maintain that state of calm, passive concentration necessary for a favorable re-entry. That is why so many recognition-points are given. If you fail on one, it is always possible, up to the very end, to succeed on another. Hence these teachings should be read carefully and remembered well.[...]

Methods of Choosing the Post-Session Personality

Choosing the post-session ego is an extremely profound art and should not be undertaken carelessly or hastily. One should not return fleeing from hallucinated tormentors. Such re-entry will tend to bring the person to one of the three lower levels. One should first banish the fear by visualizing one's protective figure or the Buddha, then choose calmly and impartially.

The limited foreknowledge available to the voyager should be used to make a wise choice. In the Tibetan tradition each of the levels of game-existence is associated with a particular color and also certain geographical symbols. These may be different for [...] Westerners. Each person has to learn to decode his own internal road map. The Tibetan indicators may be used as a starting point. The purpose is clear: one should follow the signs of the three higher types and shun those of the three lower. One should follow light and pleasant visions and shun dark and dreary ones.[...]

Use your foresight to choose a good post-session robot. Do not be attracted to your old ego. Whether you choose to pursue power, or status, or wisdom, or learning, or servitude, or whatever, choose impartially, without being attracted or repelled. Enter into game existence with good grace, voluntarily and freely. Visualize it as a celestial mansion, i.e., as an opportunity to exercise game-ecstasy. Have faith in the protection of the deities and choose. The mood of complete impartiality is important since you may be in error. A game that appears good may later turn out to be bad. Complete impartiality, freedom from want or fear, ensure that a maximally wise choice is made.

As you return, you see spread out before you the world, your former life, a planet full of fascinating objects and events. Each aspect of the return trip can be a delightful discovery. Soon you will be descending to take your place in worldly events. The key to this return voyage is simply this: take it easy, slowly, naturally. Enjoy every second. Don't rush. Don't be attached to your old games. Recognize that you are in the re-entry period. Do not return with any emotional pressure. Everything you see and touch can glow with radiance. Each moment can be a joyous discovery."[1]

This excerpt, from 'The Psychedelic Experience. A Manual Based on the Tibetan Book of the Dead', is presented here to illustrate the stages/layers of inner experience available during psychedelic experiences. To find out more about these stages and their detailed descriptions, please read the entire manual. Also, the processes described in 'The Psychedelic Experience. A Manual Based on the Tibetan Book of the Dead' are not generally valid. For example, the kundalini spike through the spine is not the only way of activating the high-synchrony in the energy body layer. After the energy body layer has been harmonized through various practices, the high-sync can be activated all at once; no upward flow is necessary.

And remember that in intentional visionary experiences, there is a greater degree of choice, as compared to the psychedelic-induced experiences. In psychedelic experiences, the usual 'safe' way is to prepare the set and the setting, and then to let go and let the plants do the work. My view is that we can consciously co-participate in the psychedelic experience flow, while we maintain a flexible-fluid configuration.

Intentional vs. psychedelic-induced visionary experiences

Is it possible that the intentional visionary experiences (without psychedelics) may involve the same brain mechanisms as the psychedelic-induced visionary experiences? What does modern neuroscience say about this topic? A possible answer is provided by Michael J. Winkelman, in research titled 'The Mechanisms of Psychedelic Visionary Experiences: Hypotheses from Evolutionary Psychology', where he explores two hypotheses: (1)—The effects of psychedelics in producing visionary experiences involve the same mechanisms, elicited by other non-drug mechanisms, for altering consciousness and producing visionary experience; and (2)—These mechanisms involve a dis-inhibition of regulatory mechanisms of the brain that release a number of innate modules, operators or intelligences, especially the mirror neuron system.

In his paper, Winkelman writes: "Neuropharmacological effects of psychedelics have profound cognitive, emotional, and social effects that inspired the development of cultures and religions worldwide. Findings that psychedelics objectively and reliably produce mystical experiences press the question of the neuropharmacological mechanisms by which these highly significant experiences are produced by exogenous neurotransmitter analogs.

Humans have a long evolutionary relationship with psychedelics, a consequence of psychedelics' selective effects for human cognitive abilities, exemplified in the information rich visionary experiences. Objective evidence that psychedelics produce classic mystical experiences, coupled with the finding that hallucinatory experiences can be induced by many non-drug mechanisms, illustrates the need for a common model of visionary effects. Several models implicate disturbances of normal regulatory processes in the brain as the underlying mechanisms responsible for the similarities of visionary experiences produced by psychedelic and other methods for altering consciousness.

Similarities in psychedelic-induced visionary experiences and those produced by practices such as meditation and hypnosis and pathological conditions such as epilepsy indicate the need for a general model explaining visionary experiences. Common mechanisms underlying diverse alterations of consciousness involve the disruption of normal functions of the prefrontal cortex and default mode network. This interruption of ordinary control mechanisms allows for the release of thalamic and other lower brain discharges that stimulate a visual information representation system and release the effects of innate cognitive functions and operators.

Converging forms of evidence support the hypothesis that the source of psychedelic experiences involves the emergence of these innate cognitive processes of lower brain systems, with visionary experiences resulting from the activation of innate processes based in the mirror neuron system.[...]

The differences in psychedelic-induced mystical and shamanic experiences illustrate that while these substances reliably produce certain kinds of experience, the forms of experience may vary considerably—one agent, variable experiences. Secondly, the similarity of psychedelic and non-psychedelic mystical experiences suggests that the explanation of psychedelic experiences is not through mechanisms unique to psychedelics, but rather through shared mechanisms affected by non-drug procedures.[...]

The repeatable effects of psychedelics in producing such visions and mystical experiences make them an unparalleled tool for the examination of the operation of this cognitive-affective system that is an innate aspect of the human brain-mind. Psychedelics consequently can serve as tools to provoke and expose this system, facilitating the examination of an area of human knowledge that has remained marginalized because of its notoriously subjective qualities. Through the use of psychedelics, we can come to better understand the nature of some of the ancient symbolic and conceptual capacities of the human brain, and the kind of experiences that generate the human quest for transcendent knowledge and spirituality."[2]

Afterword

In my explorations, after many years of practice, I admit that I don't intentionally pay attention, very much, to the detailed methodologies and processes that I describe in this study. When I navigate through intentional visionary experiences, the techniques are by now automatic tools, and in each now-moment, there are various tools that become available, and in the next moment, other tools make themselves available, and so on. Choosing them is more like a dance, not a process of cognitive analysis. I just live through the experience, adapting and adjusting the flowing, based on what I can do, and on what is being offered to me[3]. Without reason to fear, I know I am never lost, and the tools always appear when needed. The more I use a tool, the easier it is to use it in the next inner art session. With time, the tools are transformed into choices. And when no tool shows up, I just relax and abandon the no-tool configuration and flow further. I don't know where I am going, but I trust that I have a satisfactory amount of samskaras to deliver me safely to the next self-identity shape, after the intentional visionary experience ends.

Good journeys!

References and notes

1 Leary, T., Metzner, R., & Alpert, R. (1965). *The Psychedelic Experience. A Manual Based on the Tibetan Book of the Dead* (3rd Printing ed.). University Books.

2 Winkelman, M. J. (2017). The Mechanisms of Psychedelic Visionary Experiences: Hypotheses from Evolutionary Psychology. *Frontiers in Neuroscience*, 11. https://doi.org/10.3389/fnins.2017.00539

3 Further reading: Brazdău, O. (2019, February 27). *Entheogenic Insights I: Psychology of DMT/Ayahuasca Experience.* Consciousness Quotient Institute. Retrieved January 14, 2022, from
https://www.consciousness-quotient.com/psychology-of-dmt-ayahuasca-experience

References and Notes

2

Baars, B. J., & Geld, N. (2019). *On Consciousness: Science & Subjectivity – Updated Works on Global Workspace Theory*. Nautilus Press.

Baars, B. J., Banks, W. P., & Newman, J. B. (2003). *Essential Sources in the Scientific Study of Consciousness*. A Bradford Book.

Block, N. (2007). Consciousness, accessibility, and the mesh between psychology and neuroscience. *Behavioral and Brain Sciences*, 30(5–6), 481–499. https://doi.org/10.1017/s0140525x07002786

Chalmers, D. J. (1997). *The Conscious Mind: In Search of a Fundamental Theory* (Philosophy of Mind) (Revised ed.). Oxford University Press.

Cohen, J. D., & Schooler, J. W. (1996). *Scientific Approaches to Consciousness (Carnegie Mellon Symposia on Cognition Series)* (1st ed.). Psychology Press.

Dennett, D. C. (1992). *Consciousness Explained* (1st ed.). Back Bay Books.

Hameroff, S. R., Kaszniak, A. W., & Chalmers, D. (1999). *Toward a Science of Consciousness III: The Third Tucson Discussions and Debates (Complex Adaptive Systems)*. A Bradford Book.

Imants, B., & Mossbridge, J. (2016). *Transcendent Mind: Rethinking the Science of Consciousness* (1st ed.). American Psychological Association.

Koch, C. (2017). *Consciousness: Confessions of a Romantic Reductionist* (1st ed.). The MIT Press.

Lau, H. (2022). *In Consciousness we Trust: The Cognitive Neuroscience of Subjective Experience*. Oxford University Press.

Natsoulas, T. (1992). Is Consciousness What Psychologists Actually Examine? *The American Journal of Psychology*, 105(3), 363. https://doi.org/10.2307/1423193

Penrose, R. (1996). *Shadows of the Mind: A Search for the Missing Science of Consciousness* (Reprint ed.). Oxford University Press.

Seth, A. (2021). Being You: A New Science of Consciousness. Dutton.

3

Russell, W. (1994). *The Secret of Light* (3rd ed.). University of Science and Philosophy.

4a

Personal communication, as cited in Brazdău, O. (2019, February 27). *Entheogenic insights I: Psychology of DMT/Ayahuasca Experience.* Consciousness Quotient Institute. Retrieved January 13, 2021, from
https://www.consciousness-quotient.com/psychology-of-dmt-ayahuasca-experience

4b

Grossberg, S. (2017). Towards solving the hard problem of consciousness: The varieties of brain resonances and the conscious experiences that they support. *Neural Networks*, 87, 38–95. https://doi.org/10.1016/j.neunet.2016.11.003

Hunt, T. (2019). Calculating spatial boundaries and phenomenal capacity of conscious resonating structures in General Resonance Theory. *Authorea.*
https://doi.org/10.22541/au.156245363.39461026

Hunt, T., & Schooler, J. W. (2019). The Easy Part of the Hard Problem: A Resonance Theory of Consciousness. *Frontiers in Human Neuroscience*, 13. https://doi.org/10.3389/fnhum.2019.00378

5a

Steriade, M. (2006). Grouping of Brain Rhythms in Corticothalamic Systems. *Neuroscience*, 137(4), 1087-1106. https://doi.org/10.1016/j.neuroscience.2005.10.029

5b

Ho, M. (2009). Quantum Jazz: Liquid Crystalline Water Music of the Organism. *Subtle Energies & Energy Medicine Journal Archives*, 20(1), 37-52.

6a

Walla, P. (2011). Non-Conscious Brain Processes Revealed by Magnetoencephalography (MEG). In E.W. Pang (Ed.). *Magnetoencephalography*. IntechOpen. https://doi.org/10.5772/28211

6b

Josipovic, Z., & Miskovic, V. (2020). Nondual Awareness and Minimal Phenomenal Experience. Frontiers in Psychology, 11. https://doi.org/10.3389/fpsyg.2020.02087

Kitazawa, S. (2002). Where conscious sensation takes place. *Consciousness and Cognition*, 11(3), 475–477. https://doi.org/10.1016/s1053-8100(02)00031-4

Lo, S. Y. (2017b). Attention without awareness: Attentional modulation of perceptual grouping without awareness. *Attention, Perception, & Psychophysics*, 80(3), 691–701. https://doi.org/10.3758/s13414-017-1474-7

Maier, A., & Tsuchiya, N. (2020). Growing evidence for separate neural mechanisms for attention and consciousness. *Attention, Perception, & Psychophysics*, 83(2), 558–576. https://doi.org/10.3758/s13414-020-02146-4

6c

Herzog, M. H., Drissi-Daoudi, L., & Doerig, A. (2020). All in Good Time: Long-Lasting Postdictive Effects Reveal Discrete Perception. *Trends in Cognitive Sciences*, 24(10), 826–837. https://doi.org/10.1016/j.tics.2020.07.001

Klemperer, F. (1992). Preconscious perceptual processing. *British Journal of Psychiatry*, 161(3), 420. https://doi.org/10.1192/bjp.161.3.420a

Kouider, S., de Gardelle, V., Sackur, J., & Dupoux, E. (2010). How rich is consciousness? The partial awareness hypothesis. *Trends in Cognitive Sciences*, 14(7), 301–307. https://doi.org/10.1016/j.tics.2010.04.006

Lamme, V. A. (2003). Why visual attention and awareness are different. *Trends in Cognitive Sciences*, 7(1), 12–18. https://doi.org/10.1016/s1364-6613(02)00013-x

Michel, M., & Doerig, A. (2021). A new empirical challenge for local theories of consciousness. *Mind & Language*. https://doi.org/10.1111/mila.12319

Paré, D., & Llinás, R. (1995). Conscious and pre-conscious processes as seen from the standpoint of sleep-waking cycle neurophysiology. *Neuropsychologia*, 33(9), 1155–1168. https://doi.org/10.1016/0028-3932(95)00055-8

Singer, W. (2007). Phenomenal Awareness and Consciousness from a Neurobiological Perspective. *NeuroQuantology*, 4(2). https://doi.org/10.14704/nq.2006.4.2.94

Soto, D., & Silvanto, J. (2016). Is conscious awareness needed for all working memory processes? *Neuroscience of Consciousness*, 2016(1), niw009. https://doi.org/10.1093/nc/niw009

van Gaal, S., & Lamme, V. A. F. (2011b). Unconscious High-Level Information Processing. *The Neuroscientist*, 18(3), 287–301. https://doi.org/10.1177/1073858411404079

6d

Blumenfeld, H. (2021). Brain Mechanisms of Conscious Awareness: Detect, Pulse, Switch, and Wave. *The Neuroscientist*, 107385842110493. https://doi.org/10.1177/10738584211049378

Bratzke, D., Bryce, D., & Seifried-Dübon, T. (2014). Distorted subjective reports of stimulus onsets under dual-task conditions: Delayed conscious perception or estimation bias? *Consciousness and Cognition*, 30, 36–47. https://doi.org/10.1016/j.concog.2014.07.016

Cohen, M. A., Dennett, D. C., & Kanwisher, N. (2016). What is the Bandwidth of Perceptual Experience? *Trends in Cognitive Sciences*, 20(5), 324–335. https://doi.org/10.1016/j.tics.2016.03.006

Ortinski, P., & Meador, K. J. (2004). Neuronal Mechanisms of Conscious Awareness. *Archives of Neurology*, 61(7). https://doi.org/10.1016/j.tics.2016.03.006

Pockett, S. (2002). On Subjective Back-Referral and How Long It Takes to Become Conscious of a Stimulus: A Reinterpretation of Libet's Data. *Consciousness and Cognition*, 11(2), 144–161. https://doi.org/10.1006/ccog.2002.0549

Pockett, S. (2006). The great subjective back-referral debate: Do neural responses increase during a train of stimuli? *Consciousness and Cognition*, 15(3), 551–559. https://doi.org/10.1016/j.concog.2005.04.001

6e

Madl, T., Baars, B. J., & Franklin, S. (2011). The Timing of the Cognitive Cycle. *PloS one*, 6(4), e14803. https://doi.org/10.1371/journal.pone.0014803

7a

Goldman-Rakic, P. (1997). Space and time in the mental universe. *Nature*, 386(6625), 559–560. https://doi.org/10.1038/386559a0

Roselli, A. (2018). How Long is Now? A New Perspective on the Specious Present. *Disputatio*, 10(49), 119–140. https://doi.org/10.2478/disp-2018-0009

Szymaszek, A., Sereda, M., Pöppel, E., & Szelag, E. (2009). Individual differences in the perception of temporal order: The effect of age and cognition. *Cognitive Neuropsychology*, 26(2), 135–147. https://doi.org/10.1080/02643290802504742

Zahavi, D. (2008). *Subjectivity and Selfhood: Investigating the First-Person Perspective*. A Bradford Book (MIT Press).

7b

Wittmann, M. (2011). Moments in Time. *Frontiers in Integrative Neuroscience*, 5. https://doi.org/10.3389/fnint.2011.00066

7c

Craddock, T. J. A., Priel, A., & Tuszynski, J. A. (2014). Keeping time: Could quantum beating in microtubules be the basis for the neural synchrony related to consciousness? *Journal of Integrative Neuroscience*, 13(02), 293–311. https://doi.org/10.1142/s0219635214400019

Hameroff, S. (2007). Orchestrated Reduction of Quantum Coherence in Brain Micro-tubules: A Model for Consciousness. *NeuroQuantology*, 5(1). https://doi.org/10.14704/nq.2007.5.1.114

Sahu, S., Ghosh, S., Hirata, K., Fujita, D., & Bandyopadhyay, A. (2013). Multi-level mem-ory-switching properties of a single brain microtubule. *Applied Physics Letters*, 102(12), 123701. https://doi.org/10.1063/1.4793995

8

Brazdău, O. (2014). Witnessing awareness and modes of cognitive awareness. A termi-nology proposal for the psychological assessment of witnessing and (meta)cognitive ex-periences. In D. Chopra (Ed.), *Brain, Mind, Cosmos: The Nature of Our Existence and the Universe (Sages and Scientists Series Book 1). Kindle Edition* (1st ed., chapter 4). Chopra Foundation.

Deikman, A. J. (1966). De-automatization and the Mystic Experience. *Psychiatry*, 29(4), 324–338. https://doi.org/10.1080/00332747.1966.11023476

Forman, R. K. C. (1997). *The Problem of Pure Consciousness: Mysticism and Philosophy*. Ox-ford University Press.

Travis, F., & Pearson, C. (2000). Pure Consciousness: Distinct Phenomenological and Phys-iological Correlates of 'Consciousness Itself'. *International Journal of Neuroscience*, 100(1–4), 77–89. https://doi.org/10.3109/00207450008999678

9

Bečev, O. (2019). Meta-awareness as a solution to the problem of Awareness of Intention. *E-Logos*, 26(2), 35–47. https://doi.org/10.18267/j.e-logos.466

Dunne, J. D., Thompson, E., & Schooler, J. (2019). Mindful meta-awareness: sustained and non-propositional. *Current Opinion in Psychology*, 28, 307–311. https://doi.org/10.1016/j.copsyc.2019.07.003

Gorman, P. F. (2018). *Awareness Itself: Being Aware of Awareness Itself Is the Key*. Vine Press.

Hussain, D. (2015). Meta-Cognition in Mindfulness: A Conceptual Analysis. *Psychological Thought*, 8(2), 132–141. https://doi.org/10.5964/psyct.v8i2.139

Loper, A. B., & Hallahan, D. P. (1982). Meta-Attention: The Development of Awareness of the Attentional Process. *The Journal of General Psychology*, 106(1), 27–33. https://doi.org/10.1080/00221309.1982.9710970

Naccache, L. (2018). Why and how access consciousness can account for phenomenal consciousness. *Philosophical Transactions of the Royal Society B: Biological Sciences*, 373(1755), 20170357. https://doi.org/10.1098/rstb.2017.0357

Schooler, J. W. (2002). Re-representing consciousness: dissociations between experience and meta-consciousness. *Trends in Cognitive Sciences*, 6(8), 339–344. https://doi.org/10.1016/s1364-6613(02)01949-6

Schooler, J. W., Smallwood, J., Christoff, K., Handy, T. C., Reichle, E. D., & Sayette, M. A. (2011). Meta-awareness, perceptual decoupling and the wandering mind. *Trends in Cognitive Sciences*. https://doi.org/10.1016/j.tics.2011.05.006

Spira, R. (2017). Being Aware of Being Aware (*The Essence of Meditation Series*). Sahaja.

12

Alzetta, N. (2021). The attentional episode: (smallest) interval of attended conscious experience. *SSRN Electronic Journal*. https://doi.org/10.2139/ssrn.3917433

de Brigard, F. (2012). The Role of Attention in Conscious Recollection. *Frontiers in Psychology*, 3. https://doi.org/10.3389/fpsyg.2012.00029

Kiefer, M., Ansorge, U., Haynes, J. D., Hamker, F., Mattler, U., Verleger, R., & Niedeggen, M. (2011). Neuro-cognitive mechanisms of conscious and unconscious visual perception: From a plethora of phenomena to general principles. *Advances in Cognitive Psychology*, 7(1), 55–67. https://doi.org/10.2478/v10053-008-0090-4

Marchetti, G. (2012). Against the View that Consciousness and Attention are Fully Dissociable. *Frontiers in Psychology*, 3. https://doi.org/10.3389/fpsyg.2012.00036

Posner, M. I. (1994). Attention: the mechanisms of consciousness. *Proceedings of the National Academy of Sciences*, 91(16), 7398–7403. https://doi.org/10.1073/pnas.91.16.7398

Searle, J. R. (1993). Consciousness, attention and the Connection Principle. *Behavioral and Brain Sciences*, 16(1), 198–203. https://doi.org/10.1017/s0140525x00029642

Sklar, A. Y., Kardosh, R., & Hassin, R. R. (2021). From non-conscious processing to conscious events: a minimalist approach. *Neuroscience of Consciousness*, 2021(2). https://doi.org/10.1093/nc/niab026

13

Fehmi, L., Fehmi, S. S., & Beauregard, M. (2021). *The Open-Focus Life: Practices to Develop Attention and Awareness for Optimal Well-Being*. Shambhala.

15

Cox, M. V. (1978). Order of the acquisition of perspective-taking skills. *Developmental Psychology*, 14(4), 421–422. https://doi.org/10.1037/0012-1649.14.4.421

Mattan, B. D., Rotshtein, P., & Quinn, K. A. (2016). Empathy and visual perspective-taking performance. *Cognitive Neuroscience*, 7(1–4), 170–181. https://doi.org/10.1080/17588928.2015.1085372

McHugh, L., Stewart, I., & Williams, M. (2012). *The Self and Perspective Taking*. Amsterdam University Press.

Niccolai, V., Klepp, A., Schnitzler, A., & Biermann-Ruben, K. (2021). Neurophysiological mechanisms of perspective-taking: An MEG investigation of agency. *Social Neuroscience*, 16(5), 584–593. https://doi.org/10.1080/17470919.2021.1974546

Ruby, P., & Decety, J. (2003). What you believe versus what you think they believe: a neuroimaging study of conceptual perspective-taking. *European Journal of Neuroscience*, 17(11), 2475–2480. https://doi.org/10.1046/j.1460-9568.2003.02673.x

17

Brazdău, O., Ahuja, S., Opariuc, C. D., Jones, V., Sharma, S., Monsanto, C., Andrews, S., & Fiveson, K. (2021). An Exploratory Analysis of Collective Patterns of Conscious Experience Using a Self-Report Questionnaire. *Frontiers in Psychology*, 12:634677. https://doi.org/10.3389/fpsyg.2021.634677

18

Sivananda, S. (n.d.). Vasanas. The Divine Life Society. Retrieved January 14, 2022, from https://www.sivanandaonline.org

19

Duncan, T., & Semura, J. (2004). The Deep Physics Behind the Second Law: Information and Energy as Independent Forms of Bookkeeping. *Entropy*, 6(1), 21-29. https://doi.org/10.3390/e6010021

23

Monsanto, C. (2013, July). *The Language of Emotions. A Social Developmental Strategy* [Paper presentation]. Conference of the Association of Caribbean Social Work Educators, Willemstad, Curacao.

24

Fujimoto, A. (2018). Sati (mindfulness) and Sampajañña (awareness). *Journal of Indian and Buddhist Studies (Indogaku Bukkyogaku Kenkyu)*, 66(2), 899–895. https://doi.org/10.4259/ibk.66.2_899

26a

Cvetkovic, D., & Cosic, I. (2011). *States of Consciousness: Experimental Insights into Meditation, Waking, Sleep and Dreams (The Frontiers Collection)* (2011th ed.). Springer.

Gackenbach, J. (1988). *From Sleep Consciousness to Pure Consciousness*. Sawka.com. Retrieved January 15, 2022, from http://www.sawka.com/spiritwatch/from.htm

Garay, A., & Trovato, M. (2009). Analysis of reports from different experiences of consciousness during wakefulness, sleep and transitional states. *Sleep Medicine*, 10, S6. https://doi.org/10.1016/s1389-9457(09)70024-3

26b

Alexander, C. N. (1987). Dream Lucidity and Dream Witnessing: A Developmental Model Based on the Practice of Transcendental Meditation. *Lucidity Letter*, 6(2), 1-11.

27

Fehmi, L. (2003). Attention to Attention. In J. Kamiya (Ed.). *Applied Neurophysiology and EEG Biofeedback*. Future Health.

29

Baumeister, R. F. (2011). *Public Self and Private Self (Springer Series in Social Psychology)* (Softcover reprint of the original 1st ed. 1986 ed.). Springer.

Bernstein, M. J., & Elizabeth, H. (2018). The self as a central tenet of our psychology: New perspectives on the self. *Self and Identity*, 17(4), 367–370. https://doi.org/10.1080/15298868.2018.1440627

Georgalis, N. (2007). First-Person Methodologies: A View From Outside the Phenomeno-logical Tradition. *The Southern Journal of Philosophy*, 45(S1), 93–112. https://doi.org/10.1111/j.2041-6962.2007.tb00115.x

Gore, J. S., & Cross, S. E. (2014). Who Am I Becoming? A Theoretical Framework for Un-derstanding Self-Concept Change. *Self and Identity*, 13(6), 740–764. https://doi.org/10.1080/15298868.2014.933712

Hood, B. (2013). *The Self Illusion: How the Social Brain Creates Identity* (Reprint ed.). Oxford University Press.

Leary, M. R., & Tangney, J. P. (2013). *Handbook of Self and Identity* (Second ed.). The Guil-ford Press.

Oppenheimer, L. (2002). Self or Selves? *Theory & Psychology*, 12(1), 97–128. https://doi.org/10.1177/0959354302121006

Petitmengin, C. (2009). *Ten Years of Viewing from Within: The Legacy of Francisco Varela* (Journal of Consciousness Studies) (Illustrated ed.). Imprint Academic.

Swann, W. B. (1999). *Resilient Identities: Self, Relationships, And The Construction Of Social Reality*. Basic Books.

Wittmann, M., Hurd, P., & Rowat, G. (2019). Altered States of Consciousness: Experiences Out of Time and Self. Brilliance Audio.

32, 33

Brazdău, O., Ahuja, S., Opariuc, C. D., Jones, V., Sharma, S., Monsanto, C., Andrews, S., & Fiveson, K. (2021). An Exploratory Analysis of Collective Patterns of Conscious Experience Using a Self-Report Questionnaire. *Frontiers in Psychology*, 12:634677. https://doi.org/10.3389/fpsyg.2021.634677

Macdonald, D. A., & Friedman, H. L. (2002). Assessment of Humanistic, Transpersonal, and Spiritual Constructs: State of the Science. *Journal of Humanistic Psychology*, 42(4), 102–125. https://doi.org/10.1177/002216702237126

41

Maslow, A. H. (1998). *Toward a Psychology of Being*, 3rd Edition (3rd ed.). Wiley.

42

Vyasa (n.d.). *The Bhagavad Gita – Chapter 14 – The Yoga of the Distinction of the Three Gunas*. Santhosa.Com. Retrieved January 14, 2022, from https://www.santosha.com/philosophy/gita-chapter14.html

52a

Glaze, J. A. (1928). Psychological Effects of Fasting. *The American Journal of Psychology*, 40(2), 236. https://doi.org/10.2307/1414486

Tart, C. (2001). *States of Consciousness* (Illustrated ed.). iUniverse.

Tart, C. (1972). *Altered States of Consciousness* (1st ed.). Doubleday.

Warren, J. (2007). *The Head Trip: Adventures on the Wheel of Consciousness* (First Edition). Random House.

52b

Yetman, D. (2020, October 26). *What Is Hypnagogia, the State Between Wakefulness and Sleep?* Healthline. Retrieved January 14, 2022, from https://www.healthline.com/health/hypnagogia

53a

Beck, D. E., & Cowan, C. C. (2005). *Spiral Dynamics: Mastering Values, Leadership and Change*. Wiley-Blackwell.

Cook-Greuter, S. R. (2000). Mature ego development: A gateway to ego transcendence. *Journal of Adult Development*, 7(4), 227–240. https://doi.org/10.1023/a:1009511411421

Graves, C. W. (1970). Levels of Existence: an Open System Theory of Values. *Journal of Humanistic Psychology*, 10(2), 131–155. https://doi.org/10.1177/002216787001000205

Grof, S. (1988). *The Adventure of Self-Discovery: Dimensions of Consciousness and New Perspectives in Psychotherapy and Inner Exploration*. State University of New York Press.

Kegan, R. (1982). *The Evolving Self: Problem and Process in Human Development* (Reprint ed.). Harvard University Press.

Loevinger, J. (1976). *Ego Development: Conceptions and Theories (Jossey-Bass Behavioral Science Series)* (1st ed.). Jossey-Bass.

O'Fallon, T. (2020). States and STAGES: Waking Up Developmentally. *Integral Review*, 16(1), 13-38

Torbert, W. R. (2004). *Action Inquiry: The Secret of Timely and Transforming Leadership*. Berrett-Koehler Publishers.

Wade, J. (1996). *Changes of Mind: A Holonomic Theory of the Evolution of Consciousness*. State University of New York Press.

Washburn, M. (1995). *The Ego and the Dynamic Ground: A Transpersonal Theory of Human Development*. State University of New York Press.

Wilber, K. (2000). *Integral Psychology: Consciousness, Spirit, Psychology, Therapy*. Shambhala.

53b

deVos, C. (2018, May 22). A New Republic of the Heart: The Art and Practice of Sacred Activism. *Integral Life*. Retrieved January 14, 2022, from https://integrallife.com/a-new-republic-of-the-heart-the-art-and-practice-of-sacred-activism

54

Brazdău, O., Ahuja, S., Opariuc, C. D., Jones, V., Sharma, S., Monsanto, C., Andrews, S., & Fiveson, K. (2021). An Exploratory Analysis of Collective Patterns of Conscious Experience Using a Self-Report Questionnaire. *Frontiers in Psychology*, 12:634677. https://doi.org/10.3389/fpsyg.2021.634677

Further reading:
Brown, B. C. (2006, April 3). An Overview of Developmental Stages of Consciousness. In-

tegral Without Borders. Retrieved January 16, 2022, from https://integralwithoutborders.org/sites/default/files/resources/Overview%20of%20De velopmental%20Levels.pdf

55a

Cook-Greuter, S. (2013). *Nine Levels of Increasing Embrace in Ego Development: A Full-Spectrum Theory of Vertical Growth and Meaning Making*. Retrieved March 01, 2021, from http://www.cook-greuter.com/Cook-Greuter%209%20levels%20paper%20new%201.1%2714%2097p%5B1%5D.pdf

55b

O'Fallon, T. (2020). States and STAGES: Waking Up Developmentally. *Integral Review*, 16(1), 13-38.

56a

O'Fallon, T., Polissar, N., Neradilek, M. B., & Murray, T. (2020). The Validation of a New Scoring Method For Assessing Ego Development Based on Three Dimensions of Language. *Heliyon*, 6(3), e03472. https://doi.org/10.1016/j.heliyon.2020.e03472

56b

Barta, K. (2020). Seven Perspectives on the STAGES Developmental Model. *Integral Review*, 16(1), 69-148.

59

Cook-Greuter, S. (2013). *Nine Levels of Increasing Embrace in Ego Development: A Full-Spectrum Theory of Vertical Growth and Meaning Making*. Retrieved August 01, 2021, from http://www.cook-greuter.com/Cook-Greuter%209%20levels%20paper%20new%201.1%2714%2097p%5B1%5D.pdf

60

Joye, S. R. (2021). *Tantric Psychophysics: A Structural Map of Altered States and the Dynamics of Consciousness* (2nd Edition, Revised ed.). Inner Traditions.

Maslow, A. H. (1994). *Religions, Values, and Peak-Experiences*. Penguin Books.

McFetridge, G., Hardt, J., Aldana, J., & Slavinski, Z. (2004). *Peak States of Consciousness: Theory and Applications, Volume 1: Breakthrough Techniques for Exceptional Quality of Life*. Institute for the Study of Peak States Press.

Wilson, C. (2009). *Super Consciousness: The Quest for the Peak Experience*. Watkins.

62a

Lynam, A. (2020). Principles and Practices for Developmentally Aware Teaching and Mentoring in Higher Education. *Integral Review*, 16(1), 149-186.

62b

O'Fallon, T. (2020). States and STAGES: Waking Up Developmentally. *Integral Review*, 16(1), 13-38.

79

Dixon, J. E. (2020). *Biology of Kundalini: Exploring the Fire of Life*. Emancipation Unlimited LLC.

80a

Albini, E. (2020). *Myofascial Training: Intelligent Movement for Mobility, Performance, and Recovery* (First ed.). Human Kinetics.

80b

Long, L. (2021, July 27). *Fascia, Connections and Consciousness*. Freeman+Taylor Yoga. Retrieved January 14, 2022, from https://www.richardfreemanyoga.com/from-the-sangha/2021/july-fascia-connections-and-consciousness

83

Silverman, L. K. (2002). *Upside-Down Brilliance: The Visual-Spatial Learner* (1st ed.). DeLeon Publishing.

84a

Rodrigues, H. (2010, June 3). *Samyama*. Mahavidya – Scholarly Resources for the Study of Hinduism. Retrieved January 16, 2022, from http://www.mahavidya.ca/2010/06/03/samyama

84b

Sinha, S. (2017). *Prajna-Paramita-Hridaya/The Heart Sutra Bhagavati, the Heart of Transcendental Knowledge*. SSRN Electronic Journal. https://doi.org/10.2139/ssrn.3058606

86

Lynam, A. (2020). Principles and Practices for Developmentally Aware Teaching and Mentoring in Higher Education. *Integral Review*, 16(1), 149-186.

88

Leary, T., Metzner, R., & Alpert, R. (1965). *The Psychedelic Experience. A Manual Based on the Tibetan Book of the Dead* (3rd Printing ed.). University Books.

89

Osho. (1975). *Life Has No Beginning and No End* (excerpt from Tao: The Three Treasures, Vol. 4). Retrieved January 14, 2022, from https://www.osho.com/osho-online-library/the-books

90

Aron, E. (2022). *The Highly Sensitive Person*. Retrieved January 14, 2022, from https://hsperson.com

91

Bearman, S. (2014, September 6). *Depression, Anxiety, and the Mismanagement of Aliveness*. Interchange Counseling Institute. Retrieved January 14, 2022, from http://www.interchangecounseling.com/blog/depression-anxiety-and-the-mismanagement-of-aliveness

92a

Waldman, J. D. (2007). Thinking systems need systems thinking. *Systems Research and Behavioral Science*, 24(3), 271–284. https://doi.org/10.1002/sres.828

92b

O'Fallon, T. (2015, March). *The Evolution of the Human Soul: Developmental Practices in Spiritual Guidance*. Terri O'Fallon | The Marriage of States, Stages & Shadow. Retrieved January 14, 2022, from https://www.terriofallon.com/wp-content/uploads/2015/08/The-Evolution-Of-The-Human-Soul-10.pdf

93

Jonas, K. J. (2013). Automatic Behavior – Its Social Embedding and Individual Consequences. *Social and Personality Psychology Compass*, 7(9), 689–700. https://doi.org/10.1111/spc3.12060

94

James, M. (2013, July 30). Conscious of the Unconscious. *Psychology Today*. Retrieved January 14, 2022, from https://www.psychologytoday.com/intl/blog/focus-forgiveness/201307/conscious-the-unconscious

95

Barta, K. (2020). Seven Perspectives on the STAGES Developmental Model. *Integral Review*, 16(1), 69-148.

98

Tillier, B. (1995, October 26). *The Theory of Positive Disintegration by Kazimierz Dąbrowski*. Positive Disintegration. Retrieved January 14, 2022, from http://www.positivedisintegration.com/#overview

102a

Hanson, R. (2011). *Just One Thing: Developing a Buddha Brain One Simple Practice at a Time*. New Harbinger Publications.

102b

Hisamatsu, E., & Pattni, R. (2015). Yoga and the Jesus Prayer: A Comparison between aṣṭānga yoga in the Yoga Sūtras of Patañjali and the Psycho-Physical Method of Hesychasm. *Journal of Hindu-Christian Studies*, 28(1). https://doi.org/10.7825/2164-6279.1606

103

Lynam, A. (2020). Principles and Practices for Developmentally Aware Teaching and Mentoring in Higher Education. *Integral Review*, 16(1), 149-186.

106

Sharma, B., & Cook-Greuter, S. (2010). *Polarities and Ego Development: Polarity Thinking in Ego Development Theory and Developmental Coaching*. Integrales Forum. Retrieved January 14, 2022, from https://www.integralesforum.org/attachments/Sharma%20Cook-Greuter%20paper%20EAIF%20SUNY.pdf

107

O'Fallon, T. (2015). *StAGES: Growing Up is Waking Up: Interpenetrating Quadrants, States and Structures*. Pacific Integral. Retrieved January 14, 2022, from https://www.terriofallon.com/stages-growing-up-is-waking-up-interpenetrating-quadrants-states-and-structures

108

Puhakka, K. (2007). Nonduality: A Spontaneous Movement To and Fro. In J. J. Prednergast, & G. K. Bradford (Eds.), *Listening from the Heart of Silence: Nondual Wisdom and Psychotherapy, Volume 2 (Nondual Wisdom & Psychotherapy)* (1st ed., pp. 151–169). Paragon House.

112a

Morgan, C. J., Rothwell, E., Atkinson, H., Mason, O., & Curran, H. V. (2010). Hyper-priming in cannabis users: A naturalistic study of the effects of cannabis on semantic memory function. *Psychiatry Research*, 176(2–3), 213–218. https://doi.org/10.1016/j.psychres.2008.09.002

112b

Wentura, D., Moritz, S., & Frings, C. (2008). Further evidence for "hyper-priming" in thought-disordered schizophrenic patients using repeated masked category priming. *Schizophrenia Research*, 102(1–3), 69–75. https://doi.org/10.1016/j.schres.2008.04.016

114

Crosthwait, A. (2019, July 28). *What it feels like to change*. Alison Crosthwait. Retrieved January 14, 2022, from https://www.alisoncrosthwait.com/blog/what-it-feels-like-to-change

116a

Fehmi, L. (2003). Attention to Attention. In J. Kamiya (Ed.). *Applied Neurophysiology and EEG Biofeedback*. Future Health.

116b

American Psychiatric Association. (2022). *Diagnostic and Statistical Manual of Mental Disorders, 4th Edition (DSM-IV)* (4th ed.). American Psychiatric Association.

118

Satprem, S. (2008). *Sri Aurobindo or the Adventure of Consciousness*. Mira Aditi.

121

Christi, N. (2021). *Love, God, and Everything: Awakening from the Long, Dark Night of the Collective Soul*. Bear & Company.

Foley, M. (2019). *The Dark Night: Psychological Experience and Spiritual Reality*. ICS Publications.

Lounibos, J. B. (2011). *Self-Emptying of Christ and the Christian: Three Essays on Kenosis*. Wipf & Stock.

Md, G. M. G. (2009). *The Dark Night of the Soul: A Psychiatrist Explores the Connection Between Darkness and Spiritual Growth* (Reprint ed.). HarperOne.

Meadow, M. J. (1984). *The dark side of mysticism: Depression and "the dark night".* Pastoral Psychology, 33(2), 105–125. https://doi.org/10.1007/bf01086371

Rodd, J. (2020). *Selfless. Turiya: Beyond the Dark Night of the Soul.* Inlandia Inst.

123

Welwood, J. (2014, February 1). *Human Nature. Buddha Nature. On Spiritual Bypassing, Relationship, and the Dharma. An interview with John Welwood by Tina Fossella.* John Welwood. Retrieved January 14, 2022, from https://www.johnwelwood.com/articles/TRIC_interview_uncut.pdf

125

Bick, P. A., & Kinsbourne, M. (1987). Auditory hallucinations and subvocal speech in schizophrenic patients. *American Journal of Psychiatry*, 144(2), 222–225. https://doi.org/10.1176/ajp.144.2.222

128

American Center for the Integration of Spiritually Transformative Experiences. (2015, August 6). *Cultural Competency Guidelines for Professionals Working with Clients Who Report Issues Related to Their Spiritually Transformative Experience.* ACISTE. Retrieved January 14, 2022, from https://aciste.org/competency-guidelines-for-professionals

129

Puhakka, K. (2007). Nonduality: A Spontaneous Movement To and Fro. In J. J. Prednergast, & G. K. Bradford (Eds.), *Listening from the Heart of Silence: Nondual Wisdom and Psychotherapy, Volume 2 (Nondual Wisdom & Psychotherapy)* (1st ed., pp. 151–169). Paragon House.

130a

Grof, S. (2000). *Psychology of the Future: Lessons from Modern Consciousness Research (Suny Series in Transpersonal and Humanistic Psychology)* (1st ed.). State University of New York Press.

130b

Turner, R. P., Lukoff, D., Barnhouse, R. T., & Lu, F. G. (1995). A Culturally Sensitive Diagnostic Category in the DSM-IV. *The Journal of Nervous and Mental Disease*, 183(7), 435–444. https://doi.org/10.1097/00005053-199507000-00003

130c

von Peter, S., Bergstrøm, T., Nenoff-Herchenbach, I., Hopfenbeck, M. S., Pocobello, R., Aderhold, V., Alvarez-Monjaras, M., Seikkula, J., & Heumann, K. (2021). Dialogue as a Response to the Psychiatrization of Society? Potentials of the Open Dialogue Approach. *Frontiers in Sociology*, 6. https://doi.org/10.3389/fsoc.2021.806437

130d

Mackler, Daniel. (2014, April 8). *Healing Homes: recovery from psychosis without medication* [Video]. YouTube. https://www.youtube.com/watch?v=JV4NTEp8S2Q

130e

Perry, J. W. (1998). *Trials of the Visionary Mind (SUNY Series in Transpersonal and Humanistic Psychology)*. State University of New York Press.

131

Warren, J. (2016, May 10). *The Promise and Peril of Spiritual Belief*. Jeff Warren. Retrieved January 14, 2022, from https://jeffwarren.org/articles/promise-peril-spiritual-belief

134a

Moors, P., Wagemans, J., & de-Wit, L. (2017). Causal events enter awareness faster than non-causal events. *PeerJ*, 5, e2932. https://doi.org/10.7717/peerj.2932

134b

Brazdău, O. (2019, February 27). *Entheogenic Insights I: Psychology of DMT/Ayahuasca Experience*. Consciousness Quotient Institute. Retrieved January 14, 2022, from https://www.consciousness-quotient.com/psychology-of-dmt-ayahuasca-experience

143

Monroe, R. (n.d.). *The H Band*. All About Heaven. Retrieved January 14, 2022, from https://allaboutheaven.org/observations/monroe-robert-out-of-body-003602/221

152

Zimmer, C. (2010, October 27). *The Brain: "Ringing in the Ears" Actually Goes Much Deeper Than That*. Discover Magazine. Retrieved January 14, 2022, from http://discovermagazine.com/2010/oct/26-ringing-in-the-ears-goes-much-deeper

153

Leary, T., Metzner, R., & Alpert, R. (1965). *The Psychedelic Experience. A Manual Based on the Tibetan Book of the Dead* (3rd Printing ed.). University Books.

155

Brazdău, O. (2019, February 27). *Entheogenic Insights I: Psychology of DMT/Ayahuasca Experience*. Consciousness Quotient Institute. Retrieved January 14, 2022, from https://www.consciousness-quotient.com/psychology-of-dmt-ayahuasca-experience

156

Andrews, S. (2019, September 16). *Sharing Awareness Consciously Together*. Consciousness Quotient Institute. Retrieved January 14, 2022, from https://www.consciousness-quotient.com/knowing-sharing-awareness-consciously-together

Further reading:

Linklater, A. (2009). Human Interconnectedness. *International Relations*, 23(3), 481–497. https://doi.org/10.1177/0047117809340483

Atkinson, R. (2017). *The Story of Our Time: From Duality to Interconnectedness to Oneness*. Sacred Stories Publishing.

Kauffman, J. P. (2015). *Conscious Collective: An Aim for Awareness*. Conscious Collective, LLC.

Hanh, N. T. (2006). *One Buddha is Not Enough: A Story of Collective Awakening* (Illustrated ed.). Parallax Press.

Diehl, K. M. (2009). *The Collective Awakening: Messages Along the Path of Awareness*. Gateway to Being.

160

Lonczak, H. S. (2015, June 9). *What is Positive Parenting? A Look at the Research and Benefits*. PositivePsychology.Com. Retrieved January 14, 2022, from https://positivepsychology.com/positive-parenting

162a

Jenkins, T. (2021, February 4). *Discovering Your Company's Higher Purpose*. Conscious Revolution. Retrieved January 14, 2022, from https://www.consciousrevolution.biz/discovering-your-companys-higher-purpose

162b

Conscious Capitalism. (2021, August 24). *Conscious Capitalism Philosophy*. Retrieved January 14, 2022, from https://www.consciouscapitalism.org/philosophy

163a

Jones, V. (2012). *In Search of Conscious Leadership: A Qualitative Study of Postsecondary Educational Leadership Practices* (Doctoral dissertation). State University, San Diego.

163b

Lieberman, S. (2020, December 22). *What Business Ghosting Says About Your Leadership, and Why Real Leaders Don't Ghost*. Multi Briefs: Exclusive. Retrieved January 14, 2022, from http://exclusive.multibriefs.com/content/what-business-ghosting-says-about-your-leadership-and-why-real-leaders-dont/business-management-services-risk-management

164

Gerndt, U. (2014). *Frederic Laloux – "Reinventing organizations"*. Reinventing Organizations. Retrieved January 14, 2022, from https://www.reinventingorganizations.com/uploads/2/1/9/8/21988088/1403

165

Further reading: University of Michigan. (1997, January 13). *Physics offers glimpse into the universe's dark era*. University of Michigan News. Retrieved January 14, 2022, from https://news.umich.edu/physics-offers-glimpse-into-the-universe-s-dark-era

166

Melodysheep (John D. Boswell). (2020, October 7). *Life Beyond II: The Museum of Alien Life* (*4K*) [Video]. YouTube. https://www.youtube.com/watch?v=ThDYazipjSl

170

Everett, D. L. (2009). *Don't Sleep, There Are Snakes: Life and Language in the Amazonian Jungle* (Vintage Departures) (Illustrated ed.). Vintage.

172

Stewart, J. (2000). *Evolution's Arrow: The Direction of Evolution and The Future of Humanity.* The Chapman Press.

173

Stewart, J. (2020, October 10). The Emergence of Intentional Evolutionaries. Consciousness Quotient Institute. Retrieved January 14, 2022, from https://www.consciousness-quotient.com/the-emergence-of-intentional-evolutionaries

174

Stewart, J. (2020, November 4). *The Evolutionary Awareness in a Planetary Society Based on Cooperation.* Consciousness Quotient Institute. Retrieved January 14, 2022, from https://www.consciousness-quotient.com/the-evolutionary-awareness-in-a-planetary-society-based-on-cooperation

Also available

In a waking dream, we inhabit the dreamworld with an awareness of doing so-as sometimes happens upon waking from sleep when a dream continues to feel present alongside an awareness of lying in bed.

Taking perspectives from transpersonal psychology, ecotherapy, complexity theory, and fractal geometry, this book develops new possibilities within waking dream practice (also known as "active imagination" and "guided imagery") to show:

- how the in-between waking/dreaming experience allows us to become aware of not just what we imagine but also the process of how we imagine-a process that reveals the principles and skills of image-based transformation and healing.
- how a broad understanding of imagination-as present in all perceptions, actions, and relationships (not just as pictures "inside the mind")-allows for an image-centric approach to psychotherapy and everyday life as an ongoing "eyes-wide-open" waking dream.

The result is an experiential and theoretical appreciation of imagination, not just as a means to rational insight but as a creative ability at the heart of human potential.

isbn 978-1-912-618-08-0 (print) / 978-1-912618-09-7 (ebook)

TransPersonal
Press

Also available

To celebrate its 30 years of pioneering work in the fields of counselling and psychotherapy training, the Re-Vision Centre for Transpersonal & Integrative Therapy has brought together a selection of writing by practitioners and teachers who have worked at the heart of the organization.

The chapters address a social and cultural crisis which, at this point in the history of our planet, needs new ways of looking at therapy and how it relates to the world beyond the consulting room. Just as 'the personal is political' was a way of seeing individual issues within the context of a wider political field, so we now need to see that the soul is a different kind of agency from that of the ego – one that is both internal and external, individual and cultural. The world may have lost connection with soul in its obsession with merchandise and control, but soul has not lost connection with us. These chapters offer an integrative perspective that both gives a place to the troubles of the modern world and also develops a well-tuned craft to firstly attend to our painful wounds and ultimately transform their bitterness into the salt of wisdom.

This book is a compelling work for psychotherapists, counsellors, trainees, and anyone interested in how psychotherapy influences and is influenced by the state of the planet, by imagination and by the reality of how politics impact on our daily lives.

ISBN 978-1-912-618-02-8 (print) / 978-1-912618-03-5 (ebook)

TransPersonal
Press

Also available

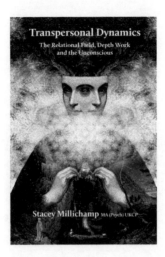

Transpersonal Dynamics offers approaches to the therapeutic encounter from the leading edge of quantum physics field theory and integrative psychology.

Transpersonal Dynamics is the culmination of over 20 years of feedback about 'what works', gathered through delivering integrative and transpersonal training to counsellors, coaches, psychologists and psychotherapists who work with organisations, adults, couples, families, young people and children.

Using down-to-earth language in a practical way, this book addresses some of the gritty aspects of the therapeutic relationship, with the aim to inspire and support practitioners to take more risks to bring a collaborative, relational quality to their work.

Stacey Millichamp is a trainer on the Masters Degree in Psychotherapy and the Diploma in Integrative and Transpersonal Clinical Supervision at the Psychosynthesis Trust *in London, and teaches on the Diploma in Supervision with Soul at the* Re-Vision Centre for Integrative Psychosynthesis *in London. She is the Director of* Entrust Associates, *which provides counselling to staff and students of secondary and primary schools in London.*

isbn 978-1-912-618-00-4 (print) / 978-1-912618-00-1 (ebook)

TransPersonal
Press

Also available

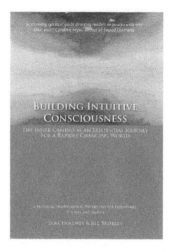

Are you looking to make real and lasting change in your life? *Building Intuitive Consciousness* offers a reliable and effective method to support such change by guiding readers on an inner pilgrimage to awaken to their Intuitive Consciousness.

It has been said that no problem can be solved from the same level of consciousness that created it. We believe that by awakening to the Intuitive Consciousness within ourselves, we are able to transcend old patterns and habitual behaviours that may be limiting us in some way from being able to take our next steps forward.

Using the wisdom of ancient spiritual practice and modern psychology, *Building Intuitive Consciousness* is both a practical and mystical manual to guide you on this journey. By delving deep into our psychology and expanding up into the heights of our numinous or spiritual potential, this unsentimental book offers a roadmap to access our true inner wisdom, free from the restraints and distortions of our ego.

Packed with immediately applicable insights and accessible exercises, this second edition now includes notes that are relevant for professionals, making it the perfect manual for psychologists, therapists, managers or anyone on a journey of self-discovery.

isbn 978-1-912-618-04-2 (print) / 978-1-912618-05-9 (ebook)

TransPersonal
Press

Also available

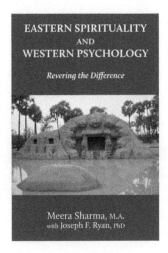

Eastern Spirituality and Western Psychology offers a practical path to harmony between spirituality and Western psychology, between heart and mind.

This book:
- challenges basic assumptions of Western psychology
- demystifies Vedic psychology
- presents how Eastern spirituality can enhance Western psychology

It guides readers by clarifying the relationship between spirituality and psychological growth, and demonstrates that psychotherapy and spirituality are complementary aspects of human development, with both essential for optimum mental, existential, and spiritual growth. It is up to everyone to take responsibility for making the changes that enable us to contribute to the well-being of the whole.

In this insightful book, the authors reflect on this revolution and consider how it is likely to evolve in the future. It paves the way for those interested in the transpersonal, whether psychologists, psychotherapists, Orientalists, or spiritual practitioners.

isbn 978-1-912-618-06-6 (print) / 978-1-912618-07-3 (ebook)

TransPersonal
Press

Lightning Source UK Ltd.
Milton Keynes UK
UKHW010416260422
402059UK00012B/332

9 781912 698103